ISSUES IN ENVIRONMENTAL ECONOMICS

Issues in Environmental Economics

Edited by

Nick Hanley and Colin Roberts

Blackwell Publishers

© 2002 by Blackwell Publishers Ltd
a Blackwell Publishing company

First published as a special issue of *Journal of Economic Surveys*, 2001

Editorial Offices:
108 Cowley Road, Oxford OX4 1JF, UK
Tel: +44 (0)1865 791100
Osney Mead, Oxford OX2 0EL, UK
Tel: +44 (0)1865 206206
350 Main Street, Malden, MA 02148-5018, USA
Tel: +1 781 388 8250
Iowa State University Press, a Blackwell Publishing company, 2121 S. State Avenue, Ames, Iowa 50014-8300, USA
Tel: +1 515 292 0140
Blackwell Munksgaard, Nørre Søgade 35, PO Box 2148, Copenhagen, DK-1016, Denmark
Tel: +45 77 33 33 33
Blackwell Publishing Asia, 54 University Street, Carlton, Victoria 3053, Australia
Tel: +61 (0)3 347 0300
Blackwell Verlag, Kurfürstendamm 57, 10707 Berlin, Germany
Tel: +49 (0)30 32 79 060
Blackwell Publishing, 10, rue Casimir Delavigne, 75006 Paris, France
Tel: +331 5310 3310

First published 2002 by Blackwell Publishers Ltd

Library of Congress Cataloging-in-Publication Data has been applied for

ISBN 0-631-23569-8

A catalogue record for this title is available from the British Library.

Typeset by Mathematical Composition Setters Ltd, Salisbury, Wiltshire
Printed and bound in Great Britain by MPG Books Ltd, Bodmin, Cornwall

For further information on
Blackwell Publishers visit our website:
www.blackwellpublishers.co.uk

CONTENTS

CHAPTER 1

ISSUES IN ENVIRONMENTAL ECONOMICS: AN OVERVIEW

Nick Hanley

University of Glasgow

Colin Roberts

University of Edinburgh

The field of Environmental and Natural Resource Economics (ENRE) has developed rapidly since its modern birth in the early 1970s — for an excellent, brief history of environmental and resource economics, see Crocker (1999).

Whilst much of the writing of classical economists such as Mill, Ricardo and Malthus was concerned with natural resource issues, the subject then largely disappeared from economics until the resurgence in environmental awareness in the 1960s, and the increasing awareness of possible resource scarcity limits in the early 1970s (as evidenced in 'The Limits to Growth' (Meadows *et al.*, 1972)).

Modern ENRE was a response to these concerns, partly in order to demonstrate the limited ability of a market economy to handle scarcity, and partly as a way of extending conventional economics in order to be able to address environmental issues. Later in the 1970s, the issue of how to estimate the value of changes in non-market environmental goods and services grew in importance. This valuation literature expanded rapidly in response to rising interest on the part of governments in extending cost-benefit analysis to environmental policy making, and in response to the fact that environmental economics was now part of the legal process over environmental damage claims in the US.

Within the field of pollution economics, which had started with Pigou in the 1920s, attention switched away from traditional point sources of pollution, such as factories, and towards non-point, diffuse sources, such as farmland. This occurred in response to changing priorities for pollution control in North America and Europe. Another type of pollution problem raised its head in the 1980s, namely transboundary pollution such as acid rain and global warming. Now focus had to shift to the conditions under which international treaties could be successfully negotiated for such pollutants — one of the many ways in which game theory has been taken up in ENRE (see Hanley and Folmer, 1998). Within natural resource economics, interest in efficient depletion programmes for renewable and non-renewable resources was supplemented with investigations into the management of natural capital, more broadly defined.

In this special issue of *Journal of Economic Surveys*, we have assembled a collection of specially commissioned papers which try to address some of these frontiers in environmental and resource economics. What are not included here are contributions on the economics of sustainable development. Whilst some of the papers do address sustainability issues, the editors felt that the field of sustainable development is now so large as to possibly justify a special issue all to itself. Instead, we present papers centred around three themes: the economics of pollution control, resource economics, and valuation.

With regard to pollution, the change in emphasis away from point sources to non-point sources was noted above. In their paper, Jim Shortle and Richard Horan summarise the main advances that have been made in this literature. They focus on both theoretical and empirical work, noting the extent to which these have been tied together. Non-point pollution poses very difficult problems to policy makers, due to reasons of imperfect information, spatial variability and the large number of potential polluters. Shortle and Horan explain how academic advances in this area have contributed to resolutions to these policy challenges.

A recent innovation in pollution control policy in the US and Europe has been the introduction of non-mandatory programmes. Conventional wisdom used to be that pollution control imposed private costs on firms in return for social benefits, so that firms could not be relied on to take voluntary action to reduce pollution. However, a growing theoretical literature now suggests a surprisingly wide range of cases where firms can be encouraged to cut emissions or otherwise improve the environmental performance of their activities, as Madhu Khanna explains. Empirical findings on factors motivating self-regulation are explored. Khanna surveys the non-mandatory approaches now in place world-wide, and reviews evidence on the performance of these schemes.

Climate change is one of the major environmental issues of our time. Under the yet-to-be ratified Kyoto Protocol, governments set themselves targets for reducing emissions of carbon dioxide, and two economic instruments likely to play some part in this effort are carbon taxes and carbon trading. A number of countries world-wide have recently introduced carbon or energy taxes (e.g. the UK Climate Change Levy, introduced this year), whilst carbon trading was effectively written into the Kyoto protocol. Paul Ekins and Terry Barker provide a comprehensive and critical review of the recent economic literature covering both of these instruments. The paper sets out the theoretical basis of both, with special reference to revenue-recycling and distributional impacts. Finally, the paper reviews the evidence on the likely costs of such schemes (and how cost predictions depend on modelling strategy), **and** on their environmental effectiveness.

The Kyoto Protocol is one example of an international environmental agreement (IEA), aimed at reducing an environmental public bad at the global scale. Many serious environmental problems have this global public bad nature, for instance, ozone depletion and biodiversity loss. Game theory tools have increasingly been applied to the study of IEAs, as the paper by Ulrich Wagner explains. Since the sovereignty of states precludes external enforcement, such agreements must be self-enforcing. Game theory models explain why rewards and punishments generally fail to achieve full co-operation (which is typically the pareto optimal outcome). Wagner reviews the types of provision which can enhance incentives for participation in IEAs, and the factors which influence their effectiveness.

Tropical rain forests are a vital part of the world's natural capital stock, yet they are being depleted at an alarming rate. Explaining why this is, and what to do about it, has become an important new focus for resource economists. Ed Barbier and Jo Burgess provide a comprehensive overview of this literature, including both empirical and theoretical explanations. They also report some new results on a cross-country comparison of depletion rates, which shows that agricultural expansion is the most important factor driving deforestation. Income effects are variable: in other words, an environmental 'Kuznets curve' for deforestation does not always seem to exist. What emerges is a country-specific vector of causes, amongst which institutional factors can be very important.

The final paper in this special issue is concerned with a very different topic: that of estimating monetary values for non-market environmental amenities. As mentioned above, this field of enquiry has grown very rapidly over the last 20 years. Amongst stated preference valuation methods, contingent valuation has dominated. Nick Hanley, Susana Mourato and Robert Wright outline an alternative approach to stated preference valuation, known as choice modelling. This has become well-established in the fields of market research and transport research, and since the mid 1990s has been used by environmental economists. Choice modelling defines environmental amenities in terms of their attributes, and seeks to estimate marginal values for these. The different types of choice models are explained, and their relative abilities assessed. An application to rock-climbing sites in Scotland is used for illustrative purposes. The paper concludes by asking whether choice modelling solves any of the 'big' problems with contingent valuation, and what challenges choice modellers still face.

The editors hope that you the reader find these papers stimulating. They represent a cross-section of 'frontiers' in environmental and resource economics. They also represent a cross-section of authors, from well-established scholars to rising talent, and show that ENRE enters the 21st century in good form, but with many challenges still to be met.

References

Crocker, T. (1999) A brief history of environmental and resource economics. In J. van den Bergh (ed.) *Handbook of environmental and natural resource economics*. Cheltenham: Edward Elgar.

Hanley, N. and Folmer, H. (1998) *Game Theory and the Environment*. Cheltenham: Edward Elgar.

Meadows, D., Meadows, D., Randers, J. and Behrens, W. (1972) *The Limits to Growth*. New York: Universe Books.

CHAPTER 2

THE ECONOMICS OF NONPOINT POLLUTION CONTROL

James S. Shortle

Pennsylvania State University

Richard D. Horan

Michigan State University

Abstract. A timely literature on the design of economic incentives for nonpoint pollution control has been emerging. We describe the nonpoint pollution control problem, some of the peculiar challenges it poses for policy design, and the policy-related contributions of the theoretical and empirical literature on the economics of nonpoint pollution.

Keywords. Nonpoint pollution; Environmental policy: Economic incentives

1. Introduction

The merits of alternative pollution control policy instruments has been a major topic in the environmental economics literature since the 1960s. The static efficiency advantages of economic incentives (especially emissions charges) over the 'command and control' approaches often selected in practice were described early on by Kneese and others, and economists have been singing the praises of economic instruments for pollution control ever since (Bohm and Russell, 1985; Russell and Powell, 1999). The growing interest in and use of economic instruments in the U.S., Europe, and elsewhere indicates that the case has had some impact (Hahn, 2000; Opschoor *et al.*, 1994; U.S. EPA, 2001). But how robust are the underlying theory and results?

The literature on pollution control instruments is largely focused on the design and performance of emissions-based instruments (e.g. emissions charges, emissions standards, emission trading) (Russell and Powell, 1999). This focus reflects the conclusion that emissions are the preferred base for the application of economic incentives when pollution sources can be identified and their emissions metered with a reasonable degree of accuracy at a reasonable cost, and when the emissions do not have a significant stochastic component (Beavis and Walker, 1983; Oates, 1995). These conditions are reasonably well satisfied by the conventional point sources of pollution, but are uncharacteristic of nonpoint sources.

Point sources of pollution, exemplified by large industrial facilities or sewage treatment plants, are those that emit pollutants into the environment from a fixed and readily identifiable point, such as an outfall or pipe. Emissions from nonpoint sources are, in contrast, diffuse. They are exemplified by emissions from mobile sources, leaching and runoff of pollutants from farm fields, and runoff from parking lots or streets. The diffuse nature of nonpoint emissions makes routine observation and accurate metering of them (given current monitoring technology) prohibitively costly. In consequence, emissions-based instruments are not appropriate for the nonpoint problem (Griffin and Bromley, 1982; Segerson, 1988; Shortle and Dunn, 1986).

Growing recognition of the importance of nonpoint pollution problems in the U.S. and Europe has stimulated economic interest in the design of environmental policy instruments for nonpoint sources.[1] Our goals here are to describe the nonpoint pollution control problem, some of the challenges it poses for policy design, and the policy-related contributions of the theoretical and empirical literature on the economics of nonpoint pollution. Our treatment of these issues mirrors the focus of current applied research and policy in that we emphasize nonpoint water pollution. Examples of nonpoint sources of water pollution include agriculture, urban areas, mines, forests, and deposition of atmospheric pollutants. The importance of different sources varies from location to location, but problems related to agricultural and urban sources are pervasive, and a major focus of nonpoint policy development.

2. The nonpoint pollution management problem

The economics literature on nonpoint pollution control instruments has largely been concerned with three broad questions. One is who, among the set of suspected nonpoint polluters, to target. That nonpoint emissions are unobservable leads to uncertainty about the contributions of individual nonpoint sources. This uncertainty can be profound when the number of nonpoint candidates is large. A second question is the optimal basis for defining and measuring compliance with environmental regulations. Specifically, given that emissions-based instruments are not optimal, then what compliance measures ought to be used instead? The third question is how best to induce changes in production and pollution control practices to achieve environmental quality objectives given a particular choice or mix of compliance measures. The menu for this question includes the usual fare, including (1) education programs (moral suasion and technical assistance), (2) research and development programs to create environmentally friendly and profitable innovations, (3) direct regulations, and (4) economic incentives. Major options in the latter category are taxes or liability for damages to discourage environmentally harmful activities, subsidies to encourage pro-environment behaviors, tradeable permits to ration environmentally harmful activities, and contracts in which environmental authorities purchase specified pro-environmental actions.

With respect to the question of who to target, it seems obvious enough that instruments ought to be directed at those who are directly responsible for nonpoint emissions. Within this set, concern for monitoring, enforcement, and pollution control costs would suggest focusing control efforts based on contributions to ambient pollution concentrations, and abatement costs. Unobservable nonpoint emissions and the large number of small contributors typical of nonpoint problems result in a significant moral hazard problem that complicates targeting polluters based on their contributions. Expanding the set of those who must comply with pollution controls increases public monitoring and enforcement costs, and increases the chances of regulating agents who cause little or no problem, thus increasing compliance costs without increasing benefits. Yet failure to target broadly enough diminishes effectiveness and limits opportunities for cost-effective allocations. The efficiency gains from careful targeting are a major focus of empirical research on nonpoint pollution control.

It is important to note that answers to the 'who to target' question need not be limited to the actual source of emissions. Agriculture and transport emissions are examples. Environmental impacts of pesticides are managed in large part by regulations limiting the pesticides that chemical manufacturers can market to farmers and other users. Similarly, mobile source emissions in developed countries are managed in large degree through regulations of vehicle manufactures. In both cases, regulation of a comparatively small number of chemical manufacturers or vehicle manufactures is easier politically and administratively than regulation of the many households and small businesses that actually cause environmental harm.

With respect to what to target, economically and ecologically desirable candidates for compliance bases will be more or less (1) correlated with environmental conditions, (2) enforceable, and (3) targetable in time and space (Braden and Segerson, 1993). The nonpoint literature has focused on three basic options. One option is emissions proxies (e.g. estimates of field losses of fertilizer residuals to surface or ground waters) or other site-specific environmental performance indicators that are constructed from observations of site-specific data. Such indicators are often available, and can vary form formulae that aggregate over a few variables to data intensive and computationally demanding computer models (Novotny and Olem, 1994). Examples of performance indicators for agriculture are annual average gross soil loss, for managing sediment pollution, and the excess of nutrient inputs to crop and/or livestock production over the nutrients contained in farm products, for managing nutrient pollution (National Research Council, 1993). Another option for bases that has received significant attention is inputs or practices that are correlated with pollution flows. In agricultural nonpoint pollution control, for example, these would include polluting inputs such as fertilizers and pesticides, and farming practices that affect the movement of these chemicals into the environment. The third option that has received considerable interest from economists is the ambient concentrations of pollutants in environmental media.

The alternative mechanisms can be combined with alternative compliance measures to define a range of instruments for nonpoint pollution control.

Examples are presented in Table 1. The listing emphasizes policy mechanisms that have received significant attention in the economics literature and which we describe in this paper. Education programs have been implemented in many locations for encouraging and facilitating the adoption of environmentally friendly practices (e.g. OECD, 1998; Coburn, 1994). There are many examples of

Table 1. Nonpoint pollution control instruments.

Mechanism	Compliance Measure		
	Inputs/Practices	Emissions proxies	Ambient concentrations
Taxes/Subsidies	Charges on fertilizer or pesticide purchases	Charges on modeled nutrient loadings	Ambient taxes
	Changes on manure applications	Charges on nutrient applications in excess of crop needs	
	Cost-sharing or other subsidies for inputs or practices that reduce pollution	Charges on estimated net soil loss	
	Crop land retirement subsidies		
Standards	Pesticides registration	Restrictions on modeled nutrient loadings	
	Restrictions on fertilizer application rates	Regulations on nutrient applications in excess of crop needs	
	Mandatory use of pollution control practices		
Markets	Input trading	Estimated emissions trading	
Contracts/Bonds	Land retirement contracts		
	Contracts involving the adoption of conservation or nutrient management practices		
Liability rules	Negligence liability rules		Strict or negligence liability rules

Source: Horan and Shortle (forthcoming).

product and design standards. Pesticide registration is the principal method for protecting the environment, workers, and consumers from pesticide hazards in developed countries, and is used increasingly in developing countries (Dinham, 1993; OECD, 1986). Standards governing the amount and timing of manure applications, and restrictions on the numbers of farm animals are used to control ammonia, phosphorous, and nitrogen pollution from agriculture are found in the E.U. and U.S. (Hanley forthcoming; Ribaudo forthcoming). Architectural standards are used to control urban runoff. Economic incentives applied to inputs and practices are also a dimension of nonpoint water pollution control programs. Subsidies for adoption of pollution control practices in agriculture and some other sectors are found in many countries as are charges emissions proxies and the use of polluting inputs (e.g. pesticides and fertilizers) (OECD, 2001; U.S. EPA, 2001; Hanley forthcoming; Ribaudo forthcoming). Dutch livestock producers are assessed charges based on surplus phosphates from manure (Hanley forthcoming). The City of Denver in the U.S. state of Colorado levies charges on owners of developed parcels of land based on the impervious surface area. The purposes of such levies is often to raise revenues for pollution control and other programs rather than to directly discourage environmentally harmful activities (OECD, 1994, 1999). Contracts, under which producers agree to implement a negotiated set of practices, including converting crop land to less environmentally harmful uses, for a specified time interval in return for payments, are used to control agricultural nonpoint pollution in the U.S. (USDA, 1997). Liability rules for protecting water quality from nonpoint pollution have drawn interest at both the U.S. state and federal levels (ELI, 1997; Ribaudo forthcoming). Pollution trading, in which individual sources of pollution are provided with limited rights to pollute and allowed to trade these rights in markets, is drawing significant interest as means for agricultural nonpoint pollution control in the U.S., with a number of pilot programs underway or on the drawing boards (Horan forthcoming).

3. A model of nonpoint pollution

A formal model of nonpoint pollution is useful for highlighting differences between the archtype point source pollution problem and the nonpoint problem, and for providing a framework for illustrating developments in the literature. Our model (which is drawn from Shortle and Abler, 1997), and most of the economic research on nonpoint pollution, is static. There are, however, a few important studies that look at dynamic issues, most notably Dosi and Morretto (1993, 1994), and Xepapadeas (1992). See Tomasi et al. (1994) for an especially comprehensive treatment.

Consider a watershed in which emissions from both point and nonpoint sources contribute to water quality impairments. Emissions by the kth point source ($k = 1, ..., s$) are denoted e_k, and these emissions are taken to be nonstochastic and observable at minimal cost without error.[2] In contrast, nonpoint source emissions are stochastic and cannot be measured directly at an acceptable cost.

Nonpoint firms can only control the distribution of probable emissions outcomes through their production and pollution control choices. Accordingly, modeling nonpoint pollution management requires attention to the underlying production and pollution control decisions. For this purpose, we assume the existence of a physical model of the relationship between nonpoint emissions and polluters' choices.[3] Polluting emissions from the ith nonpoint source ($i = 1, ..., n$) are given by $r_i = r_i(x_i, \alpha_i, \nu_i, \theta_i)$, where r_i is nonpoint emissions, x_i is a $(1 \times m)$ vector of production and pollution control choices (inputs), α_i represents site characteristics (e.g. soil type and topography), ν_i represents stochastic environmental variables (e.g. rainfall) that affect nonpoint emissions, and θ_i represents parameters of pollution processes for site i.

By our assumption that nonpoint emissions cannot be directly measured, we mean that the r_i cannot be observed directly. An indirect method of observation would involve plugging observations of polluters' choices and the environmental drivers into the nonpoint emissions function. If perfect forecasts could be obtained from this approach, then emissions-based instruments would be available. However, perfect forecasts are not possible under the current state of the art.

Ambient pollution concentrations are a function of point and nonpoint emissions, natural background levels of the pollutant, ζ, watershed characteristics, ψ, fate and transport parameters, φ, and stochastic environmental variables, δ, i.e., $a = a(r_1, ..., r_n, e_1, ..., e_s, \zeta, \psi, \delta, \vartheta)$ $(\partial a/\partial r_i \geqslant 0 \ \forall i, \partial a/\partial e_k \geqslant 0 \ \forall k)$. We refer to the relation $a(\bullet)$ as the fate and transport function.

Polluters are assumed to be risk-neutral, profit maximizers, and to have no collective influence on the prices of inputs or outputs. The change in producers' quasi-rents (profits less fixed costs) is then an appropriate measure of the costs of pollution controls (Just *et al.*, 1982). Denote the ith nonpoint source's expected profit for any choice of inputs by $\pi_{Ni}(x_i)$. This function can be thought of as a restricted profit function where the restrictions apply to inputs affecting nonpoint emissions (Shortle and Abler, 1997). Similarly, point source profits, restricted on emissions, are denoted $\pi_{Pk}(e_k)$. The social cost of pollution, D, is an increasing, convex function of the ambient pollution concentration and economic parameters, ς, i.e. $D = D(a, \varsigma)(\partial D/\partial a > 0, \partial^2 D/\partial a^2 \geqslant 0)$.

Expected net benefit maximization

Given these specifications, an (ex ante) efficient allocation of resources for production and pollution control activities is the solution to the following problem:

$$\underset{x_{ij}, e_k}{\text{Max}} \ NB = \sum_{i=1}^{n} \pi_{Ni}(x_i) + \sum_{k=1}^{s} \pi_{Pk}(e_k) - E\{D(a, \varsigma)\} \tag{1}$$

where E is the expectations operator over all stochastic variables. With appropriate continuity and convexity assumptions, first order necessary conditions for the ex ante efficient or *first-best* allocation are

$$\frac{\partial \pi_{Ni}}{\partial x_{ij}} = E \left\{ \frac{\partial D}{\partial a} \frac{\partial a}{\partial r_i} \frac{\partial r_i}{\partial x_{ij}} \right\} \quad \forall i, j \tag{2}$$

$$\frac{\partial \pi_{Pk}}{\partial e_k} = E \left\{ \frac{\partial D}{\partial a} \frac{\partial a}{\partial e_k} \right\} \quad \forall k \tag{3}$$

The point source condition (3) requires that the marginal cost of emissions reductions (i.e. the forgone quasi-rents due to emissions abatement) equal the expected marginal benefit (i.e. the reduction in pollution damage costs). If the emissions from point sources are uniformly mixed (i.e. $\partial a / \partial e_k = \partial a / \partial e_l \ \forall k \neq l$), condition (3) would reduce to familiar 'equi-marginal' principle (Hanley *et al.*, 1997; Baumol and Oates, 1988). The nonpoint conditions (2) take a very different form in that they involve comparisons of the expected marginal costs and benefits of underlying production and pollution control decisions.

Conditions (2) and (3) pertain to the choice of practices and emissions by point and nonpoint sources. An efficient allocation of control efforts requires not only that those who are producing in given locations make optimal choices, but also that the number and location of producers is optimal (Baumol and Oates, 1988). For sake of brevity, we do not present these conditions here, although they can be found elsewhere (Shortle *et al.*, 1998; Horan *et al.*, 1998). Conditions (2)–(3), along with appropriate entry/exit conditions, characterize the point and nonpoint polluter behaviors that reduce pollution problems with maximum performance. We denote the first-best solution by $x_{ij}^* \forall i, j, n^*, e_k^* \forall k$ and s^*.

Cost-effectiveness

Given limited data on the costs of environmental degradation, and limited political acceptance of benefit-cost analysis for determining environmental goals (Hanley *et al.*, 1997; Hahn, 2000), an alternative and widely used criterion for assessing pollution control allocations is to minimize the social cost (exclusive of damages) of achieving a pre-specified environmental objective (Baumol and Oates, 1988). Useful notions of cost-effectiveness must consider the variability of nonpoint loadings (Braden *et al.*, 1991; Braden and Segerson, 1993; Milon, 1987; Shortle, 1987; Segerson, 1988; McSweeny and Shortle, 1990; Byström *et al.*, 1998, 2000). There are several possibilities. The simplest is a combination of point and nonpoint pollution control efforts that minimizes costs subject to an upper bound on the expected ambient concentration. For instance, if the ambient target is a_0, then the proposed allocation minimizes costs (maximizes expected profits) subject to $E\{a(\cdot)\} \leq a_0$. Much of the empirical literature on cost-effective nonpoint pollution control takes this mean-based approach. However, the resulting allocation may have undesirable properties because it does not explicitly constrain the variation in ambient pollution (Shortle, 1990). If the damage cost function is linear in the ambient concentration, then expected damages are as well. A given mean concentration will then imply a given expected damage cost. If, however, damages are nonlinear, then expected damages will depend on moments of the distribution of the ambient concentration in addition to the mean. Accordingly, gains from reductions in average ambient concentrations could be offset by losses due increased variability.

An approach that addresses this issue uses probabilistic constraints of the form $\text{Prob}(a \geqslant a_0) = \Phi(a) \leqslant \alpha(0 < \alpha < 1)$. This 'safety-first' approach has received attention in economic research on pollution control when ambient concentrations are stochastic and is consistent with regulatory approaches to drinking water quality and other types of environmental protection (Beavis and Walker, 1983; Lichtenberg and Zilberman, 1988; Lichtenberg et al., 1989). Studies show that least-cost allocations and control costs for achieving probabilistic standards can be much different than those obtained for simple bounds on expected concentrations (Milon, 1987; McSweeny and Shortle, 1990; Byström et al., 1998, 2000; Shortle et al., 1999; Horan et al., 2001). We will discuss this issue in greater detail in the section on pollution trading.

The economically most interesting cost-effectiveness concept when a is stochastic is an upper bound on expected damage costs (provided the damage function is known). Only in this case will allocations that achieve the target at least cost be unambiguously more efficient than allocations that achieve the target at higher cost (Shortle, 1990; Horan, 2001).

Nonpoint pollution control instruments

The theory of environmental policy has largely addressed the design of instruments that can satisfy condition (3). In the following sections we discuss various instruments intended to satisfy the nonpoint condition (2), or both the point and nonpoint conditions, (2) and (3). The former include instruments that substitute firm level emissions proxies for metered emissions, and instruments that target firms' choices of inputs or practices. The latter include ambient based instruments, and various types of point-nonpoint trading schemes. We address these options beginning with a look at the theoretical contributions on instrument design and then turning to empirical research.

4. Emissions proxies

In a pioneering study on the economics of nonpoint pollution control, Griffin and Bromley (1982) examined economic incentives and regulatory standards applied either to polluters' production and pollution control practices or to nonpoint emissions estimates constructed from observations of these choices. The estimates are obtained by plugging observations of input choices into the nonpoint emissions functions that we assumed in the previous section, and can be thought of as hydrologic models that simulate or estimate pollution loads from agricultural, forest, urban or other land uses given characteristics of the land resources, climate, land uses, and production and pollution control practices. Griffin and Bromley described the construction of taxes and standards for the emissions estimate that could produce the first-best outcome. Essential for their results, however, is that the estimate is a perfect substitute for measured emissions (i.e. there is no forecasting error), and that emissions are not stochastic (i.e. they assume the parameters of the nonpoint emissions functions are known and that there are no stochastic processes).

Building on Griffin and Bromley's work, Shortle and Dunn (1986) examined the same types of instruments under the more realistic assumptions that physical models do not eliminate uncertainty about nonpoint loads. They demonstrated that the first-best allocation could not be obtained using a tax on an unbiased emissions estimator except under highly restrictive conditions. A deeper understanding of the importance of properly characterizing polluters' choices and their impacts on environmental risks when modeling and analyzing nonpoint instruments can be had by examining this argument further.

Let t_i denote a firm-specific tax rate applied to the estimated emissions from the ith site. The environmental agency announces the relationship $E\{r_i\}$ (where E represents the agency's expectations operator) so that polluters can understand how to compute their tax liability. After-tax profit is given by $\pi_{Ni}(x_i) - t_i E\{r_i\}$. The first order necessary conditions for input use are (for an interior solution),

$$\frac{\partial \pi_{Ni}}{\partial x_{ij}} - t_i E \left\{ \frac{\partial r_i}{\partial x_{ij}} \right\} = 0 \quad \forall i, j \qquad (4)$$

Comparison of condition (4) to condition (2) implies that the following condition (after some manipulation) must hold to obtain the least-cost allocation:

$$t_i = \frac{E \left\{ \dfrac{\partial D^*}{\partial a} \dfrac{\partial a^*}{\partial r_i} \dfrac{\partial r_i^*}{\partial x_{ij}} \right\}}{E \left\{ \dfrac{\partial r_i^*}{\partial x_{ij}} \right\}} = E \left\{ \frac{\partial D^*}{\partial a} \frac{\partial a^*}{\partial r_i} \right\} + \frac{\text{cov} \left\{ \dfrac{\partial D^*}{\partial a} \dfrac{\partial a^*}{\partial r_i}, \dfrac{\partial r_i^*}{\partial x_{ij}} \right\}}{E \left\{ \dfrac{\partial r_i^*}{\partial x_{ij}} \right\}} \quad \forall i, j \quad (5)$$

In general, equation (5) is overdetermined as the tax rate t_i is determined by m equations. Accordingly, if $m > 1$, there will not, in general, exist a t_i that will satisfy all m equations in (5) The intuition here is straightforward. A charge on estimated emissions only provides polluters an incentive to control mean emissions levels. However, choices that cost-effectively reduce $E\{r_i\}$ do not necessarily reduce $E\{D\}$ cost-effectively when D is nonlinear (Shortle and Dunn, 1986; Shortle, 1990). Only when a single input influences emissions (i.e. $m = 1$) or when the covariance between marginal damages and marginal emissions, $\text{cov}\{(\partial D^*/\partial a)(\partial a^*/\partial r_i), \partial r_i^*/\partial x_{ij}\}$, is zero for each input for each firm (e.g. when $D = \sum E\{r_i\}$) do the choices that cost-effectively reduce mean emissions also cost-effectively reduce expected damages (Horan et al., 1998).

This result on the inefficiency of taxes on estimated emissions applies to other mechanisms, such as contracts, regulations, and also pollution trading markets, that measure performance and compliance in terms of estimated or mean emissions.[4] While there is no direct research on the matter, it is clear that achieving a first best solution using incentives applied to firm-level environmental indicators would require the use of a suite of indicators composed of the mean, variance, and other relevant moments of a firm's impacts on ambient conditions.

A second best-incentive for estimated emissions

Although they cannot be used to bring about a first-best outcome, incentives applied to emission proxies and other firm-level environmental performance indicators are not without economic merit, and are of considerable real world interest. An optimal, but necessarily second-best, charge on a nonpoint emissions proxy would maximize social expected net benefits subject to firm responses to the tax. Unless nonpoint firms are identical in terms of cost structure, the relations characterizing emissions, and marginal ambient impacts of emissions, then the resulting rates would necessarily be firm-specific. For simplicity, let us assume identical nonpoint firms. Then the nonpoint charge will be uniform across sources and, dropping the subscript i, can be expressed as:

$$
t_r^* = \frac{\sum_{j=1}^{m}\left[E\left\{\dfrac{\partial D^*}{\partial a}\right\}E\left\{\dfrac{\partial a^*}{\partial r}\right\}E\left\{\dfrac{\partial r^*}{\partial x_j}\right\} + \text{cov}\left\{\dfrac{\partial D^*}{\partial a},\dfrac{\partial a^*}{\partial r}\right\}E\left\{\dfrac{\partial r^*}{\partial x_j}\right\} + \text{cov}\left\{\dfrac{\partial D^*}{\partial a}\dfrac{\partial a^*}{\partial r},\dfrac{\partial r^*}{\partial x_j}\right\}\right]\kappa_j^*}{\sum_{j=1}^{m} E\left\{\dfrac{\partial r^*}{\partial x_j}\right\}\kappa_j^*}
\tag{6}
$$

where $\kappa_j^* = (\partial x_j^*/\partial t_r)/(\sum_{j=1}^{m}\partial x_j^*/\partial t_r)$ and r_i^* and a^* are functions of e_k^* and x_{ij}^*, which are the solutions to the second-best problem described above given this particular type of tax. Interpreting κ_j as a weight (since $\sum_{j=1}^{m}\kappa_j = 1$), the numerator of the expression for t_r^* is the expected marginal social cost of input use, averaged across all inputs. The denominator is the expected marginal contribution of input use in emissions production, averaged across all inputs. The second-best tax, t_r^*, does not give firms incentives to adjust their input choices to reflect differences in their environmental risk-effects. The risk-effects are represented by the covariance terms on the RHS of (6). Where damages are convex in a, the covariance term $\text{cov}\{\partial D^*/\partial a, \partial a^*/\partial r\}$ is of the same sign as $\partial \text{Var}(a^*)/\partial r$.[5] Thus, if increased loadings increase the variance of ambient pollution and hence damages, then average risk is increased and t_r^* is larger, other things equal. Similarly, if damages are convex in loadings, then the covariance term $\text{cov}\{(\partial D^*/\partial a)(\partial a^*/\partial r), \partial r^*/\partial x_j\}$ is of the same sign as $\partial \text{Var}(r^*)/\partial x_j$. Thus, if increased input use increases the variance of nonpoint emissions and hence damages (on average across inputs), then average risk is increased and t_r^* is larger, other things equal.[6]

How does the second-best nonpoint 'emissions' charge compare to a 'Pigouvian' charge on point source emissions?[7] Assuming as above that emissions from each point source have identical marginal ambient impacts, then the optimal tax on point source emissions is uniform across sources and of the form

$$t_e = E\left\{\frac{\partial D^*}{\partial a}\right\} E\left\{\frac{\partial a^*}{\partial e}\right\} + \text{cov}\left\{\frac{\partial D^*}{\partial a}, \frac{\partial a^*}{\partial e}\right\} \qquad (7)$$

Risk is represented by the covariance terms on the RHS of (7), which is of the same sign as $\partial \text{Var}\{a^*\}/\partial e$ when D is convex in a. In the absence of any risk-effects, the taxes in (6) and (7) differ only according to marginal ambient impacts of point sources relative to nonpoint sources. The source with the greatest contribution at the margin optimally faces a larger tax. When risk-effects are introduced, however, the relative magnitudes become less clear as both mean and variance components are important. Thus, a source having a greater expected marginal contribution could face a lower tax if the risk-effects of the other source are significant. The comparisons become even more complex when sources have different marginal ambient impacts. These issues emerge again in our discussion of point/nonpoint trading.

5. Inputs and practices

Economists have long recognized input-based instruments as possible substitutes for direct taxes on negative externalities (see e.g. Plott, 1966; Holtermann, 1976; Common, 1977). There is considerable evidence that input-based incentives could be effective in bringing changes in resource allocation. Agricultural firms, for example, respond to changes in the costs of inputs, increasing the use of those that become relatively cheap, while conserving on those that become relatively expensive (Shumway, 1995). In the long run, input price responsiveness is even greater, as technologies are developed and adopted to further conserve on more expensive inputs and expand the use of those that are cheaper (Hayami and Ruttan, 1985). Thus policy makers, if they are willing to use taxes or subsidies at levels that will have an impact, can expect results from input-based incentives. The challenge is designing input-based incentives that achieve environmental goals at reasonable cost.

Griffin and Bromley (1982) described the design of input-based nonpoint pollution control instruments using information contained in the nonpoint production functions on the relationships between production choices and emissions. They demonstrated that taxing inputs that increase a nonpoint externality and subsidizing inputs that reduce it could replicate the results of a tax on the externality. Similar results for nonstochastic nonpoint externalities are obtained by Stevens (1988) and Dinar *et al.* (1989). Shortle and Abler (1994) and Shortle *et al.* (1998) extend Griffin and Bromley's work to examine the design of input tax/subsidy schemes with stochastic and imperfectly estimated emissions. Both demonstrate that the first-best solution can be obtained by this approach.

A formal look at an optimal tax/subsidy structure is a useful starting point for understanding the significant real-world challenges in designing an input tax/subsidy scheme that could fulfill the theoretical promise. Let the tax rate on input j of firm i be τ_{ij} so that expected after-tax profit is $\pi_{Ni}(x_i) - \sum_{j=1}^{m} \tau_{ij}x_{ij}$. Given that producers choose inputs to maximize after-tax profits, the optimal marginal input tax rates (after some manipulation) are

$$\tau_{ij} = E\left\{\frac{\partial D^*}{\partial a}\right\} E\left\{\frac{\partial a^*}{\partial r_i}\right\} E\left\{\frac{\partial r_i^*}{\partial x_{ij}}\right\} + E\left\{\frac{\partial D^*}{\partial a}\right\} \text{cov}\left\{\frac{\partial a^*}{\partial r_i} \frac{\partial r_i^*}{\partial x_{ij}}\right\}$$

$$+ \text{cov}\left\{\frac{\partial D^*}{\partial a}, \frac{\partial a^*}{\partial r_i} \frac{\partial r_i^*}{\partial x_{ij}}\right\} \quad \forall i, j \tag{8}$$

The optimal tax rate for input j for firm i equals expected marginal damages, times the expected marginal increase in ambient pollution levels from firm i's emissions, times the expected increase in emissions from increased use of input j at the margin, plus two covariance terms that act as risk premiums or rewards, depending on the signs. The tax rate may be positive or negative depending on the signs and relative magnitudes of the three RHS terms in equation (8). The sign of the first RHS term will be positive for pollution-increasing inputs and negative for pollution-decreasing inputs. The signs of the risk terms are ambiguous without further specification. If a is convex (concave) in emissions, then the first covariance term is of the same (opposite) sign as $\partial \text{Var}(r_i^*)/\partial x_{ij}$. Thus, when a is convex (concave), risk and hence τ_{ij} are increased (decreased) when an increase in the use of the input increases the variance of emissions. Similarly, when $\partial D/\partial a > 0$, risk and hence τ_{ij} are increased when an increase in the use of the input increases the variance of a.

The tax/subsidy scheme described above is designed to only satisfy condition (2). There is no guarantee that the set of producers and locations will be cost-effective. It is therefore necessary to use additional instruments that are designed to influence entry and exit without distorting input choices. One such instrument is a lump sum tax/subsidy charged to extra-marginal producers, should they decide to produce. The design of the lump sum charge is described in Shortle *et al.* (1998).

Information issues in the design of input-based instruments

Analogous to Pigouvian emission charges, the input tax/subsidy in (8) is a nice theoretical prescription for obtaining the first-best allocation, but unrealistic. The scheme is exceptionally information intensive and complex (from the regulatory agency's perspective) in that all choices that affect environmental outcomes are subject to incentives, with the tax/subsidy rates being firm-specific to reflect the differential environmental impacts of inputs on polluting emissions, and pollution emissions on ambient environmental conditions from one location to another. While purchases of potentially harmful inputs or investments in pollution control structures can be easily tracked in some instances, many management decisions having a large impact on the environment can be very costly to monitor (Braden and Segerson, 1993). Also, firm-specific input-based incentives, beyond being inherently information intensive, could lead to significant enforcement problems because they would encourage 'under the table' input arbitrage between firms facing different rates (Helfand and House, 1995). In practice, uniform rates, at least within regions where such arbitrage could easily occur, would be required. Finally, the scheme is designed assuming that public planners know private control costs. The more likely case is asymmetric information.

Several questions arise at this point. One is how to address the moral hazard problem resulting from costly monitoring of production and pollution control practices. Some options include (individually or in combination) (A) modifying the tax/subsidy system to include incentives for accurate self-reporting of production and pollution control practices; (B) reducing the input tax/subsidy base to a subset of choices that are both relatively easy to observe and highly correlated with ambient impacts; and (C) shifting the basis for compliance monitoring from the many input choices of many individual nonpoint source firms to some more easily observed alternative. While the design of mechanisms for self-reporting compliance with emission standards has received considerable attention in the literature (e.g. Harford, 1987; Malik, 1993), there has been little attention to option (A) in the literature on input-based nonpoint pollution controls. An exception is Huang (1994) who examines a state-dependent penalty system for agricultural nonpoint sources. The second option is examined in a growing literature on the design of second-best input-based incentives. Because this literature is largely empirical, we defer a review of results to a later section. Included within the third option would be shifting compliance to (C1) the manufacturers of polluting products used by nonpoint sources, (C2) the collectively determined ambient concentration of pollutants, or (C3) the output of industries that are nonpoint sources. Option (C3) has been received some attention in the theoretical literature but is so crude that it garners little enthusiasm (see e.g. Braden and Segerson, 1993). Option (C1) has been an important method for dealing with nonpoint pollution problems. Examples are the use of pesticide registration to mitigate environmental and other risks associated with pesticides and vehicle emission standards imposed on manufacturers for reducing mobile source emissions. This option can have merit as part of a portfolio of instruments, but the tool is also so crude that economists continue to advocate the use of additional mechanisms that signal individual nonpoint sources (e.g. farmers, drivers) about the external costs of their choices (see e.g. Lichtenberg, 1992; Porter, 1999). Option (C2) is the subject of some important advances in the theory of nonpoint pollution control. We address the literature on ambient based instruments in the next section.

The question of how to deal with asymmetric information about pollution control costs in the design of input based instruments is addressed in several studies. Tomasi *et al.* (1994) divide information about nonpoint sources into two categories. One is a polluter's profit or control-cost type, pertaining to the returns to a firm from its production and pollution control choices, or equivalently, the costs to the firm from changes in resource allocation for pollution control. Typically, firms are assumed to have better information about their profit type than do government planners.[8] Following a common approach, our model can be easily modified to include asymmetric information about profit types. We rewrite nonpoint profits for firm i as $\pi_{Ni}(x_i, \varphi_i)$ where φ_i represents the firm's profit type. Similarly, we rewrite point source profits for firm k as $\pi_{ek}(e_k, \varphi_k)$ where φ_k represents the firm's profit type. Under asymmetric information about firm types, each firm knows its type parameter but government planners do not. Consequences of asymmetric information about profit types include *ex ante* uncertainty about how firms will respond to environmental instruments that allow firms some flexibility in how they comply, and about their compliance costs.

The second type of information is polluters' environmental types, pertaining to information about the impacts of a firm's choices on ambient concentrations. In the terms of our model, a firm's environmental type will depend on its nonpoint emissions function, and characteristics of the fate and transport function. The first determines the emissions that result, in combination with other variables, from a firm's choices of inputs, and the second determines the impacts of the firm's emissions on the ambient concentration. The various parameters of the those functions can be thought of as defining environmental types (i.e. for the nonpoint emissions functions, these parameters include. ζ, ψ, and ϑ; the parameters for fate and transport are α_i and θ_i). The costs of reducing ambient pollution from any particular source depends both on its control-cost and environmental type.

The performance of some instruments, such as the liability rules and ambient based instruments discussed in the next section, depend on firms' knowledge of their (and possibly others') environmental types. Other instruments, such as the input tax/subsidy schemes we have been discussing in this section, require no knowledge on the part of firms about their environmental types. While firms are reasonably assumed to know their profit types, they may have limited or no knowledge of their environmental types. There may be some bits of information relevant to defining environmental types that is private, but on the whole we expect environmental authorities because of their greater access to the engineering and scientific expertise required to define pollution types, to generally have greater knowledge about environmental types than the small businesses and households that are typical of nonpoint sources. Accordingly, instruments that require firms to know their types may be limited in their applicability to cases in which environmental relationships are fairly simple or to cases in which it is reasonable to expect that polluters can be trained. We will return to this issue below.

We emphasize relative knowledge about environmental types, because while environmental planners may have greater knowledge on the whole, there is still significant public uncertainty about environmental types. Like uncertainty about profit types, one result is *ex ante* uncertainty about the environmental outcomes of policy initiatives. Assuming environmental parameters such as α_i, θ_i, ζ, ψ, and ϑ are uncertain with a known joint probability density function and that firms and the regulatory agency have symmetric information about this distribution, then the instruments we have considered to this point are consistent with having been designed under the assumption that profit types are known, but that environmental types are not.

Similarly, with asymmetric information about profit types, environmental instruments can be designed based on the environmental authority's expectations about profit types. In this case, assuming no transactions costs from observing inputs and emissions, we can express the objective function as

$$
\text{Max } E\{NB\} = E\left\{ \sum_{i=1}^{n} \pi_{Ni}(x_i, \varphi_{Ni}) + \sum_{k=1}^{s} \pi_{Pk}(e_k, \varphi_{ek}) - D(a, \varsigma) \right\} \quad (9)
$$

where the expectation is formed using the joint density function for all uncertain variables, including profit and environmental types. For policies that do not exhaust firms' degrees of freedom in how they may respond, the input and emission quantities must be replaced by economic behavioral functions that include policy parameters (e.g. input tax rates) and firm profit types. This approach is exemplified in the literature on emissions-based instruments by research comparing the efficiency of emission charges and quantity controls under asymmetric information (e.g. Stavins, 1996; Weitzman, 1974), and Spence and Roberts (1976) work on the design of a mixed system of emissions charges, reductions subsidies, and tradeable permits. An extension of Weitzman's analysis to the nonpoint problem is Shortle's (1984) comparison of charges and quantity controls applied to noisy emissions proxies. An extension of the Roberts and Spence approach is Shortle and Abler's (1994) design of a mixed system of taxes, subsidies, and tradeable permits for polluting nonpoint source inputs.

Alternatively, environmental regulators can use mechanism design techniques to address the adverse selection problem. There is an growing literature on the use of nonlinear pricing rules and direct revelation mechanisms to design input-based incentives for nonpoint pollution control. Shortle and Dunn (1986) describe a nonlinear input tax/subsidy scheme that can obtain the first-best solution under asymmetric information about profit types in the limiting case of a single nonpoint polluter and zero transactions costs. In a model with multiple polluters, Shortle and Abler (1994) showed the first-best solution could be obtained using a Groves (1973) version of the Shortle and Dunn nonlinear input tax. Smith and Tomasi (1995) demonstrate that only second-best solutions are obtainable with direct revelation mechanisms when there are transactions costs related to the collection of tax revenues. The result clearly applies to cases in which there are multiple sources. Wu and Babcock (1995,1996) develop a contract to induce land-based nonpoint polluters to choose second-best input vectors for their land type. The contract requires the environmental agency to know the distribution of land types, and pays polluters based on the land area they put under contract. Their model assumes that land types define both environmental and profit types. Analogous to Smith and Tomasi, Wu and Babcock include the social costs of tax revenue collection, in this case for funds to pay to nonpoint polluters. Each of the above mentioned studies focuses on the adverse selection problem, and assumes that input choices can be observed costlessly. There is limited research on the design of input based instruments taking into account both moral hazard about one or more input choices and asymmetric information about profit types.

6. Ambient pollution taxes and liability rules

The approaches discussed above involve monitoring the inputs and practices of polluters who are suspected of contributing to environmental degradation. Segerson's (1988) pathbreaking study led researchers to explore an alternative approach that involves shifting monitoring from the choices of suspected polluters to the ambient concentration of pollutants in environmental media. The approach directly addresses the moral hazard problem. The regulatory agency only monitors ambient pollution concentrations and firms' tax payments. If ambient concentrations can be monitored with reasonable accuracy and at a lower cost than inputs, then the ambient tax offers a clear advantage in this regard. Furthermore, ambient instruments can provide a unified approach to the control of point and nonpoint sources, since both types can be regulated through the same mechanism (Hanley et al., 1997).

Segerson's ambient tax works as follows. Firm-specific taxes (subsidies) are charged (paid) when the ambient pollution concentration rises above (falls below) an exogenously determined target. The tax portion of this incentive can be written $t_i a + k_i$ where t_i is the ambient tax rate for firm i and k_i denotes a firm-specific lump sum tax or subsidy. Assuming expected profit maximization, firm i will choose its inputs to maximize after-tax profits, $V_i = \pi_{Ni}(x_i) - E_i\{t_i a\} - k_i$ where E_i represents the firm's expectations operator over all uncertain and stochastic variables. As above, firms may have uncertainties about how their choices affect environmental processes (i.e. their environmental types). In addition, since each firm's tax depends on the environmental impacts of other firms' choices, the expectations operator is also defined over the ambient impacts of other firms' choices (Horan et al., 1999; Cabe and Herriges, 1992). In general, E_i may differ from $E_j \, \forall \, j \neq i$ and also from the government's expectations as denoted by E (e.g. as in conditions (2) and (3)).

Assuming that firms believe that the input choices of others are independent of their own decisions (Nash conjectures), then firm i's profit maximizing conditions for input use in an interior solution are

$$\frac{\partial \pi_{Ni}}{\partial x_{ij}} = E_i \left\{ t_i \frac{\partial a_i}{\partial x_{ij}} \right\} \quad \forall i, j$$

Thus, each firm equates its marginal profits from the use of an input to the expected marginal impact the input will have on the firm's tax. The first-best tax is determined by equating the RHS of (10) with the RHS of (2). For the special case in which $E_i = E$ $\forall i$ and $m = 1$, the optimal tax rate is firm-specific and of the form $t_i = E\{(\partial D^*/\partial a)(\partial a^*/\partial x_{il})\}/E\{\partial a^*/\partial x_{il}\}$ $\forall i$ (Segerson 1988). Implementation of this tax will yield the first-best outcome as a Nash equilibrium given that the profit, nonpoint emissions, and fate and transport functions, and other essential information are common knowledge. The tax rate t_i is state-independent because it does not depend on the realized values of random variables — it is defined as an expectation over all possible values. However, when $E_i = E$ $\forall i$ and $m > 1$, it can be shown that a state-independent tax rate cannot be first-best (Horan et al., 1998), for the same reasons that a tax on estimated nonpoint emissions cannot be first-best. An alternative that can bring about an efficient outcome is a linear state-dependent tax rate of the form $t = \partial D^*/\partial a$, which is applied uniformly across firms (Horan et al., 1998). Note this rate is not defined in terms of an expected value as is the rate defined above. Thus, the realized values of the stochastic variables will influence t, and so t is a random variable when firms make their decisions. Accordingly, the tax they face is $E\{ta\}$ as opposed to $tE\{a\}$. Another alternative that can bring about efficiency is a nonlinear tax of the form $E\{D(a)\}$ (i.e. each person pays total damages) (Horan et al., 1998; Hansen, 1998).[9]

The discussion above is based on the assumption that $E_i = E$ $\forall i$. This turns out to be an important assumption. Because an ambient tax penalizes or reward firms according to their collective performance, a polluter's response to an ambient tax will depend on its own expectations about the impact of its choices, the choices of others, and natural events on ambient conditions. In other words, it will depend on the polluter's conjectures about its own environmental type and about the profit and environmental types of all other firms. This makes polluters' expectations (or conjectural variations) about other polluters' behavior, and the regulator's knowledge of these expectations, critical to the actual design and performance of ambient based instruments. Thus, the regulator's information requirements are not necessarily reduced relative to input-based instruments. Moreover, polluters' information requirements are not trivial and are much greater than under an input-based instrument. Given that the typical polluter has limited technical information and capacity in this area, it is not obvious that this information burden makes good economic sense.

Cabe and Herriges (1992) and Horan et al. (1999) explore the consequences of asymmetric prior information about profit types and environmental types. If $E_i \neq E$, and $E_i \neq E_j$ $\forall i \neq j$, then incentives designed on the assumption that they are the same will not have the desired properties. For instance, a polluter may perceive no impact of its choices on pollution. In this case, an ambient tax may have either no impact, or it will result in a decision to escape the tax entirely by ending the suspect activity. The regulator has a choice between adjusting the incentives for the mismatch, educating the polluter, or a combination of both. The data collection and program design issues involved in systematically measuring mismatches, developing educational programs that would effectively close them, and adjusting incentives for their effects could be enormous.

Segerson's ambient tax has inspired several intriguing extensions. One extension that aims to eliminate the moral hazard problem is a system of subsidies and random fines developed by Xepapadeas (1991). The incentive system works as follows. The regulatory agency monitors ambient pollution levels. If ambient pollution becomes larger than a pre-determined target level, then one polluter is chosen at random and fined. Meanwhile, the other producers receive a portion of the fine minus the damages to society. Herriges *et al.* (1994) illustrates that such an incentive system could be effective at increasing the expected costs of shirking if polluters are sufficiently risk-averse.

In some cases, observed ambient conditions may be more a function of past choices than contemporary actions. For instance, nitrates and pesticides may take years to move from fields to wells (Kim *et al.*, 1993). Accordingly, contemporary changes in ambient conditions may bear little relationship to current behavior. The challenge of designing ambient taxes when ambient condition is a stock that evolves in response to emissions and stochastic shocks is examined by Xepapadeas (1992).

The feasibility of ambient instruments is clearly limited by the feasibility and costs of monitoring. Monitoring ambient conditions can be highly costly and subject to considerable error. This is illustrated by the uncertainty that exists about ground water quality in many areas. There may also be political limitations (Shortle and Abler, 1997; Xepapadeas, 1999). In particular, individuals who take costly actions to improve their environmental performance could find themselves subject to larger rather than smaller penalties due to environmental shirking on the part of others, natural variations in pollution contributions from natural sources, or stochastic variations in weather. Conversely, individuals who behave badly may end up being rewarded by the good actions of their neighbors or nature.

These and other considerations lead Weersink *et al.* (1998), in the case of agricultural nonpoint water pollution, to suggest that ambient taxes may be best suited to managing environmental problems in small watersheds in which agriculture is the only source, farms are relatively homogeneous, water quality is readily monitored, and there are short time lags between polluting activities and their water quality impacts. We would add in addition, especially until there is significant real or experimental evidence on how individuals respond to ambient incentives, that the scope of environmental problems should be limited. The theory has been developed for a single pollutant, and asks for fairly complex decisions in response to expectations about the pollutant. With multiple pollutants, particularly if they interact, the decision environment would be much more complex.

Liability rules

Closely related to the concept of an ambient tax is a joint and several liability rule (Miceli and Segerson, 1991). Under such a rule, polluters can be sued for the total amount of damages incurred, even if the polluter was one of many contributors. Any polluter who is found liable would then have the right to sue other polluters for their contributions.

Liability rules create incentives that are similar to the ones created by an ambient tax (since the decision to sue will depend on the level of environmental quality). However, liability rules differ from traditional ambient-based incentives in several respects. First, they are only imposed if a suit is privately or publicly initiated, and if a court of law rules in favor of the damaged parties. Thus, firms have added uncertainty about whether or not they will be successfully sued for damages, which could limit the effectiveness of this approach. For instance, the dispersion of harm and the inability to identify sources and prove responsibility could make the probability of a producer being sued and held liable very small under strict liability rules (Braden and Segerson, 1993). A negligence rule in which liability is based on compliance with 'accepted management practices' may be more appropriate in these cases. Under such a rule, a producer would liable unless she was not in compliance with acceptable practices. Finally, an important drawback of heavy reliance on liability rules is that the litigation process for liability may be expensive relative to other regulatory methods. This expense may prevent individuals from attempting to claim damages, letting polluters go unregulated (Shavell, 1987).

Due to these considerations, liability rules are not likely to be first-best, and are probably best suited for the control of pollution related to the use of hazardous materials, or for non-frequent occurrences such as accidental chemical spills (Lichtenberg, 1992; Menell, 1991; Wetzstein and Centner, 1992). Liability may also be beneficial when used in conjunction with other instruments, as we discuss in a separate section below.

7. Point-nonpoint trading

The approaches that we have discussed to this point have only implicitly incorporated point source controls. In recent years, there has been a push in the U.S. and elsewhere to better coordinate the pollution control efforts of both point and nonpoint sources. One approach that would accomplish this goal is to provide individual point and nonpoint sources of pollution with limited rights to pollute and allow them to trade these rights in markets.

Pollution trading has gained popularity in a number of other settings and is increasingly accepted as a cost-effective approach for achieving environmental quality goals (U.S. EPA, 2001). The main appeal of trading is its potential to achieve environmental goals at lower social cost than the 'command and control' instruments that have been the dominant approach to pollution control (see e.g. Montgomery, 1972; Hahn, 1989; Tietenberg, 1990). In 'text book' form, polluters receive (through an endowment, auction, purchase, or some other means) a number of pollution permits that specify allowable emissions for the permit holder. Permits can be traded subject to rules governing trades. Pollution sources having greater marginal pollution control costs will purchase permits from sources having smaller marginal costs. The result is that firms having lower control costs emit less, firms having greater control costs emit more, and the maximum total allowable level of pollution is met at lower cost than if trading was not allowed.

While there may be significant potential gains from reallocating pollution control between point and nonpoint sources, there are also significant challenges in the design of point-nonpoint trading systems that can realize these gains. Trading between point and nonpoint sources entails a fundamental departure from text book tradeable discharge markets (Malik *et al.*, 1993; Shortle, 1987). Trades involving nonpoint sources cannot be based on actual nonpoint emissions due to the stochastic and unobservable nature of these emissions. Thus, the question of the appropriate basis for measuring nonpoint performance (i.e. what it is that will be traded) remains. Point-nonpoint systems that have been developed to date involve point sources trading increases in emissions for reductions in estimated loadings from nonpoint sources (where loadings can be thought of as represented by the term r_i is the model described above) (Horan forthcoming).

An alternative to trading mean loadings would be to trade inputs that are correlated with pollution flows (e.g. trading point source emissions permits for agricultural permits restricting the use of polluting inputs such as fertilizers). Systems have been proposed in which point source emissions could be traded for reductions in the use of fertilizers and/or reductions of cropland in fertilizer-intensive uses (Hanley *et al.*, 1997).

In addition to the question of what to trade, another fundamental issue is the rate at which nonpoint allowances are traded for point source allowances (Letson, 1993; Malik *et al.*, 1993; Shortle, 1987). Because nonpoint inputs and estimated loadings are imperfect substitutes for point source emissions, trades should not occur at a one-to-one ratio.

Below we outline two types of trading systems. One involves trades of point source emissions for estimated nonpoint source loadings. The second involves trades of point source emissions for nonpoint source inputs. Theoretical research has demonstrated that emissions-for-inputs trading (E-I) systems can be designed to provide greater economic efficiency, transactions costs aside, than emissions-for-estimated loadings trading (E-EL) systems because they are better able to manage the variability of nonpoint loads (Shortle and Abler, 1997). The reason, as we discussed previously, is that estimated loadings are suboptimal as a basis for nonpoint pollution control. However, under 'real world' conditions, an E-EL trading system may well outperform an E-I system. We will return to this issue later.

Emissions for estimated emissions trading

An emissions-for-estimated loadings trading system would consist of two categories of permits: point source permits, p^*, and nonpoint source permits,

r^*. The former are denominated in terms of emissions while the latter are denominated in terms of estimated loadings. Firms must have a combination of both types at least equal to their emissions, in the case of point sources, or estimated loadings in the case of nonpoint sources.[10]

In most existing programs, permits are traded at a rate of $1:1$ within source categories and a trading ratio, $t = dr^*/de^*$, defines how many nonpoint permits substitute for one emissions permit for trades between source categories. This restriction of $1:1$ trading within categories reduces cost-effectiveness when firms' emissions (or loadings) have differential marginal environmental impacts because uniform trading ratios do not give firms incentives to exploit differences in their relative marginal environmental impacts as a differentiated system would (Tietenberg, 1995). However, this restriction could provide a net economic gain if it reduces program administrative and other transactions costs. The same is true for a uniform trading ratio that does not vary depending on the locations of sources involved in a trade. Most existing point-nonpoint programs do operate with a single trading ratio, although the ratio is spatially differentiated for a few newer programs such as the ones in Michigan and Idaho (GLTN, 2000).

A trading ratio equal to one implies indifference at the margin between the source of control. Ratios in excess of one imply a high cost of nonpoint control relative to point source control and thus a marginal preference for point source reductions. The reverse is true for ratios less than one. Little can be said *a priori* about the magnitude of an optimally set trading ratio, although theory suggests that factors such as the relative marginal contributions of point and nonpoint sources, the degree of environmental risk impacts, correlations between key environmental and cost relationships, the overall level of heterogeneity associated with point and nonpoint sources, and the relative marginal transactions costs associated with implementing point and nonpoint controls could all play a role (Horan *et al.*, 2000a; Shortle, 1987; Malik *et al.*, 1993). For instance, the trading ratio will optimally be smaller (hence, nonpoint permits are relatively cheap for point sources to purchase) when nonpoint source pollution is an important source of environmental risk.

Emissions for inputs trading

Now consider an emissions-for-inputs (E-I) trading system. As above we assume two main categories of permits: point and nonpoint. PS permits are denominated in terms of emissions as in the E-EL system. In contrast, NPS permits are differentiated further and denominated in terms of specific inputs. As with the E-EL system, we assume an efficiency-reducing restriction of $1:1$ trading of permits within source categories, with trading ratios applicable for trades between source categories and for different inputs. Additional inefficiencies may arise for E-I trading systems where only a subset of inputs are traded, although this is likely to be a practical consideration because it will likely be difficult and costly to monitor all inputs (Shortle *et al.*, 1998).

Trades involving pollution-reducing inputs (i.e. those inputs for which increased use reduces pollution) are characterized by some interesting features. Specifically, permits for these inputs may define minimum required input use in some situations, since firms would tend to under-use pollution-reducing inputs in the absence of environmental policy. When this occurs, then cost-effective trading ratios involving these inputs will be negative (i.e. a reduction in emissions is traded for an *increase* in pollution-reducing inputs) and the economic effect will be to create an opportunity cost associated with reduced use of pollution-reducing inputs.

Second-best E-I trading ratios, given the 1 : 1 trading restriction and restrictions on the number of inputs requiring permits, are derived by Horan *et al.* (2000a), although little can be said *a priori* about their magnitudes. As with the E-EL ratio, the E-I ratios can be greater than, less than, or equal to one, and will likely be influenced by similar factors. One difference between E-I and E-EL trading, however, is the impact of input substitution. Specifically, if permits requiring an increase in pollution-reducing inputs also have the effect of increasing the producers' demand for pollution-increasing inputs, then damages could increase as a result. In such cases, trading ratios involving pollution-reducing inputs would be increased to encourage greater control of point sources and to encourage reduced use of pollution-increasing inputs. Accordingly, trading ratios involving pollution-reducing inputs will not necessarily be negative.

One important difference between the two types of trading systems is that E-I trading allows for differential targeting of inputs whereas E-EL trading does not. Differential treatment of inputs may provide advantages in terms of a better ability to fine tune input risk-effects (i.e. the impact of different inputs on the variance and other moments of environmental outcomes). However, these advantages are diminished with uniform instruments and when instruments are only applied to a limited number of inputs. If the risk-effects associated with the use of inputs are very small, then there should be little difference in the performance of the two trading systems, given that instruments are applied to all inputs that affect loadings. Given that the risk-effects are small, we would expect the relative performance of E-EL trading to improve relative to E-I trading as inputs that affect loadings are excluded. Conversely, if risk effects are important, then E-I trading may be comparatively advantageous provided that the set of inputs in the targeted set is not overly restricted.

Another important difference between the two trading systems, in the case of uniform trading ratios, is that E-EL trading has the advantage of transmitting more site-specific information to producers about their environmental pressures (i.e. mean loadings) relative to E-I trading. The extent of this advantage is likely to depend on the correlation between key environmental and cost relationships. Well-constructed proxies can better correlate with environmental quality impacts than individual inputs when loadings are a function of more than one choice variable. For instance, in the case of nitrogen losses, the residual nitrogen available for leaching into ground water is more highly correlated with the manageable nitrogen excess than with the fertilizer application (National Research Council, 1994).

8. Mixed approaches

We have ordered our presentation of instruments thus far by the compliance base. We have shown, for a variety of compliance bases, the conditions under which an efficient solution could emerge when a single instrument is applied to a single compliance base. In each case, we have indicated that the conditions, in terms of the model assumptions or in the way the instruments would have to be implemented, are quite restrictive. As these conditions are relaxed, the ability of a single instrument applied to a single compliance base to yield an efficient outcome is reduced. An emerging theme in the nonpoint literature is that mixed approaches may best address the informational challenges of nonpoint problems (Laffont, 1994; Braden and Segerson, 1993). A mixed approach could include any combination of mechanisms and compliance bases.

Braden and Segerson (1993) discuss mixing input taxes with liability rules. Input taxes cannot be efficient when only some polluting inputs can be monitored. Likewise, liability rules may be inefficient when a polluter may not be held liable due to difficulties in identifying the source and proving responsibility. An approach that mixed these two instruments could improve efficiency in such a situation. Horan *et al.* (1999) demonstrate that ambient taxes cannot achieve first-best outcomes when polluters are risk averse, but develop an approach mixing input taxes with an ambient tax to obtain the first-best solution. Xepapdeas (1995) examines a mix of effluent taxes and ambient taxes for a case in which polluters know their emissions but the regulator does not without costly monitoring. A pure effluent tax would require costly monitoring. Augmenting it with an ambient tax would lead polluters to reveal all or part of their emissions, thus reducing enforcement costs.

9. Empirical research on nonpoint instruments

There is a substantial empirical literature addressing questions about how best to design particular types of nonpoint water pollution control instruments, and the economic merits of alternative approaches. This research is largely characterized by two features. First, it is almost exclusively addressed to the control of agricultural nonpoint sources in North America and Western Europe. Second, most analyses explore the impacts of policy from an ex ante point of view. That is, the studies are simulations of the likely impacts of policies that have not yet been implemented as opposed to an analysis of actual policies that are in place.

In this section, we describe important empirical findings in the context of the three questions we raised earlier: who to target? what to target? and what mechanism to use? As we do this, it is important to keep in mind the inherent difficulties in making comparisons among results from different studies. This is because the assumptions underlying different studies vary widely, and they also often differ significantly from those of the model we presented above. An ideal model would include the economic behavior of all farms contributing to a particular problem, as well as the environmental consequences of that behavior.

Yet, not all studies model more than a single producer and/or the environmental impacts of on-farm decisions. For those studies that do model multiple polluters and environmental impacts, the theoretical literature indicates that comprehensive studies of nonpoint pollution instruments should include stochastic pollution processes, heterogeneity among the environmental impacts of different pollution sources, and asymmetric information between the regulatory agency and polluters about polluters' control costs. Yet very few empirical studies model more than one of these features simultaneously. Heterogeneity is the most common theme while only a few studies consider the impacts of stochastic pollution and asymmetric information.

Finally, comprehensive answers to each of the three questions requires a look at transactions costs differences. There is, however, little research on this crucial issue. Noteworthy exceptions are Carpentier and Bosch (1998), McCann and Easter (1999), and Weinberg and Wilen (1997). These studies indicate that transactions costs are not trivial, and can vary substantially across approaches.

Who to target?

In theory, a first-best solution involves targeting all suspected polluters. However, the transactions costs associated with such a broad and highly targeted approach may be extensive. Thus, at one extreme, the answer to the question of who to target may involve targeting one polluter (or group of polluters) but not another. At the other extreme, the answer involves targeting each polluter in the same manner by applying instruments uniformly. In between these extremes, polluters may optimally be targeted differentially, to varying degrees depending on their cost structures and environmental impacts. We address the range of targeting possibilities in this section.

The problem of excluding one or more polluters from the targeted set has received very limited attention in the empirical literature. Horan *et al.* (2000b) explore this problem in the context of whether it is optimal to control both point and nonpoint sources of pollution. That study compares various first-best and second-best point-nonpoint trading systems for the Susquehanna River Basin in Pennsylvania, where trades could occur between agricultural nonpoint sources and municipal and industrial point sources of pollution. They find that the majority of control costs optimally fall on nonpoint sources, indicating that having substantial point source controls relative to nonpoint controls yields excessive costs. For instance, one trading system involves trading point source emissions for nonpoint permits based on how much land is brought into production. Significant nonpoint controls are too costly to undertake in this system. But even so, little is optimally reallocated back to point sources. Instead, the optimal level of control is small and expected social costs are not reduced significantly. More control is attained under alternative trading systems, but the costs primarily fall on nonpoint sources in those cases as well. In the case of trading point source emissions for estimated nonpoint loads, the optimal trading ratio is less than one (indicating a preference at the margin for nonpoint controls) under a wide variety of watershed conditions. Such small ratios are much smaller than ratios found in existing markets.

A number of studies analyze the welfare costs of applying instruments uniformly across nonpoint polluters as opposed to optimally differentiated. For instance, Helfand and House (1995) compare several instruments for reducing nitrate leaching by 20% from two soils used for lettuce production in California's Salinas Valley (US). Nitrate leaching in their model is deterministic and is increasing in the amounts of nitrogen fertilizers and irrigation water applied, and is unaffected by any other inputs. Accordingly, the instruments they consider are taxes and restrictions on nitrogen inputs, and taxes and restrictions on irrigation water inputs. Their analysis is especially interesting for its comparison of first-best and second-best specifications of the input-based instruments. Specifically, they compare the costs of achieving the target reduction under several scenarios involving combinations of taxes (or restrictions) on one or both inputs, with the rates (restrictions) being either uniform or differentiated across soils. They find the cost-effectiveness of uniform applications of the instruments to be only slightly less than that of differentiated applications. In contrast, they find that cost-effectiveness may be significantly reduced (relative to the first-best outcome) when only a subset of production decisions are targeted by a uniform policy. It is difficult to determine the extent to which this result is due to the instruments being applied uniformly or due to the instruments being applied to only a subset of choices. The two effects cannot easily be separated out. At a minimum, it would be necessary to also know the costs associated with applying farm-specific instruments to the same subset of choices, and these results were not reported. Thus, all we can say is that uniformity could be more of a factor when the instrument base is sub-optimal. Indeed, there is evidence that the welfare loss from uniform treatment may vary significantly depending on the chosen instrument base (Horan et al., 2000b).

Given the limited amount of heterogeneity in Helfand and House's model (only two soils), their results for the case of uniform instruments applied to each input should not be generalized. Most empirical studies show that, transactions costs aside, highly targeted, information intensive strategies for nonpoint pollution control policies outperform undifferentiated strategies, often by a substantial margin (e.g. Babcock et al., 1997; Flemming and Adams, 1997; Carpentier et al., 1998; Claassen and Horan, 2001). This may be especially true when market prices are impacted by producer responses to environmental policy. At the farm level, a tax on the use of one input (e.g. a chemical) may increase the demand for alternative, non-targeted inputs (e.g. other chemicals) that could also be harmful to the environment. At the market level, a tax could impact input and output prices and alter the demand for non-targeted inputs in ways that could be environmentally damaging. It is optimal to consider such impacts when choosing among bases and setting instrument levels so that any adverse impacts are not too great. For example, a first-best tax would be negative for inputs that reduce emissions. However, the optimal second-best tax for a pollution-decreasing input will be positive if an increase in the use of the input is associated with increased demand for the use of pollution-increasing inputs, resulting in adverse environmental consequences. For further discussion of substitution effects, see e.g. Braden and Segerson (1993), Claassen and Horan (2001), Hrubovcak *et al.* (1989), Schnitkey and Miranda (1993), Shogren (1993).

What to target?

The empirical literature is largely addressed to the design and performance of instruments applied to agricultural input or practices, or farm-level emissions proxies. Ambient–based instruments, while of significant interest, have received little attention in empirical research.

A number of studies support the conclusion that the choice of instrument base can significantly influence the cost-effectiveness of agri-environmental policy (e.g. Larson *et al.*, 1996; Weinberg and Kling, 1996; Weinberg *et al.*, 1993). For instance, Helfand and House (1995) and Larson *et al.* (1996) examine various input-based instruments to limit nitrate leaching from lettuce production in the Salinas Valley (US). Both studies find that instruments based on irrigation water were more cost-effective than instruments based on nitrogen use because irrigation water was more highly correlated with nitrate leaching. The implication is that the appropriate instrument base may not be the chemicals or nutrients responsible for pollution, but rather the choices that are most highly correlated with pollution flows.

Although we demonstrated above that first-best input-based instruments will outperform instruments based on emissions proxies, this conclusion need not hold when the comparison is between for second-best input instruments and emissions proxies. In the imperfect real world of nonpoint pollution control, instruments that use emissions proxies may well outperform input based instruments. Comparisons involving inputs and estimated nonpoint emissions or other performance bases is limited and more work is needed in this area. There are several studies that show that taxes or standards applied to nitrogen emissions proxies (e.g. excess nitrogen or expected nitrate leachate) are more cost-effective than taxes or standards applied to nitrogen inputs (Fontein *et al.*, 1994; Johnson *et al.*, 1991; Huang and LeBlanc, 1994; Moxey and White, 1994; Shortle *et al.*, 1993). However, these studies have not considered the input related risk effects which are important in a first-best context.

Horan *et al.* (2000b) take risk effects into account when they compare trading systems based on estimated nonpoint loadings with systems based on various nonpoint inputs. In comparing systems in which uniform trading ratios are applied, they find that trading programs for which nonpoint permits are defined in terms of estimated loadings are less costly than those based on input use and perform almost as well as the first-best approach. This result occurs largely because loadings are a better indicator of environmental pressures than are inputs. In contrast, programs in which allowances are defined in terms of nonpoint inputs are more costly due to the restriction of uniform trading ratios within source categories. This result indicates that differential treatment among sources is likely to improve performance for input-based trading systems, but not for trading systems based on estimated loadings. Finally, they find that the choice of input permit base matters a great deal in terms of program performance.

What mechanism?

It is well-known that appropriately designed taxes, subsidies, and regulations can each produce the same desired economic and environmental outcomes when producers and the government have symmetric information regarding firms' cost types. However, this equivalence result breaks down when producers have better information about cost types than the government. There is very little empirical literature on the performance of alternative agricultural pollution control instruments under conditions of public uncertainty about polluters' control costs. One exception is Abrahams and Shortle (2000), who compare several tax and standard policies for reducing nitrate pollution in the United States using a model that captures public uncertainty about the costs and benefits of nitrate pollution control. They also compute the value of information that would accrue from resolving the uncertainty about key economic and environmental parameters and the sensitivity of the instruments policy performance to market distortions created by agricultural price and income policies.[11] First-best nitrate policy choices were found to be sensitive to commodity programs and uncertainty. In particular, they found tax policies to be more cost-effective than quantity controls in the presence of public uncertainty, but with perfect information the quantity instruments are as cost-effective as the tax instruments.

10. Conclusions

Although nonpoint pollution has been long recognized as an important cause of environmental degradation, nonpoint pollution control is only now becoming a major priority in developed countries with advanced environmental protection policies. At the same time, there is growing interest in the use of economic instruments for addressing environmental problems, and a timely literature on the design of economic incentives for nonpoint pollution control. It would seem that economists may have a significant opportunity to have a positive impact on policy design in the nonpoint arena.

The theoretical literature on nonpoint pollution control is largely addressed to identifying instruments with economically appealing properties given the especially challenging informational issues inherent in the problem. These include various incentive mechanisms, including charges and subsidies, trading, and contracts, applied to inputs or practices, emissions proxies, and ambient concentrations. This literature, although still evolving, already provides a rich basis for innovative approaches.

A number of areas of further theoretical development can be identified. Input-based instruments, and instruments applied to emissions proxies have long been of interest for nonpoint pollution control. Additional research addressing problems of moral hazard and adverse selection in the design on input based instruments is needed. So too is research on monitoring and enforcement mechanisms, the behavior of individuals under collective penalty (or reward) mechanisms, and multiple instruments (see also Xepapadeas, 1999; Tomasi et al., 1994). There is little literature on dynamic incentive properties, and while there is much nodding to the importance of transactions costs, there is little formal attention to this most fundamental problem.

The greatest advances in economic research are to be made through empirical work. The empirical literature has focused largely on input-based taxes and standards. There are still many issues raised in the theoretical literature that have not been adequately researched or tested empirically. For instance, the theoretical literature has stressed the importance of the stochastic nature of nonpoint pollution for policy design and performance. Yet very few empirical studies even model stochastic elements.[12] Empirical work to test the importance of this feature and to provide detailed guidance for policy design is essential. The same holds true for asymmetric information and other complexities of nonpoint problems. There is also need for an experimental literature to test the design and performance of more novel ideas such as ambient-based instruments. Finally, while much is made of the importance of transactions costs, there is little research on their magnitude or tradeoffs between these costs and other dimensions of instrument performance.

Notes

1. For a sampling of assessments of the nonpoint pollution problems, see e.g. Duda (1993); OECD (1998a); U.S. EPA (2000).
2. Point sources emissions can be costly to monitor and exhibit random variations. Our assumption is consistent with the usual treatment in the economic literature and is useful for contrast between the point and nonpoint sources.
3. Numerous models are available for modeling agriculture, urban, and other nonpoint sources (Novotny and Olem, 1994).
4. Smith and Tomasi (1999) argue to the contrary for a particular type of contract designed using mechanism design theory.
5. Let $f = f(q)(f', f'' > 0)$, where $q = q(h, v)$, h is deterministic and v is a stochastic variable. Then $\text{cov}\{f'(q), \partial q/\partial h\}$ is of the same sign as $\text{cov}\{q, \partial q/\partial h\} = 0.5(\partial \text{ var}\{q\}/\partial h)$, where this equality follows from: $\partial \text{var}\{q\}/\partial h = \partial(E\{q^2\} - E\{q\}^2)/\partial h = 2(E\{q\partial q/\partial h\} - E\{q\}E\{\partial q/\partial h\}) = 2 \text{ cov}\{q, \partial q/\partial h\}$. If $f'' < 0$, then $\text{cov}\{f'(q), \partial q/\partial h$ will have the opposite sign relative $\partial \text{ var}\{q\}/\partial h$. This result is used throughout the paper, although with different definitions for f, q, and h.
6. As Malik et al. (1993) point out, the impacts of input use on the variance of nonpoint emissions may stem from either objective or subjective uncertainty. Impacts related to objective uncertainty arise when changes in input use affect how stochastic processes influence emissions. Impacts related to subjective uncertainty may arise when changes in input use have uncertain impacts to emissions due to society's limited experience with controlling nonpoint source pollution.
7. By 'Pigouvian', we mean that the tax rate is set equal to the expected marginal cost of pollution in the optimal solution. In this context, however, because the nonpoint

charge is second-best, the optimal solution refers to a second-best allocation rather the first-best allocation normally associated with a Pigouvian tax.

8. The expectation that firms know more about their control costs than government is a major basis for economic critique of command and control policies that reduce firms' flexibility to use their specialized knowledge. The issue is a bit more problematic for typical nonpoint sources than for large industrial polluters or municipalities with access to engineering expertise. Because of their size and the fixed costs of acquiring information, the small businesses and households that typify nonpoint sources may not invest much in information on techniques for limiting pollution. Public agencies may have significantly better information about pollution control or pollution prevention practices. Disseminating such knowledge could provide environmental improvements if this knowledge encourages individuals to behave in more environmentally friendly ways — either with existing methods and technologies or by adopting alternative technologies.

9. In each case, the variable portion of the tax may be quite large and could potentially drive firms out of business. To prevent this from occurring, the tax may have to be combined with a lump sum component, k_i, that refunds at least part of the tax. The lump sum component can also be used to induce optimal entry and exit. Entry and exit considerations are particularly important in the case of an ambient tax because the number and location of firms affecting ambient pollution levels impact the tax that each firm faces. Thus, if too many or too few firms operate, then the marginal conditions faced by all other firms are likely to be affected and the resulting levels of input use will be sub-optimal.

10. In existing programs that include agricultural sources, agricultural sources are not required to have permits. Instead, these sources have an implicit, initial right to pollute, which is consistent with initially having permits equal to unregulated estimated loadings levels.

11. The value of information in this context is the expected increase in the expected net benefits that would result from improved policy design.

12. In early empirical studies in this area, stochastic fluctuations were probably ignored due to the relatively unsophisticated software that was available at the time. However, today's software is increasingly sophisticated in its ability to model stochastic events and other forms of uncertainty.

References

Abrahams, N., and Shortle, J. S. (2000) Uncertainty and the Choice between Compliance Measures and Instruments in Nitrate Nonpoint Pollution Control. Working Paper, Department of Agricultural Economics and Rural Sociology, Pennsylvania State University, University Park.

Anderson, R. C., Lohof, A. Q. and Carlin, A. (1997) The United States Experience with Economic Incentives in Environmental Pollution Control Policy. U.S. Environmental Protection Agency, Washington, D.C.

Babcock, B. A., Lakshminarayan, P. Wu, J. and Zilberman, D. (1997) Targeting Tools for the Purchase of Environmental Amenities. *Land Economics*, 73, 3, 325–339.

Baumol, W. and Oates, W. (1988) *The Theory of Environmental Policy*. Cambridge: Cambridge University Press.

Beavis, M. and Walker, M. (1983) Achieving Environmental Standards with Stochastic Discharges. *Journal of Environmental Economics and Management*, 10, 103–111.

Bohm, P. and Russell, C. (1985) Comparative Analysis of Alternative Policy Instruments.

In A. Kneese and J. Sweeny (eds), *Handbook of Natural Resource and Energy Economics Vol. 1* Amsterdam: Elsevier Science Publishers.

Braden, J. B., Bozaher, A, Johnson, G. and Miltz, D. (1989) Optimal Spatial Management of Agricultural Pollution. *American Journal of Agricultural Economics*, 71, 404–413.

Braden, J. B., Larson, R. and Herricks, E. (1991) Impact Targets vs Discharge Standards in Agricultural Pollution Management. *American Journal of Agricultural Economics*, 73, 388–397.

Braden, J. B. and Segerson, K. (1993) Information Problems in the Design of Nonpoint Pollution. In C. S. Russell and J. F. Shogren (eds), *Theory, Modeling and Experience in the Management of Nonpoint-Source Pollution*, Dordrecht: Kluwer Academic Publishers.

Byström, O. (1998) The Nitrogen Abatement Costs of Wetlands. *Ecological Economics*, 26, 321–331.

Byström, O., Andersson, H. and Gren, I-M. (2000) Economic Criteria for Restoration of Wetlands Under Uncertainty. *Ecological Economics*. 35: 35–45.

Byström, O. and Bromley, D. W. (1998) Contracting for Nonpoint-Source Pollution Abatement. *Journal of Agricultural and Resource Economics*, 23, 1, 39–54.

Cabe, R. and Herriges, J. (1992) The Regulation of Nonpoint-Source Pollution Under Imperfect and Asymmetric Information. *Journal of Environmental Economics and Management*, 22, 34–146.

Camacho, R. (1991) Financial Cost-Effectiveness of Point and Nonpoint Source Nutrient Reduction Technologies in the Chesapeake Bay Basin, ICPRB Report, 91–8.

Carpentier, C. L., Bosch, D. J. and Batie, S. S. (1998) Using Spatial Information to Reduce Costs of Controlling Nonpoint Source Pollution. *Agricultural and Resource Economics Review*, 27, 72–84.

Claassen, R., *et al.* (2001) Agri-Environmental Policy at the Crossroads: Guideposts on a Changing Landscape. By Roger Claassen, LeRoy Hanse, Mark Peters, Vince Breneman, Marca Weinberg, Andrea Cattaneo, Peter Feather, Dwight Gadsby, Daniel Hellerstein, Jeff Hopkins, Paul Johnson, Mitch Morehart, and Mark Smith. Economic Research Service, U. S. Department of Agriculture. Agricultural Economic Report No. 794. January.

Claassen, R., and Horan, R. D. (2001) Uniform and Non-Uniform Second-Best Input Taxes: The Significance of Market Price Effects on Efficiency and Equity. *Environmental and Resource Economics*.

Claassen, R. and Horan, R. D. (2000) Environmental Payments to Farmers: Issues of Program Design'. Agricultural Outlook, AGO-272, 15–18, June.

Coburn, J. (1994) Cleaning Up Urban Stormwater: The Storm Drain Stenciling Approach (Or Getting to the Nonpoint Source). *Journal of Soil and Water Conservation*, 49, 312–316.

Common, M. (1977) A Note on the Use of Taxes to Control Pollution. *Scandanavian Journal of Economics*, 79, 345–349.

Crutchfield, S. R., Letson, D. and Malik, A. S.. (1994) Feasibility of Point-Nonpoint Source Trading for Managing Agricultural Pollutant Loadings to Coastal Waters. *Water Resources Research*, 30, 2825–2836.

Dinar, A., Knapp, K. C. and Letey, J. (1989) Irrigation Water Pricing to Reduce and Finance Subsurface Drainage Disposal. *Agricultural Water Management*, 16, 155–171.

Dinham, B. (1993) *The Pesticide Hazard: A Global Health and Environmental Audit*, London: Zed Books.

Dosi, C. and Moretto, M. (1993) NPS Pollution, Information Asymmetry, and the Choice of Time Profile for Environmental Fees. In C. S. Russell and J. F. Shogren (eds), *Theory, Modeling and Experience in the Management of Nonpoint-Source Pollution*, Dordrecht: Kluwer Academic Publishers.

—— (1994) Nonpoint Source Externalities and Polluter's Site Quality Standards Under Incomplete Information. In T. Tomasi and C. Dosi (eds), *Nonpoint Source Pollution Regulation: Issues and Policy Analysis*, Dortrecht: Kluwer Academic Publishers.

Duda, A. M. (1993) Addressing Nonpoint Sources of Water Pollution Must Become and International Priority. *Water Science and Technology*, 28, 3–5.

Elmore, T., Jaksch, J. and Downing, D. (1985) Point/Nonpoint Source Trading Programs for Dillon Reservoir and Planned Extensions for Other Areas. In Perspectives on Nonpoint Source Pollution, EPA, Washington, D.C.

Environmental Law Institute. (1997) *Enforceable State Mechanisms for the Control of Nonpoint Source Water Pollution*. Washington, DC.

Faeth, P. (2000) Fertile Ground: Nutrient Trading's Potential to Cost-Effectively Improve Water Quality. Washington, DC: World Resources Institute.

Flemming, R. A. and Adams, R. M. (1997) The Importance of Site-Specific Information in the Design of Policies to Control Pollution. *Journal of Environmental Economics and Management*, 33, 347–358.

Fontein, P. F., Thijssen, G. J., Magnus, J. R. and Dijk, J. (1994) On Levies to Reduce the Nitrogen Surplus: The Case of the Dutch Pig Farm. *Environmental and Resource Economics*, 4, 445–478.

GLTN (Great Lakes Trading Network) (2000) Summary of Program and Project Drivers and other Presentation Materials. *Markets for the New Millennium: How Can Water Quality Trading Work For You?, Conference and Workshop*, Chicago Illinois, May 18–19.

Griffin, R. C. and Bromley, D. W. (1982) Agricultural Runoff as a Nonpoint Externality: A Theoretical Development. *American Journal of Agricultural Economics*, 64, 547–552.

Groves, T. (1973) Incentives in Teams. *Econometrica*, 41, 617–31.

Hahn, R. (1989) Economic Prescriptions for Environmental Problems: How the Patient Followed the Doctors Orders. *Journal of Economic Perspectives*, 3, 95–114.

—— (2000) The Impacts of Economics on Environmental Policy. *Journal of Environmental Economics and Management*, 39, 375–400.

Hanley, N., Shogren, J. F. and White, B. (1997) *Environmental Economics in Theory and Practice*, New York: Oxford University Press.

Hanley, N. (forthcoming). Policy on Agricultural Pollution in the European Union. In J. Shortle and D. Abler (eds), *Environmental Policies for Agricultural Pollution Control*. Wallingford U.K.: CAB International.

Hanson, L. G. (1998) A Damage Based Tax Mechanism for Regulation of Non-Point Emissions. *Environmental and Resource Economics*, 12, 1, 99–112

Harford, D. (1987) Self-reporting of Pollution and the Firm's Behavior Under Imperfectly Enforceable Regulations. *Journal of Environmental Economics and Management*, 14, 293–303

Hayami, Y. and Ruttan, V. W. (1985) *Agricultural Development: An International Perspective*. Baltimore: Johns Hopkins University Press.

Helfand, G. E. and House, B. W. (1995) Regulating Nonpoint Source Pollution Under Heterogeneous Conditions. *American Journal of Agricultural Economics*, 77, 1024–1032.

Herriges, J. R., Govindasamy, R. and Shogren, J. (1994) Budget-Balancing Incentive Mechanisms. *Journal of Environmental Economics and Management*, 27, 275–285.

Holtermann, S. (1976) Alternative Tax-Systems to Correct Externalities and the Efficiency of Paying Compensation. *Economica*, 46, 1–16.

Horan, R. D., (2001) Cost-Effective and Stochastic Dominance Approaches to Stochastic Pollution Control. *Environmental and Resource Economics*.

Horan, R. D. (forthcoming). Differences in Social and Public Risk Perceptions and Conflicting Impacts on Point/Nonpoint Trading Ratios. *American Journal of Agricultural Economics*.

Horan, R. D., Abler, D. G., Shortle, J. S., Carmichael, J. and Wang, L. (2001) Probabilistic, Cost-Effective Point/Nonpoint Management in the Susquehanna River Basin. Presented at the Integrated Decision-Making for Watershed Management Symposium, Chevy Chase, MD, January.

Horan, R. D., Shortle, J. S. (forthcoming) Environmental Instruments for Agriculture. In J. Shortle and D. Abler (eds), *Environmental Policy for Agricultural Pollution Control*. Walingford U.K.: CAB International.

Horan, R. D., Shortle, J. S. and Abler, D. G. (1998) 'Ambient Taxes When Polluters Have Multiple Choices. *Journal of Environmental Economics and Management*, 36, 186–199.

—— (1999a) Green Payments for Nonpoint Pollution Control. *American Journal of Agricultural Economics*, 81, 1210–1215, December 1999.

—— (1999b) Ambient Taxes Under *m*-Dimentional Choice Sets, Heterogeneous Expectations, and Risk-Aversion. Working Paper, Department of Agricultural Economics, Michigan State University.

—— (2000b) The Design and Comparative Economic Performance of Alternative Point/Nonpoint Trading Markets II: An Empirical Investigation of Nutrient Trading in the Susquehanna River Basin. Working paper, Department of Agricultural Economics, Michigan State University.

Horan, R. D., Shortle, J. S., Abler, D. G. and Ribaudo, M. (2000a) The Design and Comparative Economic Performance of Alternative Point/Nonpoint Trading Markets I: Theoretical Issues. Working paper, Department of Agricultural Economics, Michigan State University.

Huang, W., and Le Blanc, M. (1994) Market-based Incentives For Addressing Non-point Water Quality Problems: A Residual Nitrogen Tax Approach. *Review of Agricultural Economics*, 16, 427–440.

Huang, W. (1994) *Enforcement and Monitoring of Nonpoint Source Pollution Control With State-Dependent Penalty Systems*. Ph.D. Dissertation. Penn State University.

Huang, W., Shank, D. and Hewitt, T. I. (1996) 'On-Farm Costs of Reducing Residual Nitrogen on Cropland Vulnerable to Nitrate Leaching. *Review of Agricultural Economics*, 12, 325–339.

Johnson, S. L. Adams, R. M. and Perry, G. M. (1991) The On-Farm Costs of Reducing Groundwater Pollution. *American Journal of Agricultural Economics*, 73, 1063–1073.

Just, R. E., Hueth, D. L. and Schmitz, A. (1982) *Applied Welfare Economics and Public Policy*, Englewood Cliffs, NJ: Prentice Hall.

Kim, C. S., Hostetler, J. and Amacher, G. (1993) The Regulation of Groundwater Quality with Delayed Responses. *Water Resources Research*, 29, 1369–1377.

Laffont, J. (1994) Regulation of Pollution With Asymmetric Information. In C. Dosi and T. Tomasi (eds), *Nonpoint Source Pollution Regulation: Issues and Analysis*. Dordrecht: Kluwer Academic Publishers.

Larson, D., Helfand, G. and House, B. (1996) Second-Best Tax Policies to Reduce Nonpoint Source Pollution. *American Journal of Agricultural Economics*, 78, 4, 1108–1117.

Letson, D. (1992) Point/Nonpoint Source Trading: An Interpretive Survey. Natural Resources Journal, 32, 219–232.

Letson, D., S. Crutchfield, and A. Malik, 1993. Nonpoint Source Trading for Managing Agricultural Pollutant Loadings, U.S. Department of Agriculture, Economic Research Service AER-674, Washington, D. C.

Letson, D., Crutchfield, S. and Malik, A. S. (1993) Point/Nonpoint Source Trading for Controlling Pollutant Loadings to Coastal Waters: A Feasibility Study. In C. S. Russell and J. F. Shogren (eds), *Theory, Modeling and Experience in the Management of Nonpoint-Source Pollution*, Dordrecht: Kluwer Academic Publishers.

Lichtenberg, E. (1992) Alternative Approaches to Pesticide Regulation. *Northeastern Journal of Agricultural and Resource Economics*, 21, 83–92.

Lichtenberg, E. and Zilberman, D. (1988) Efficient Regulation of Environmental Health Risks. *Quarterly Journal of Economics*, 49, 167–168.

Lichtenberg, E., Zilberman, D. and Bogen, K. T. (1989) Regulating Environmental Health Risks Under Uncertainty: Groundwater Contamination in Florida. *Journal of Environmental Economics and Management*, 17, 22–34.

Malik, A. S. (1993) Self-reporting and the Design of Policies for Regulating Stochastic Pollution. *Journal of Environmental Economics and Management*, 24, 241–257.

Malik, A. S., Larson, B. A. and Ribaudo, M. O. (1994) Economic Incentives for Agricultural Nonpoint Pollution Control. *Water Resources Bulletin*, 30, 471–480.

Malik, A. S., Letson, D. and Crutchfield, S. R. (1993) Point/Nonpoint Source trading of Pollution Abatement: Choosing the Right Trading Ratio. *American Journal of Agricultural Economics*, 75, 959–967.

McCann, L. and Easter, W. K.. (1999) Transaction Costs of Policies To Reduce Agricultural Phosphorus Pollution in The Minnesota River. *Land Economics*, 75, 3, 402–414.

McSweeny, W. T. and Shortle, J. S. (1990) Probabilistic Cost Effectiveness in Agricultural Nonpoint Pollution Control. *Southern Journal of Agricultural Economics*, 22, 95–104.

Miceli, T. and Segerson, K. (1991) Joint Liability in Torts and Infra-Marginal Efficiency. *International Review of Law and Economics* 11, 235–249.

Menell, P. (1990) The Limitations of Legal Institutions for Addressing Environmental Risk. *The Journal of Economic Perspectives*, 5, 93–114.

Milon, J. W. (1987) Optimizing Nonpoint Source Controls in Water Quality. *Water Resources Bulletin*, 23, 387–396.

Montgomery, W. D. (1972) Markets in Licenses and Efficient Pollution Control. *Journal of Economics Theory* 5, 395–418.

Moxey, A. and B. White. (1994) Efficient Compliance With Agricultural Nitrate Pollution Standards. *Journal of Agricultural Economics*, 45, 27–37.

National Research Council. (1993) *Soil and Water Quality: An Agenda for Agriculture*. Washington DC: National Academy Press.

Novotny, V. and Olem, H. (1994) *Water Quality: Prevention, Identification, and Management of Diffuse Pollution*. New York: Van Nostrand Reinhold.

Oates, W. (1994) Green Taxes: Can We Protect the Environment and Improve the Tax System at the Same Time? *Southern Economic Journal*, 915–922.

OECD (Organization for Economic Cooperation and Development) (1986) *Water Pollution by Fertilizers and Pesticides*, Paris: OECD.

—— (1989) *Agricultural and Environmental Policies: Opportunity for Integration*, Paris: OECD.

—— (1993) *Agricultural and Environmental Policies Integration: Recent Progress and New Directions*, Paris: OECD.

—— (1994) *Environmental Taxes in OECD Countries*, Paris: OECD.

—— (1998) *Water Management: Performance and Challenges*. Paris: OECD.

—— (1999) *Economic Instruments for Pollution Control and Natural Resources Management in OECD Countries: A Survey*. Paris: OECD.

Opshoor, J. B., de Savornin Lohman, A. F. and Vos, H. B. (1994) *Managing the Environment: The Role of Economic Instruments*. OECD: Paris.

Plott, C. R. (1966) Externalities and Corrective Taxes. *Economica*, 33, 84–87

Rendeleman, C. M., Reinert, K. A., Tobey, J. A. (1995) Market-Based Systems for Reducing Chemical Use in Agriculture in the United States. *Environmental and Resource Economics*, 5, 51–70.

Ribaudo, M. O. and Horan, R. D.. (1999) The Role of Education in Nonpoint Source Pollution Control Policy. *Review of Agricultural Economics*, 21, 331–343, Fall/Winter.

Ribaudo, M. O. (forthcoming). Nonpoint Source Pollution Control Policy in the United States. In J. Shortle and D. Abler (eds), *Environmental Policies for Agricultural Pollution Control*. Wallingford U.K.: CAB International.

Robert, M. and Spence, M. (1976) Effluent Charges and Licenses Under Uncertainty. *Journal of Public Economics*, 5, 193–208

Russell, C. S. and Powell, P. T. (2000) Practical Considerations and Comparison of Instruments of Environmental Policy. In J. van den Bergh (ed.), *Handbook of Environmental and Resource Economics*. Chelenham UK: Edward Elgar Publishing Inc.

Schinitkey, G. D. and Miranda, M. (1993) The Impacts of Pollution Controls on Livestock-Crop Productions. *Journal of Agricultural and Resource Economics*, 18, 25–36.

Segerson, K. (1988) Uncertainty and Incentives for Non-Point Source Pollution. *Journal of Environmental Economics and Management*, 15, 87–98.

—— (1990) Liability for Groundwater Contamination from Pesticides. *Journal of Environmental Economics and Management* 19, 227–243.

Shavell, S. (1987) Liability Versus Other Approaches to the Control of Risk. In *Economic Analysis of Accident Law*, Cambridge, MA: Harvard University Press.

Shortle. J. S. (1984) The Use of Estimated Pollution Flows in Agricultural Pollution Control Policy. *Northeast Journal of Agricultural and Resource Economics*, 13, 277–285.

Shortle, J. S. (1987) Allocative Implications of Comparisons between the Marginal Costs of Point and Nonpoint Source Pollution Abatement. *Northeastern Journal of Agricultural and Resource Economics*, 16, 17–23.

—— (1990) The Allocative Efficiency Implications of Water Pollution Abatement Cost Comparisons. *Water Resources Research*, 26, 5, 793–797.

Shortle, J. S. and Abler, D. G. (1994) Incentives for Agricultural Nonpoint Pollution Control. In Graham-Tomasi, T. and C. Dosi (eds), *The Economics of Nonpoint Pollution Control: Theory and Issues*. Dortrecht, The Netherlands: Kluwer Academic Press.

—— (1997) Nonpoint Pollution. In Folmer, H., and T. Teitenberg (eds), *International Yearbook of Environmental and Natural Resource Economics*. Cheltenham, UK: Edward Elgar.

Shortle, J. S. and Dunn, J. W.. (1986) The Relative Efficiency of Agricultural Source Water Pollution Control Policies. *American Journal of Environmental Economics*, 68, 3, 668–677.

Shortle, J. S., Faichney. R., Hanley, N. and Munro, A. (1999) Least-Cost Pollution Allocations for Prabilistic Water Quality Targets to Protect Salmon on the Forth Estuary. In Steve Sorrel and Jim Skea (eds), *Pollution For Sale: Emissions Trading And Joint Implementation*. Northampton, MA: Edward Elgar.

Shortle, J. S., Horan, R. D. and Abler, D. G. (1998) Research Issues in Nonpoint Pollution Control. *Environmental and Resource Economics*, 11, 3/4, 571–585.

Shumway, R. (1995) Recent Duality Contributions in Production Economics. *Journal of Agricultural and Resource Economics*, 20, 178–194

Smith, R. B. W. and Tomasi, T. D. (1995) Transaction Costs and Agricultural Nonpoint-Source Water Pollution Control Policies. *Journal of Agricultural and Resource Economics*, 20, 277–290.

Smith, R. B. W. and Tomasi, T. D. (1999) Multiple Agents, and Agricultural Nonpoint-Source Water Pollution Control Policies. *Agricultural and Resource Economics Review*, 28, 37–44.

Smith, R. B. W. (1995) The Conservation Reserve Program as a Least-Cost Land Retirement Mechanism. *American Journal of Agricultural Economics* 77 Feb, 93–105.

Stavins, R. N. (1996) Correlated Uncertainty and Policy Instrument Choice. *Journal of Environmental Economics and Management*, 30, 218–232.

Stevens, B. (1988) Fiscal Implications of Effluent Charges and Input Taxes. *Journal of Environmental Economics and Management* 15, 285–96.

Taylor, M. L., Adams, R. M. and Miller, S. F. (1992) Farm level Response to Agricultural Effluent Control Strategies: The Case Of The Willamette Valley. *American Journal of Agricultural Economics*, 17, 1, 173–185

Tietenberg, T. H. (1995a) Tradeable Permits for Pollution Control when Emission Location Matters: What Have We Learned? *Environmental and Resource Economics*, 5, 95–113.

Tietenberg, T. H. (1999) Economic Instruments for Environmental Regulations. *Oxford Review of Economic Policy*, 6, Spring, 17–33.

Tomasi, T., Segerson, K. and Braden, J. (1994) Issues in the Design of Incentive Schemes for Nonpoint Source Pollution Control. In C. Dosi and T. Tomasi (eds), *Nonpoint Source Pollution Regulation: Issues and Analysis*, Kluwer Academic Publishers, Dordrecht (Chapter 1).

U.S. Department of Agriculture, Economic Research Service. (1997) *Agricultural Resources and Environmental Indicators* Agricultural Handbook No. 712. July.

U.S. Environmental Protection Agency. (2000) *The Quality of Our Nations Waters: A Summary of the National Water Quality.*

—— (2001) *The United States Experience With Economic Incentives for Protecting the Environment.* EPA-240-R-01-001.

Weersink, A., Livernois, J., Shogren, J. F. and Shortle, J. S. (1998) Economic Instruments and Environmental Policy in Agriculture. *Canadian Public Policy*, 24, 309–327.

Weinberg, M. and C. L., Kling (1996) Uncoordinated Agricultural Policy Making: An Application to Irrigated Agriculture in the West. *American Journal of Agricultural Economics*, 78, 65–78.

Weinberg, M., Kling, C. L. and Wilen, J. E. (1993a) Water Markets and Water Quality. *American Journal of Agricultural Economics*, 75, 278–91.

Weitzman, M. (1974) Prices vs. Quantities. *Review of Economic Studies*, 41, 477–491.

Wetzstein, M. E. and Centner, T. J. (1992) Regulating Agricultural Contamination of Groundwater Through Strict Liability and Negligence Legislation. *Journal of Environmental Economics and Management*, 22, 1–11.

Wu, J. and Babcock, B. (1996) Contract Design for the Purchase of Environmental Goods from Agriculture. *American Journal of Agricultural Economics*, 78, Nov, 935–945.

—— (1999) The Relative Efficiency of Voluntary vs Mandatory Environmental Regulations. *Journal of Environmental Economics and Management* 38, 158–175.

Xepapadeas, A. (1991) Environmental Policy Under Imperfect Information: Incentives and Moral Hazard. *Journal of Environmental Economics Management*, 20, 113–126.

—— (1992) Environmental Policy Design and Dynamic Nonpoint Source Pollution. *Journal of Environmental Economics Management*, 23, 22–39.

—— (1994) Controlling Environmental Externalities: Observability and Optimal Policy Rules. In Dosi, C., and T. Tomasi (eds), *Nonpoint Source Pollution Regulation: Issues and Policy Analysis.* Dordrecht, The Netherlands: Kluwer Academic Publishers.

—— (1997) Regulation of mineral emissions under asymmetric information. In Eirik Romstad, Jesper Simonsen and Arild Vatn (eds), *Policy Measures to Control Environmental Impacts from Agriculture in the European Union — Volume 2: Mineral Emissions*, Reading: CAB International Publishers.

—— (1999) Nonpoint Source Pollution. In J. van den Bergh. *Handbook of Environmental and Resource Economics.* Cheltenham UK: Edward Elgar.

CHAPTER 3

NON-MANDATORY APPROACHES TO ENVIRONMENTAL PROTECTION

Madhu Khanna

University of Illinois at Urbana-Champaign

Abstract. The approach to environmental protection has been evolving from a regulation-driven, adversarial 'government-push' approach to a more proactive approach involving voluntary and often 'business-led' initiatives to self-regulate their environmental performance. This has been accompanied by increasing provision of environmental information about firms and products to enlist market forces and communities in creating a demand for corporate environmental self-regulation by signaling their preferences for environmentally friendly firms. This paper provides an overview of the non-mandatory approaches being used for environmental protection and surveys the existing theoretical literature analyzing the economic efficiency of such approaches relative to mandatory approaches. It also discusses empirical findings on the factors motivating self-regulation by firms and its implications for their economic and environmental performance. It examines the existing evidence on the extent to which information disclosure is effective in generating pressures from investors and communities on firms to improve their environmental performance.

Keywords. Voluntary programs; Toxic releases; Environmental management; Stakeholder pressure; Mandatory regulations; Economic incentives

1. Introduction

Environmental regulation in the OECD countries has traditionally taken the form of mandatory command and control regulations that prescribe quantity limits on emissions of pollutants or the use of specific abatement technologies. While these regulations have improved the environment, they have resulted in a policy framework that is medium-specific, fragmented and inflexible. It has encouraged end-of-pipe pollution controls, cross-media substitution and imposed steeply rising costs of abatement on firms and regulators. Doubts about the effectiveness of increasing reliance on command and control regulations and a growing belief in the need to provide flexibility to firms to choose their least cost methods of pollution control have emerged in these countries.

As a result, economic incentives such as, taxes and tradable permits, that rely on price signals to induce pollution control and provide the needed flexibility have become much more common (NCEE, 2001; Opschoor, 1994). However, the task of designing such instruments efficiently for the hundreds of currently unregulated and high risk pollutants, for nonpoint source pollutants and for pollutants currently regulated using command and control methods would be administratively difficult, slow and costly and possibly beyond the budgets of regulatory agencies. For example, cut backs in the regulatory budget of the U.S. Environmental Protection Agency (USEPA) have limited its ability to monitor and enforce policies since the mid 1980's and there have been an increasing number of citizen enforcement actions against firms violating existing laws and against the agency for lax enforcement (Maxwell and Lyon, 1999). A desire to find cost-effective solutions to environmental problems, to substitute a co-operative approach between industry and public authorities for the prevailing adversarial approach while avoiding negative legal and political consequences associated with regulatory failure has led to a shift in the regulatory paradigm towards encouraging voluntary actions by firms to supplement (without weakening) existing regulations in the U.S and in Europe. These approaches are also being used by environmental agencies to encourage firms to take a holistic perspective towards pollution control through multi-media strategies and waste minimization without reforming the media-specific, end-of-pipe control focus of existing legislation (GAO, 1994a). This trend towards devolution of responsibility for environmental protection has been broadened beyond encouraging voluntary actions by firms to enlist market forces in creating a demand for environmental self-regulation by firms. The latter is being enabled by publicly providing environmental information about firms and products to enable citizens to make informed choices, and to signal their preferences for environmentally friendly firms. Such signals can be transmitted through the product, capital and labor markets which link buyers and employees to polluting firms and through community and citizen group pressures on firms (Tietenberg, 1998).

Since 1990, the USEPA has established over 31 voluntary programs (Mazurek, 1998b) while there are about 310 voluntary agreements in the European Union, with the majority in Netherlands and Germany (Carraro and Leveque, 1999). The environmental problems targeted by these programs include carbon emissions and toxic pollutants, waste management and water quality (Mazurek, 1998b; Borkey and Leveque, 1998). Environmental agencies in many countries have also established information disclosure programs that provide environmental information such as the Toxics Release Inventory (TRI) in the U.S. and environmental labeling programs. Even developing countries, such as Indonesia, Philippines, Mexico and India, have initiated information disclosure programs to supplement a regulatory infrastructure that is by itself weak and incapable of designing and enforcing an effective pollution control system (World Bank, 1999).

These public policy initiatives have been accompanied by a growing number of industry-led programs for self-regulation, as firms and trade associations have adopted a more proactive approach to environmental protection. These 'business-led' initiatives are in sharp contrast to the 'government-push' approach towards environmental protection that existed during the 1980s and was based on a view held by firms that efforts to control pollution were 'non-productive'. Several firms (3M, Dow Chemical, Dupont, AT&T) have developed programs to prevent pollution by redesigning products and processes, since pollution is seen by many of them as a waste of resources (Schmidheiny, 1992; Batie, 1997). Additionally, government efforts to provide information to the public have been supplemented by several non-government environmental groups, such as, the Environment Defense Fund and the Council of Economic Priorities in the U.S.[1] These groups use the media to inform the public about the risks of different toxic chemicals, identify large polluters and provide rankings of firms based on their social and environmental performance to stimulate pro-environmental actions by citizens and firms.

Thus a non-mandatory approach towards environmental protection includes both voluntary initiatives taken by polluting firms towards environmental self-regulation as well as market-based and public pressures that create a demand for self-regulation by firms. Esty and Chertow (1997) refer to this as the 'next generation' of environmental policy. This paper surveys the literature analyzing the economic issues underlying the reliance on a non-mandatory approach to environmental protection. While this approach offers regulators the opportunity to promote flexible approaches to pollution control and to avoid time-consuming regulatory development, does it increase social efficiency and lead firms to voluntarily reduce pollution beyond compliance with existing mandatory regulations? What is the economic rationale for firms to do so when traditionally such actions would have been considered to be detrimental to their goals of profitability? What is the role for mandatory regulations when firms are becoming self-motivated towards improving their environmental performance? Can non-mandatory approaches be used effectively in developing countries where traditional regulations are weak or ill enforced? This paper provides an overview of the non-mandatory approaches being used for environmental regulation in Section 2 and surveys the existing theoretical literature analyzing the issues raised above in Section 3. There is a growing empirical literature analyzing the motivations for participation by firms in voluntary programs and the role that non-mandatory approaches are playing in protecting the environment. Our survey of the empirical literature is divided into three sections. Section 4 discusses the empirical evidence on the motivations for firms to undertake voluntary initiatives, Section 5 presents the findings on the effectiveness of voluntary approaches in achieving pollution reduction and Section 6 examines the evidence on effectiveness of information based approaches in protecting the environment in developed and developing countries. Section 7 discusses the implications that can be derived from the existing literature about the potential role for a non-mandatory approach in environmental policy.

2. Examples of Non-Mandatory Approaches

Non-mandatory approaches to environmental protection encompass a diverse set of efforts aimed at environmental self-regulation by firms. These include voluntary initiatives being encouraged by regulators and undertaken by firms as well as information provision by government and non-government agencies to encourage non-mandatory efforts by the public at large to induce improved environmental performance by firms. Voluntary initiatives by firms can be classified into three broad categories, depending on the extent of government intervention involved in initiating them (Carraro and Leveque, 1999), consisting of public voluntary programs designed by regulators, negotiated agreements between a firm and the regulator, and unilateral commitments by firms to demonstrate environmental stewardship.[2] Each of these categories is described below in greater detail with examples of specific programs. These examples provide a conceptual or empirical basis for the studies surveyed in subsequent sections.

2.1. *Public voluntary programs*

These programs are established by environmental agencies to invite firms to voluntarily meet specified standards for environmental performance or adopt clean technologies. Participation in these programs is based on signing non-binding letters of agreements and progress is monitored through self-reporting. Notable examples of these programs in the U.S. include the 33/50 Program, Green Lights and the Climate Challenge Program. These programs provide public recognition, technical assistance and information subsidies to participants.

The 33/50 Program was launched by the USEPA in 1991 to encourage firms to voluntarily reduce their aggregate emissions of 17 high priority toxic chemicals at source by 33% by 1992 and by 50% by 1995 (GAO, 1994a; Davies and Mazurek, 1996). Firms had flexibility in the amount of reductions undertaken and the means used to achieve them. About 16% of the eligible firms participated in the program and the total reduction in releases of these chemicals exceeded the goal of 50% (Davies and Mazurek, 1996). Green Lights was established by the USEPA in 1991 with the aim to increase energy efficiency in lighting systems to reduce greenhouse gas emissions. Participating firms agree to survey their facilities, and to undertake lighting upgrades that could be achieved profitably without compromising lighting quality and yield an internal rate of return at least as high as 20%. The program attracted substantial participation with the number of participants growing at 7% per annum to 1700 firms by 1995 (USEPA, 1995). The Climate Challenge Program was initiated in 1994 by the U.S. Department of Energy to invite participation by electric utilities to reduce greenhouse gas emissions. Utilities had the flexibility to either participate in initiatives involving investment in renewable energy technologies and afforestation or to develop their own projects to reduce greenhouse gases to a self-specified level by 2000. By 1996, utilities responsible for over 60% of electricity generation in the U.S. had pledged participation (USDOE, 1996).

Public voluntary schemes have been used to achieve reduction in greenhouse gases by increasing energy efficiency in several countries in the EU (Storey, Boyd and Dowd, 1999). Voluntary programs in the EU provide participants with more direct regulatory relief than those in the U.S. For example, the Danish voluntary program to reduce CO_2 offers a choice of voluntarily committing to pre-identified

CO_2 reducing investment in exchange for being levied a lower tax per ton of CO_2. The Portuguese voluntary scheme with the Paper and Pulp industry offers a delay in total compliance with existing regulation and financial assistance in exchange for a precise timetable for progress in environmental performance (Borkey and Leveque, 1998).

The agricultural sector in the U.S has also relied on voluntary actions by farmers to reduce nonpoint pollution but, unlike the programs described above, it has relied on the provision of cost-share subsidies to induce those actions. Programs such as the Conservation Reserve Program (CRP) and the Environmental Quality Incentives Program provide subsidies to induce the retirement of erodible land from crop production and to adopt improved nutrient management practices to reduce chemical contamination (Ribaudo and Caswell, 1999).

2.2. *Bilateral initiatives*

Bilateral initiatives involve active negotiation between the government and the firm on abatement targets and plans. The USEPA initiated two such programs, the Common Sense Initiative and Project XL in 1994 and 1995. Both were to provide regulatory relief in exchange for pollution reductions in excess of status quo standards and integrate pollution reduction activities across different media. However, uncertainties regarding the USEPA's statutory authority to achieve regulatory reform while exempting companies from complying with current statutes and regulations have limited their scope and participation rates (Mazurek, 1998b). Project XL was established to provide flexibility to individual firms in developing pollution control strategies on a case-by-case basis. It waives certain administrative and statutory requirements for facilities that demonstrate that they can improve their environmental performance beyond that possible under compliance with existing regulations, cost-effectively and with public involvement and support. It is the only voluntary agreement in the US with legally binding provisions.[3] While site-specific regulations have the potential to stimulate greater efficiency and innovation, they also impose high transactions costs on firms for project development, determination of the baseline pollution over which improvements were to be measured, and frequent monitoring and reporting (Blackman and Mazurek, 2000). As a result of these high costs, only 15 facilities are implementing XL agreements after five years.

Negotiated agreements have been more widely used in the EU; their implementation varies across countries. Most of these agreements are legally non-binding except for the 'covenants' in the Netherlands. These are negotiated agreements between the environmental agency and the industry consisting of a quantitative abatement target for the industry and then binding contracts (operation licenses) with each firm willing to join the covenant. The abatement target for the industry is set by the parliament but the methods and timetable for abatement are negotiated with the industry. Participating firms have to prepare, in cooperation with the agencies, detailed plans about waste reduction goals and measures, timing of implementation and cost-effectiveness. The government commits to refraining from introducing new legislation, such as a standard or tax, unless the voluntary action fails to meet the agreed upon target. Firms are monitored and held liable individually; non-compliance is penalized through increased stringency of operation licenses. In contrast, agreements in Germany involve bargaining over the abatement targets and the industry is held collectively liable for implementation. If the agreement fails all firms are sanctioned independently of their abatement efforts; free riding is therefore a major problem under collective liability (Borkey and Leveque, 1998).

2.3. *Unilateral initiatives*

Unilateral initiatives by firms occur without direct government involvement and can be of three types. Firms can: (a) develop their own plans or management systems to improve their own environmental performance (b) participate in codes of conduct or guidelines developed by trade associations, and (c) meet the environmental performance standards for registering with a certifying organization, such as the International Organization for Standardization. These initiatives differ in the stringency with which they are implemented and in whether they require numeric environmental improvement goals or only the development of procedures and systems that facilitate improved environmental performance. Most of them focus only on the means (proactive efforts) for pollution control rather than the ends (actual performance improvement).

Numerous firms have adopted innovative environmental management systems that demonstrate a proactive orientation towards improving environmental performance. These systems are based on: voluntary codes of conduct on environmental issues, such as applying uniform standards to environmental practices worldwide, training and rewarding workers to find opportunities to prevent pollution, environmental auditing and applying Total Quality Management (TQM) principles to environmental management (Khanna and Anton, 2001). Many firms have also crafted comprehensive environmental programs aimed towards zero discharges and pollution prevention, such as the 3P program introduced by 3M Corporation and WRAP (Waste Reduction Always Pays) introduced by Dow Chemicals (Batie, 1997; Schmidheiny, 1992). These initiatives are self-evaluated and reported and there is no third party certification or oversight on their actual impact on environmental performance.

Additionally, many trade associations have developed codes of environmental management practices that involve concerted actions by member firms. There are 27 such industry-level initiatives in Europe and 9 such initiatives in the U.S. (Borkey and Leveque, 1998; Mazurek, 1998a and b). The best-known example of this is the Responsible Care Initiative implemented by the Chemical industry that was started in Canada in 1984 and has since spread to 40 countries. Responsible Care is a set of guiding principles and codes of management practices to ensure that facilities operate in an environmentally responsible manner, protect and promote health and safety of employees and communities and prevent pollution (Mazurek, 1998a). Responsible Care participants are allowed to use a registered trademark to promote public recognition. Participation is a condition for membership in the Chemical Industry Association of a country. Firms have discretion in the level of implementation of these practices and the specific activities they undertake. Firms are required to self-report annually on implementation progress. The Association encourages third-party verification to confirm that adequate systems are in place but has limited control over members' implementation of the codes due to anti-trust rules (Maitland, 1985). While it can revoke membership for non-compliance with the codes, in practice it has relied on offering technical assistance and peer pressure to induce firms to implement the management codes. Its approach has therefore been characterized as a 'velvet glove, but no iron fist' (Reisch, 1998).

Additionally, standards for environmental management systems have been established by the International Standards Organization (ISO 14001) that seek to provide guidelines for environmental management and eco-labeling of products. Instead of prescribing operating practices as in the case of the Responsible Care program, ISO defines procedures that firms must follow and requires third-party review and certification. These procedures are strongly influenced by the theory of TQM that encourages continuous progress towards minimizing waste in the form of defective products and pollution. Unlike Responsible Care that prescribes a common set of environmental principles, the ISO allows managers flexibility in setting their objectives. While some firms may specify goals to reduce pollution at source, others may specify training workers handling hazardous waste as their objective (Kuhre, 1995).

2.4. *Information provision*

Information disclosure strategies are being used in several ways. In the U.S, the Toxics Release Inventory (TRI) a database of releases of over 300 toxic chemicals is released publicly by the USEPA accompanied by media coverage (GAO, 1994b). The USEPA also provides the national priority list of firms potentially responsible for hazardous waste sites, the historical profile of inspections, enforcement actions and penalties assessed on all regulated facilities to the public.[4] Information about environmental lawsuits against firms by the government are often announced in the print media. The environmental agency in British Columbia, Canada publishes a list of firms not complying with environmental regulations or having poor environmental performance (Lanoie, Laplante and Roy, 1997). The environmental agency in the U.K created the Chemical Release Inventory in 1990 to provide information on annual releases of specified substances by large industrial sites. In 1995 Indonesia's environmental agency established a Program for Pollution Control, Evaluation and Rating (PROPER), for rating and publicly disclosing the environmental performance of water polluters in Indonesia (World Bank, 1999).

Environmental labeling of products is also being used increasingly to provide health and environmental information. Labeling can take the form of eco-labels (e.g. Green Seal, Blue Angel) that are voluntarily obtained 'seals of approval' certified by public or private organizations, government mandated labels (e.g. fuel efficiency ratings on automobiles) or self-declarations (e.g. manufacturer's claims about recyclability) (van Ravenswaay and Blend, 1999).

3. Motivations for Voluntary Initiatives and Efficiency

The traditional literature in environmental economics analyzing a firm's behavior under alternative environmental policies typically assumes profit-maximizing firms that take prices and regulations as given and have no incentives to control pollution in the absence of environmental regulations or go beyond compliance with existing regulations because pollution control only imposes costs that are non-productive (see the survey in Cropper and Oates, 1992). Studies analyzing environmental self-regulation by firms continue to assume that a voluntary agreement, while facilitating voluntary action with a desirable social outcome, is undertaken by firms based on their self-interest (Storey, Boyd and Dowd, 1999). These agreements are therefore self-enforcing by definition. However, these studies differ from the traditional literature in that they recognize that this self-interest in self-regulation arises because firms may be able to influence input/output prices and environmental regulations.

Participation in voluntary programs provides a variety of benefits to firms, such as public recognition through press releases, newsletters, and awards. This may enable firms to increase market share or charge higher prices for their products, now differentiated by their environmental attributes. Public opinion and improved relations with customers and the community are cited as the most important reasons by firms for participation in the Responsible Care Program (Mazurek, 1998a), for McDonald's switch from polystyrene foam containers to paper wraps and for Proctor and Gamble's introduction of a refillable fabric softener containers (USEPA, 1991). Several studies, surveyed later in the paper, also show that superior environmental performance can avoid adverse reactions from stockholders and lead to lower costs of capital for firms.

Regulators may induce participation in voluntary programs by providing firms with technical assistance to reduce their costs of learning and abatement. This assistance has consisted of information about alternative waste-reducing technologies, availability of rebates and low interest financing in the case of Green Lights program, and methods for improving efficiency of electricity transmission in the case of the Climate Challenge Program. Some programs, such as CRP and EQIP, may induce participation by providing subsidies.

Participation may provide direct regulatory relief as in the case of Project XL or an expectation of regulatory relief in the future. By undertaking proactive efforts to develop environmentally friendly products and processes, firms may be able to shape future environmental standards in their favor, gain a competitive advantage in the future and create barriers to entry by new firms. For example, the 1990 Clean Air Act Amendments list 189 hazardous air pollutants (HAP) (which include the 17 chemicals targeted by the 33/50 program) that will be subject to maximum available control technology (MACT) standards to meet National Emissions Standards for HAP from 2000 onwards. In setting the MACT standards the USEPA sets emission levels based on technology or other practices being used by the better-controlled and lower emitting sources in the industry (USEPA, 2000). Firms could therefore use the opportunity provided by participation in the 33/50 program to reduce these emissions ahead of time using flexible methods and influence the standards to be promulgated by the USEPA. Similarly, emissions reduction achieved under the Climate Challenge Program may potentially provide early credits and reduce future regulatory requirements on participating firms.[5]

Finally, self-regulation may be motivated by the potential for lowering the costs of compliance relative to those under existing mandatory regulations. The Danish program to reduce CO_2 emissions waives a part of the tax payments for firms that self-regulate and thus reduces the costs of pollution generation for firms. Programs such as the Common Sense Initiative and Project XL offer firms a multi-media permit to replace the existing media-specific permits thus reducing the overlap in reporting requirements and permit processing time.

Thus firms' incentives for environmental self-regulation can broadly be stated to be arising from the following sources: preempting the threat of mandatory regulations, shaping future regulations, technical assistance and/or financial subsidies which lower the cost of abatement, cost efficiency, and better relations with the government and with stakeholders which include, consumers, investors, communities and other firms in the industry. We categorize the theoretical studies based on their assumed motivations for voluntary action by firms and discuss their findings regarding the effectiveness of a voluntary approach to protecting the environment and its implications for social welfare.

3.1. *Preempting regulatory threats*

Several studies examine the implications of the incentives for firms to voluntarily agree to abate to preempt a threat of mandatory standards (Segerson and Miceli, 1998; Maxwell, Lyon and Hackett, 2000) or an emissions tax (Schmelzer, 1999; Hansen, 1999). Segerson and Miceli (1998) and Lyon and Maxwell (2000) consider the possibility of combining or following the threat of a mandatory policy with a subsidy to induce additional abatement.

Segerson and Miceli (1998) assume that voluntary pollution control involves lower abatement costs and transactions costs and it would be optimal for not only a cost-minimizing firm but also for a welfare maximizing regulator to choose a voluntary agreement instead of an uncertain mandatory abatement even if it results (to some extent) in a lower level of abatement. They show that as the threat of regulation increases, the firm is likely to be willing to abate more. The voluntarily achieved abatement level could be smaller than the first-best abatement level although it is always larger than the expected level under the mandatory policy. They also consider the potential of combining the threat of regulation with a subsidy and show that the optimal level of abatement is now lower than the first-best level because of the social cost of funds used to finance the subsidy. The actual level of abatement achieved depends on the allocation of bargaining power, magnitude of background threat and the social cost of funds.

Schmelzer (1999) analyzes the implications of voluntary agreement between a regulator and a single firm or an industry association, induced by a threat of an emissions tax using a two period game theoretic model. This involves a firm deciding whether or not to propose a voluntary agreement and the government deciding whether to accept or to impose a tax on pollution. As in Segerson and Miceli (1998), Schmelzer (1999) also assumes that the mandatory regulation is more costly for the regulator and hence there is an incentive for the regulator to choose a voluntary program even if it implies lower abatement levels. While in Segerson and Miceli (1998) the regulator faces a trade-off between a lower but certain level of voluntary abatement as compared to a probabilistic level under mandatory regulations, in Schmelzer (1999) a regulator with a positive discount rate faces a trade-off between a lower level of voluntary abatement in the first period and a higher but more costly and delayed level of mandatory abatement in the next period. Bargaining between the firm and the government results in a lower voluntary level of abatement but a higher level of social welfare because reductions in emissions under the voluntary program are traded off against reductions in avoided costs of monitoring and the cost of delay (due to a positive discount rate) under the mandatory policy.

Maxwell, Lyon and Hackett (2000) analyze the welfare implications of self-regulation by firms to preempt consumer groups from lobbying for more stringent mandatory abatement regulations. When it is costly for consumers to organize themselves and influence the political process, a low level of voluntary abatement by firms could be sufficient to deter consumer groups from entering the political process and could preempt more stringent mandatory regulations. Despite lower abatement levels if preemption occurs, self-regulation is welfare improving not only for firms but also for consumers. This is because if consumers were able to lobby for mandatory regulations, they would have obtained a higher level of total abatement than achieved voluntarily; hence if they allow themselves to be preempted it must be that the benefits from the improved environmental performance are lower than the costs of political and regulatory action needed to obtain higher abatement. The incentives for self-regulation to occur here arise if firms can act collusively; if firms choose voluntary abatement levels non-cooperatively then they have an incentive to free-ride and while some level of voluntary abatement would still occur to preempt regulation, it would be smaller than the level achieved collusively.

Unlike the above studies where there is only one social welfare-maximizing regulator, Hansen (1999) considers the case where the Congress is involved in policy formulation under the mandatory approach but is excluded from a voluntary agreement that is negotiated between the regulator and industry. Voluntary participation is rewarded by avoiding an emissions tax regime. Hansen (1999) shows that the voluntary and traditional process can lead to different welfare outcomes because the regulator and the Congress differ in the utility weights they attach to tax revenue and environmental damage reduction. If the regulator is more pro-firm or pro-environment than the Congress, then voluntary agreements that are beneficial to the firms and the regulator can result even if they are more costly and lead to lower social welfare and ambiguous impacts on the environmental. Hansen (1999) shows that if interest groups can punish decision makers through public criticism about environmental goals and their attainment then decision makers may agree to voluntary agreements that are neither welfare-increasing nor beneficial to the environment to evade the responsibility for environmental protection.

These studies have focused either on single firm models or assumed that the industry can act as a homogenous interest group and coordinate the allocation of abatement responsibility among member firms according to the equi-marginal principle and avoid free-riding behavior. Segerson and Miceli (1999), Dawson and Segerson (2000) and Millock and Salanie (2000) consider the case where multiple firms are involved and firms have an incentive to free-ride and reap the benefit of a voluntary agreement (avoidance of legislation) without incurring the cost. Segerson and Miceli (1999) consider two heterogeneous firms and show that the likelihood of having a voluntary agreement is higher if the agreement is implemented as long as one of the firm's accepts and the other firm is allowed to free-ride than if both firms are required to accept it. The social welfare implications of such a program with only a subset of firms participating relative to a mandatory policy requiring all firms to comply are, however, ambiguous.

In Dawson and Segerson (2000), the regulator offers an industry, consisting of multiple identical firms, the option of voluntarily meeting an aggregate abatement target to avoid an emissions-tax. Since the abatement target is industry-wide, individual firms have incentives to free-ride because all firms benefit if the target is met, while only firms that abate bear costs. Costs of abatement are assumed to be the same under the voluntary and the emissions tax policy. They show that in equilibrium at least one or more firms will be willing to voluntarily abate and meet the industry target even if other firms free-ride in order to obtain the cost-savings achieved by avoiding the tax. Voluntary participation by at least some firms is shown to be self-enforcing because they are at least as well off with participation as they would have been under the tax. Aggregate industry costs of abatement plus tax payments are lower under a voluntary program than under the tax policy since non-participating firms incur a zero cost while participating firms earn the same level of profits under both policy approaches. However, total social cost of meeting the industry abatement target is higher under a voluntary approach because of inefficient and non-uniform distribution of abatement across homogeneous firms.

In contrast to Dawson and Segerson (2000) where a few firms can compensate for free-riding behavior by others to ensure the success of a voluntary program, Millock and Salanie (2000) assume that free-riding by any firm leads to the imposition of a tax in the next period. They show that the greater and more certain the threat of a tax and the less short-sighted the firms are, the smaller the likelihood is of free-riding.

3.2. *Influencing future regulations*

Lutz, Lyon and Maxwell (2000) analyze the incentives for voluntary action by firms if it can be used to influence regulations set subsequently by the government. They consider a case where products are vertically differentiated (that is, differ in their attributes). Product differentiation allows firms to relax price competition and thus they prefer to offer distinct qualities in equilibrium. The paper shows that a high quality firm prefers to have a first-mover position and proactively commit to a quality level that is lower than would have emerged if the regulator had announced the minimum quality standard first. This induces the regulator to set a weaker standard because it cares about firms' profits that would be reduced by setting higher minimum quality standards and reducing product differentiation. Both firms therefore produce a lower quality and while this results in higher profits for them, it lowers consumers' welfare and results in lower social welfare than if the government had set the standard first.

3.3. *Technical assistance/financial incentives*

Many voluntary programs induce participation by lowering the costs of reducing waste, for example, household recycling programs provide free bins and curb-side pick up, the public voluntary programs discussed above provide technical information, a directory of rebate programs provided by energy efficient lighting companies and even direct payments in the case of some agricultural programs. Stranlund (1995) and Wu and Babcock (1999) compare the efficiency of a mandatory program relative to a voluntary program that induces participation by lowering the costs of voluntary compliance by providing public effort that can be substituted for private abatement effort. Additionally in Wu and Babcock (1999) the government also provides direct subsidy payments to offset the fixed costs of adoption. The mandatory approach in both studies consists of a fine for non-compliance and both approaches are designed to achieve the same level of compliance. While Stranlund (1995) assumes that public effort to lower costs of voluntary compliance is met through a lump-sum tax, Wu and Babcock (1999), recognize the deadweight loss associated with public expenditure. Stranlund (1995) shows that when the voluntary program provides a non-rival public good, such as technical information about pollution reducing technologies (as in the 33/50 program), the voluntary program is welfare-improving because it is more cost-efficient for the regulator to provide the public good to all than to have each individual duplicate the effort on their own. If, however, public effort is rival in nature and non-excludable, such as providing a free recycling bin to each household (whether or not they participate) to induce voluntary recycling, then a mandatory program can achieve higher social welfare because only the participants in the program would purchase the bins and incur costs. However, if the government can target its efforts and avoid provision of recycling bins to non-participants or if the price of public effort is lower than that of private effort then a voluntary program could achieve at least the same level of welfare as the mandatory program.

In Wu and Babcock (1999), the benefits of a voluntary program arise because of its lower costs of implementation or enforcement that need to be balanced with the welfare loss from financing the expenditures on a voluntary program, such as the CRP in the U.S., using socially costly public funds. As in Stranlund (1995), the comparative advantage of a voluntary program increases as participation increases since duplicated private effort is avoided by government services. Wu and Babcock (1999) show that the relative efficiency of voluntary program increases when the degree of rivalness of government services decreases, as government services become less expensive than private effort, the social costs of funds is low and the enforcement costs of the mandatory program are high. The cost-share subsidy provided here is uniform rather than differentiated across heterogeneous farmers and therefore a second best instrument. A differentiated subsidy could lead to higher welfare under a voluntary program, however, it might also reduce the advantage of the voluntary program in the form of lower costs of implementation.

Like Wu and Babcock (1999), participation in the voluntary program in Segerson (1999) is also induced using socially costly public funds, but the regulator now seeks to differentiate the subsidy payment across heterogeneous firms. Additionally, unlike the previous two studies above where the level of environmental protection achieved by both the mandatory and voluntary program is the same, the abatement level under the voluntary program in Segerson (1999) is chosen while recognizing the social costs of funds to achieve that abatement. Although costs of a given level of abatement and implementation are assumed to be the same for the voluntary and mandatory program, the benefit of a voluntary program arises when there is asymmetric information and the regulator cannot differentiate between high and low cost firms to set efficient non-uniform standards. In that case, the regulator can design a voluntary program that provides a subsidy to induce truth telling by firms. However, it achieves the first-best level of social welfare only if the social cost of public funds is zero.

Lyon and Maxwell (2000) develop a three-stage game that allows the possibility of unilateral voluntary efforts aimed at preemption of a tax. In the event that legislative efforts to impose the tax are defeated, the regulator proposes a voluntary program with an optimally determined subsidy for all firms that adopt the environmental technology unilaterally or otherwise. Both the tax and the subsidy policy impose fixed costs on the regulator and subsidy payments also involve using costly public funds. They consider a continuum of firms differentiated according to abatement costs but producing a homogeneous good and a welfare-maximizing regulator. The tax creates incentive for unilateral industry action which could preempt a tax when the costs of imposing a tax are high and the cost of raising funds for the subsidy are high. While unilateral actions that preempt a tax must be social welfare enhancing, a public voluntary agreement could be welfare-reducing relative to a tax because taxation induces inefficient firms to exit while subsidized voluntary participation does not and because it may motivate weaker unilateral action by firms so as to not preempt the subsidy program.

3.4. *Cost efficiency*

Voluntary agreements on an aggregate abatement target between an industry and a regulator allow flexibility in the allocation of abatement burden among firms within the industry. Glachant (1999) analyzes differences in transactions costs, under a voluntary and a mandatory policy (taxes or standards), due to the need to collect information to allocate this burden efficiently. Under an emissions standard policy, the regulator needs to collect information about private pollution abatement costs to set efficient non-uniform standards. Under a voluntary agreement, firms have to collect information not only about their own abatement costs but also those of other firms and incur computation costs to define their bargaining strategy. In contrast, taxes are a decentralized scheme in which firms choose their abatement levels individually in response to the price signal and firms do not need to communicate with each other or the regulator. Glachant (1999) suggests that when there is informational asymmetry and the number of firms is large, a voluntary approach is more costly than either a standards or a tax policy. It requires more intensive inter-firm communication and generates higher inter-firm rivalry since each firm's desire to reduce its abatement implies a higher level for other firms. However, when there is shared uncertainty about generic pollution abatement costs among all firms and firms are few and relatively homogeneous, voluntary approaches could be efficient because they facilitate collective learning more easily than a standard or a tax policy.

Blackman and Boyd (1999) focus on a different type of cost-efficiency that arises in the form of lower variable costs of production due to the flexibility provided by a tailored voluntary program, such as Project XL, that sets firm-specific emission standards that are assumed to be stricter but less costly than existing command and control standards. A firm participates if these cost-savings are larger than the additional fixed costs of transactions imposed by participation in the voluntary agreement. Blackman and Boyd (1999) show that participation by a monopoly unambiguously increases welfare because it results in larger production, due to lower marginal variable cost of production, and thus greater consumer surplus and monopoly profits (due to the individual rationality constraint and participation constraint). However, when a Cournot duopoly exists, offering the opportunity to participate to only one of the two firms increases the participating firm's output and market share but this occurs to some extent at the expense of the other firm. While aggregate industry output increases and consumers are better off with the tailored regulation, the net impact on producers' surplus is positive only if the tailored regulation shifts production from a firm with a low profit margin to a firm with a high profit margin. The analysis suggests that a tailored regulation can be welfare improving if it is targeted towards more profitable firms. Promoting the diffusion of the program across all firms reduces incentives for participation since it reduces the competitive advantage gained by participants.

3.5. *Improved stakeholder relations*

When polluting firms and victims or stakeholders are linked contractually through the market as buyers and sellers then victims have the potential to individually signal their environmental preferences to firms through the market in the form of adverse reputation effects and reduced demand for products, lower stock prices or high employee turnover (Tietenberg, 1998). They can thereby influence the profitability of firms and create pecuniary incentives for firms to undertake voluntary abatement. One of the underlying principles of economic theory is that perfect information among market participants is critical for the efficient operation of markets. Environmental information may be costly for individuals to obtain or individual gains from obtaining it may be small while societal gains may be large or information provided by the market may be imperfect because of moral hazard or adverse selection. Hence, there is a role for the government or other organizations in providing information that is reliable and standardized. Labeling can circumvent market inefficiencies to the extent that individuals care about the environment by removing information asymmetry or subsidizing search costs.

Investors can also create incentives for self-regulation if they prefer to hold stocks of environmentally friendly firms either because they have green preferences or believe that such firms are more likely to be profitable in the future. This could follow from a belief that pollution is a waste of purchased inputs that are not used productively or that poor environmental performance reflects poor management practices and lack of innovativeness; thus there is a potential for cost savings by reducing pollution. Additionally, poor environmental performance could be viewed as exposing the firm to greater risks of environmental liabilities, penalties and high costs of compliance in the future (Khanna *et al.*, 1998). Thus poor environmental performance of the firm can influence its stock prices.

While consumers and investors have the potential to influence firm behavior through individual action taken in their own self-interest, it is more difficult for communities to organize collectively to induce self-regulation by firms. Whether or not investors and communities react to environmental information about firms and its implications for firms and the environment is an empirical issue and the results of several empirical studies exploring these effects are discussed in the next section. Much of the theoretical literature has analyzed the welfare implications of consumer preferences for environmental quality operating by influencing the position and slope of the market demand curve for a product and creating incentives for firms to provide products differentiated by their environmental attributes.

Garvie (1997) develops a model in which identical firms produce a homogeneous good and consumers' utility, and therefore total market demand is affected not only by the aggregate quantity produced but also by the aggregate pollution generated. Consumers may therefore be willing to internalize at least some of the externalities due to their consumption decisions and this could lead to an industry demand that is lower than under the perfectly competitive equilibrium in the absence of externalities. It is then optimal for firms to undertake some voluntary abatement. However, if consumers do not fully internalize all of the environmental damage, the abatement level achieved by firms is less than the first best level. Social welfare increases with self-regulation because there is a positive relationship between abatement efforts and total quantity produced (demanded). Since consumers only care about aggregate emissions, there is incentive for firms to free-ride, unless firms can coordinate their abatement strategies and achieve a higher level of abatement and higher social welfare.

While Garvie (1997) provides an explanation for voluntary self-regulation even if all firms produce a homogeneous product, Arora and Gangopadhya (1995) develop a model to analyze the incentive for firms to differentiate their products by the way that they are produced. Consumers derive utility from buying from a firm that takes active measures to reduce pollution and their disutility from paying a higher price for it decreases as income increases. Arora and Gangopadhya (1995) show that differences in income levels segment the market by consumer types. Price competition among firms with non-homogeneous consumers gives rise to products with different environmental qualities because if they are the same then competition will ensure that profits for both firms are zero and there would be no positive level of abatement effort at which firms could make non-negative profits. The imposition of a minimum quality standard forces not only the low quality firm to raise its abatement level but the high quality firm to over meet the standard in order to differentiate itself sufficiently from the other firm.

In addition to these factors, a firm's incentives to supply green products also depend on its ability to signal improvements in their environmental performance to consumers and to successfully and credibly differentiate its products. Often sellers are better informed about quality attributes than consumers and consumers may have misperceptions of the risk and hazards of using certain products. Akerlof's (1970) seminal article showed that markets are ineffective in providing quality when sellers have good information on product quality and buyers have poor information. In this case only the lowest quality product may be sold because of the adverse selection problem: if quality cannot be signaled, higher quality products cannot get a price premium and only lower quality products will be offered for sale. In the case of experience goods where information about certain types of environmental attributes of products can be obtained by experience after buying and using the product, consumers may use the quality of products produced by the firm in the past as an indicator of present or future quality. A seller who then chooses to enter the high quality segment of the market must initially invest in his reputation by producing quality merchandise and in equilibrium must earn a premium above his costs of production if he is not to be tempted to cut quality (Shapiro, 1983). However, in a non-cooperative game between consumers and a monopolist, the reputational incentives for a monopolist to produce high quality experience goods would only be observed if there is an infinitely repeated interaction between firms and consumers (Cavaliere, 1999).

In the case of credence goods (where the environmental impact of a product cannot be ascertained by the consumer even after purchase) participation in voluntary programs provides firms with a procedure to acquire an environmentally friendly reputation to convert a credence good into an experience good. If consumers believe that it is in the self-interest of a monopolist to produce a high quality good because of a threat of entry by a competitor with a superior product or a threat of a stricter mandatory regulation then there exists a positive probability that a monopolist will produce high quality goods at least in the first period to gain a reputation but will 'milk' his reputation in the second period by producing low quality goods when consumers have been led to choose a high quality product (Cavaliere, 1999).This suggests that finite horizon voluntary agreements need to be followed by mandatory standards on quality to prevent firms from taking advantage of their reputation to sell low quality products after an agreement ends.

4. Motivations for voluntary initiatives: empirical evidence

Several studies have analyzed the decision by firms to participate in public voluntary programs such as the 33/50 program (Khanna and Damon, 1999; Celdran et al., 1996; Arora and Cason, 1995, 1996), Green Lights (DeCanio and Watkins, 1998), and Climate Challenge program (Karamanos, 2000). Videras and Alberini (2000) examine the incentives for participation in the 33/50 program, Green Lights and Waste-Wise.[6] Other studies analyze the incentives for firms to undertake unilateral initiatives by joining trade association programs (King and Lenox, 2000), adopting ISO 14001 and expanding use of personnel for environmental inspection and control (Dasgupta, Hettige and Wheeler, 2000), an environmental plan (Henriques and Sadorsky, 1996) and an environmental management system (Khanna and Anton, 2001).

Like the theoretical studies, these studies also assume that firms participate in a voluntary program or undertake unilateral initiatives if the expected net benefits or profits from doing so are larger than otherwise; participation is therefore self-enforcing. The costs and benefits from such voluntary actions are expected to vary across firms that are heterogeneous in their technologies, products, regulatory pressures and other characteristics; therefore it is rational for some firms to participate and for others not to. These studies generally use a probit or logit model to analyze the determinants of the probability of a firm undertaking a voluntary initiative; Khanna and Anton (2001) use Poisson/ordered probit methods to explain the count of environmental practices/quality of environmental management while Dasgupta, Hettige and Wheeler (2000) use ordinary least squares method to explain the adoption index for ISO 14001 management practices. Celdran et al. (1996) analyze differences in mean responses of participants and non-participants in the 33/50 program responding to a survey enquiring about the motivations for their participation decision. In the case of the Green Lights program, DeCanio and Watkins (1998) argue that the positive net benefit rule would not be a good predictor of the participation decision and test the hypothesis of the irrelevance of firm characteristics to the participation decision. This is because participation in the Green Lights Program only commits firms to make all energy efficient lighting upgrades that meet a clear profitability test and these upgrades are generic and uniform across firms and sectors and therefore differences in firm characteristics are unlikely to explain differences in the participation decision. Karamanos (2000) assumes that participation in the Climate Challenge program is based not only on profit-maximization but also to satisfy strategic managerial objectives such as satisfying employees and improving a company's image. The major findings of these studies are summarized below according to broad factors that motivate voluntary actions by firms to control pollution. Since these studies analyze very diverse samples of firms, they provide broad-based evidence on the role of external pressures from consumers, shareholders, public and government regulations as well as of firm-specific characteristics such as financial performance and size.

Stakeholder pressure

Public recognition, customer goodwill and green consumerism have been hypothesized to be among the sources of benefits to firms from undertaking voluntary actions to control pollution. Firms primarily producing final goods and in closer contact with consumers (Khanna and Damon, 1999), firms in industries with a higher advertising expenditure per unit sales and those producing larger non-33/50 releases and therefore more visible to the public (Arora and Cason, 1996) were more likely to participate in the 33/50 program and in Green Lights and WasteWise (Videras and Alberini, 2000). Consumer pressures are found to be a significant motivator for the adoption of an environmental plan (Henriques and Sadorsky, 1996) and a more comprehensive environmental management system (Khanna and Anton, 2001). Firms that were more visible or concerned about public image are also found to be more likely to participate in the 33/50 program (Celdren *et al.*, 1996) and to join Responsible Care (King and Lenox, 2000). On the other hand, Arora and Cason (1995) did not find advertising intensity to be a significant variable influencing participation in the 33/50 program, while Karamanos (2000) finds that utilities that have a larger fraction of revenues from retail consumers were more likely to participate in the Climate Challenge program but that the results were not significant.

Perceived pressures from shareholders, lobby groups, neighborhood and community groups (Henriques and Sadorsky, 1996) as well as from trade associations (Khanna and Damon, 1999) and educated employees and management (Dasgupta, Hettige and Wheeler, 2000) were found to be significant in motivating voluntary actions. Khanna and Anton (2001) find that publicly traded firms with a higher ratio of capital asset to sales and therefore more dependent on the market for capital were more likely to undertake environmental management possibly to prevent adverse reactions from stockholders. Karamanos (2000) found that utilities operating in states with high environmental group membership and poor air quality were more likely to participate in the Climate Challenge program, although only the latter effect was significant. On the other hand, Dasgupta, Hettige and Wheeler (2000) did not find a significant impact of neighbors, communities, clients and industrial associations on the adoption of ISO 14001 by Mexican firms, possibly reflecting weaker public concern in Mexico for the environment.

Competitive pressure

Several theoretical studies have suggested that voluntary agreements are more likely to occur effectively in concentrated industries with fewer firms or those with strong industry associations because of weaker incentives for free-riding (Maxwell, Lyon and Hackett, 2000), lower costs of inter-firm coordination (Glachant, 1999) and greater market power and ability to differentiate products (Garvie, 1997; Arora and Gangopadhya, 1995). The literature on the impact of market structure on innovative activity, however, suggests that competitive firms are more likely to pursue cost-reducing innovative activities than a monopolist if those activities could result in an increase in sales that reduce the price the monopolist can charge (Arrow, 1962). The empirical evidence on the impact of competitive pressure on incentives for innovative environmental management is mixed. While Arora and Cason (1995) find that firms operating under more competitive conditions, that is in less concentrated industries, were more likely to participate in the 33/50 program Khanna and Anton (2001) do not find such firms to be more likely to undertake environmental management. Instead the latter study does find that firms with a larger proportion of their facilities located in foreign countries, and thus exposed to greater global competition, were more likely to have an environmentally proactive management system. Dasgupta, Hettige and Wheeler (2000), however, did not find that a desire for international competitiveness, proxied by export orientation or multinational status, to be a significant motivator for Mexican firms to adopt ISO 14001.

Regulatory pressures

Videras and Alberini (2000), Khanna and Damon (1999) and Khanna and Anton (2001) find that the threat of liabilities, proxied by the number of Superfund sites for which firms are potentially liable, motivated participation in the 33/50 and WasteWise programs and led firms to undertake environmental management. Both Henriques and Sadorsky (1996) and Dasgupta, Hettige and Wheeler (2000) find evidence that perceived regulatory pressures by firms were important in motivating unilateral initiatives. Khanna and Anton (2001) also find that firms that belonged to highly regulated industries, as proxied by the ratio of industry-wide pollution abatement costs to sales, were more likely to adopt an environmental management system.

Past environmental performance

Several studies also find that firms that had poorer environmental performance, and thus were likely to be the target of negative campaigns by environmental groups and public pressure or exposed to larger costs of compliance/penalties in the future are more likely to undertake voluntary initiatives. Such firms may also undertake voluntary initiatives as a form of insurance against claims of environmental negligence or for altering their reputation. Firms with poorer environmental performance, proxied by high levels of releases or releases per unit sales/employees, were more likely to participate in the 33/50 program (Khanna and Damon, 1999; Arora and Cason, 1995, 1996) and join Responsible Care (King and Lenox, 2000), while utilities relying more heavily on fossil fuels for electricity generation and thus likely to be generating larger carbon emissions per unit electricity were more likely to join the Climate Challenge program (Karamanos, 2000). Khanna and Anton (2001) find that firms that had higher on-site toxic discharges per unit sales but lower off-site transfers per unit sales were more likely to undertake proactive environmental management. To the extent that low off-site transfers per unit sales indicate high costs of end-of-pipe abatement and disposal, this suggests that such firms are more likely to adopt innovative ways to reduce waste generation at source. The threat of high costs of compliance with anticipated regulations, proxied by the share of hazardous air pollutants in total releases, also led firms to participate in the 33/50 program (Khanna and Damon, 1999) and to adopt an environmental management system (Khanna and Anton, 2001).

Size

A number of studies have tested the hypothesis that larger firms are more likely to be environmentally proactive. Larger firms may experience lower marginal costs of abatement due to scale economies and have more personnel to meet the administrative and technical requirements of participation and pollution control. They may also benefit more from being environmental stewards because they are more visible and could experience an increase in demand from a larger number of consumers and have a greater ability to influence environmental regulations in the future by voluntarily over-complying. Larger firms may also be more exposed to liabilities because they have 'deeper pockets'. On the other hand, larger firms may have higher costs of coordinating employees, of training workers to detect opportunities to reduce pollution, as well as of tracking and collecting information on input flows and waste generation within the production process. Empirical evidence appears to support the former hypothesis and larger firms, measured either by total sales or number of employees, were more likely to participate in a voluntary program (Arora and Cason, 1995, 1996; DeCanio and Watkins, 1998; Karamanos, 2000; Videras and Alberini, 2000), join Responsible Care (King and Lenox, 2000) and adopt ISO 14001 practices (Dasgupta, Hettige and Wheeler, 2000).

Financial health

Some studies have hypothesized that more profitable and less risky firms are more likely to be willing to undertake investments in pollution prevention that require long term commitment. DeCanio and Watkins (1998) find that firms with higher earnings per share and higher rate of growth of earnings per share were significantly more likely to participate in the Green Lights program. On the other hand, Arora and Cason (1995) find weak evidence that profitable firms were more likely to participate in the 33/50 program. This conclusion is supported by the survey by Celdran *et al.* (1996) in which financial feasibility or cost of pollution control was not reported to be a strongly prohibitive factor for nonparticipants in the 33/50 program. Similarly, Karamanos (2000) and Henriques and Sadorsky (1996) do not find that financial health of the firm impacted its decision to undertake voluntary initiatives.

Technical feasibility

Several studies have examined the impact of technical feasibility of reducing emissions on incentives to undertake proactive initiatives. Technical feasibility can be proxied by several firm-specific characteristics, such as innovativeness measured by expenditures on research and development, age of equipment and the share of pollutants targeted for reduction relative to the total releases generated (which indicates the ease with which a firm might be able to change processes/equipment or substitute other inputs to reduce the targeted pollutants). Both Arora and Cason (1995) and Khanna and Damon (1998) do not find strong evidence that innovative firms or firms in more innovative industries were more likely to participate in the 33/50 program. However, Khanna and Anton (2001) find that innovative firms were statistically significantly more likely to adopt a comprehensive environmental management system. Firms with older equipment were also more likely to participate in the 33/50 program (Khanna and Damon, 1999) and undertake corporate environmental management (Khanna and Anton, 2001), possibly because it was less costly for them to replace old equipment with newer less pollution intensive equipment. Additionally, firms with a lower ratio of 33/50 releases to total TRI releases and thus having more options for substituting other chemicals for the 33/50 chemicals were more likely to participate in the 33/50 program. Survey responses analyzed by Celdran *et al.* (1996) also suggest that firms for whom it was technically infeasible to modify their processes were more likely to be non-participants in the 33/50 program.

5. Effect of voluntary initiatives on environmental performance

Among the empirical studies discussed above, relatively few have examined the impact of voluntary initiatives taken by firms on their environmental performance. Khanna and Damon (1999) examine the impact of participation in the 33/50 program on the releases of the 33/50 chemicals over the period 1991–93 while King and Lenox (2000) analyze the influence that participation in Responsible Care had on toxic releases of firms. Dasgupta, Hettige and Wheeler (2000) examine the implications of adoption of ISO 14001 procedures, assignment of personnel for environmental monitoring and inspection, generalized vs. specialized environmental management and worker training on the compliance record of Mexican firms. All of these studies recognize that these voluntary initiatives do not require or guarantee an improvement in environmental performance because they provided flexibility in the extent of improvement in environmental performance and lacked any sanctions for non-improvement. King and Lenox (2000) hypothesize that while participation in voluntary initiatives such as Responsible Care lead to adoption of new values, exchange of information about best practices and informal coercion to improve performance, they may also provide insurance to some firms against stakeholder pressure and reduce incentives to actually reduce pollution. In the absence of explicit coercion or sanctions for lack of improvement as in the case of the unilateral initiatives that focus on improved management practices, firms may undertake these initiatives to disguise poor performance and adopt the outward form of these initiatives but not undertake the effort required to really improve environmental performance.

To isolate the impact of a voluntary initiative on environmental performance it is important to do a with-and-without comparison of environmental performance, by controlling for other factors that could also have influenced performance. Additionally, it is also necessary to correct for self-selection bias that arises because the decision to participate in a voluntary program and the performance outcome are endogenously determined and likely to be influenced by the same observable and unobservable factors. A two-stage technique to consistently estimate the effectiveness of program participation is discussed in Khanna and Damon (1999).

After controlling for the direct effects of several factors such as existing and anticipated mandatory regulations, threat of liabilities and other firm-specific characteristics on the releases of 33/50 chemicals and using panel data methods to control for unobserved heterogeneity among firms, Khanna and Damon (1999) find that participation in the 33/50 program led to a statistically significant decline in these releases. They also find that program participation had a significant negative impact on emissions to all major media that is likely to be a consequence of the fact that the goals of the 33/50 program were not media specific and thus did not create incentives for cross-media substitution. Program participation also had a negative impact on non-33/50 releases although it was less significant than on 33/50 releases, implying that process and product changes induced by participation had scope effects that led to a reduction in releases of other chemicals as well. After correcting for sample selection bias and effects of other factors on releases, they find that although total releases by sample firms fell by 54% over 1991–93, only 28% of the reduction relative to the pre-program level could be attributed to the program.

King and Lenox (2000) analyze the impact of Responsible Care on environmental performance of firms over the period 1991–96 using pooled data and panel data methods.[7] The pooled model shows that members were improving their relative performance more slowly than non-members while the fixed effects model shows that Responsible Care had an insignificant effect on improvement. Although the environmental performance of the chemical industry as a whole improved after the inception of the program, absolute improvement among members was no faster than earlier and slower than among non-members. It should, however, be noted that this study focuses on one measure of environmental performance, toxic releases, only. It is possible that improved environmental management could have been more effective in improving other aspects of environmental performance, such as community and worker safety.

Dasgupta, Hettige and Wheeler (2000) find that adoption of ISO 14001 management practices did lead to a significant improvement in the self-reported compliance status of Mexican firms. They find that assigning a general manager to environmental work and providing environmental training to nonenvironmental workers also led to an improvement in the compliance status of these firms. Their results indicate a need for spreading training resources and managerial decision making on environmental issues widely within the firm rather than developing a specialized cadre of environmental workers/managers.

6. Effectiveness of information disclosure strategies

6.1. *Market response to environmental information*

There is some evidence that information, primarily through advertising, about the health benefits of certain products, (for example, ready-to-eat cereal) has been successful in changing purchasing patterns (Ippolito and Mathios, 1990). However, there is little scholarly research quantifying the impact of environmental labels, which differentiate goods not simply based on their use characteristics or implications for personal health or safety, but with respect to non-use characteristics or provision of public goods, on purchasing behavior of consumer and on the environment. Instead there is research on green consumerism, on consumer awareness about eco-labels and their willingness to pay a higher price for environmentally labeled products (see surveys by van Ravenswaay and Blend, 1999; Hemmelskamp and Brockman, 1997). This research provides mixed evidence about the extent to which growing environmental consciousness among consumers has led to corresponding purchasing behavior or willingness to pay a premium for products with an environmental label (Gutfield, 1991). It does show that consumer awareness about an eco-labeling program takes time and resources to develop and consumers often remain uncertain about what the environmental label implies about the environmental attributes and other qualities of a product.

In contrast to the limited empirical evidence on the impact of environmental information on the consumer goods market, several studies have analyzed the impact of information disclosure on the capital market and its effectiveness in controlling pollution. They have looked at the behavior of stock market returns in the U.S and in Canada when environmental information such as the toxics release data is first released (Hamilton, 1995; Konar and Cohen, 1997; Khanna et al., 1998), environmental law suits and violations are announced (Muoghalu et al., 1990; Laplante and Lanoie, 1994), environmental performance ratings are released (White, 1995) and strong environmental performance is rewarded (Klassen and McLaughlin, 1996). Dasgupta et al. (1998) examine the impact on stock market returns in four developing countries, Argentina, Chile, Mexico and Philippines when positive environmental news about rewards for environmental performance and negative news about spills and complaints is reported. The provision of new information about a firm's pollution level may cause abnormal changes in its stock prices if this new information diverges from the expectations that investors hold about that firm's pollution level and is perceived by them to affect the profitability of that firm (Fama, 1991). These studies use the event study methodology to analyze the reactions of a firm's stock market return to the announcement of an event on a particular day. This method is based on the assumption that in the absence of unexpected information, the relationship between stock market returns to the firm and returns on the market index should be unchanged. An abnormal return is generated on a given event-related day when unexpected information affects the return for the firm without affecting the market return. Negative abnormal returns reflect the change in investor expectations about a firm's profitability brought about by the additional information provided.

Hamilton (1995) finds that on the day that TRI was publicly released for the first time in 1989 a sample of 436 firms experienced statistically significant negative abnormal returns averaging to (−) 0.28%. These abnormal returns translated into large dollar losses amounting to $4.1 billion on average in stock market value on the event day. Konar and Cohen (1997) analyze a sample of 130 TRI emitters that also received publicity in the print media in 1989 and find that these firms received abnormal returns of (−) 0.299% on the day of the announcement while the top 40 firms with the largest abnormal returns received returns of (−) 1.32% on the event day. These studies also show that firms that were known to be large polluters beforehand were likely to receive less negative returns than other firms on the day of the event. Both studies find that firms reporting TRI releases also experienced negative and statistically significant cumulative abnormal returns over the 5-day window following the event day.

The impact of repeated provision of environmental information is examined by Khanna et al. (1998) for firms in the U.S. chemical industry over a six-year period (1989–94) and by Lanoie et al. (1997) for firms in Canada that appeared on any of 5 published lists of firms violating standards or with poor environmental performance over the period 1990–92. Firms analyzed in both these studies were already known to be large polluters and hence the first time that environmental information about them was released they did not incur statistically significant abnormal losses. However, with repeated provision of information investors could track changes in a firm's environmental performance relative to that of other firms as well as relative to its own previous levels. Khanna et al. (1998) found that firms whose releases increased relative to the previous year or whose rank rose relative to the previous year (because their pollution levels rose relative to other firms) experienced significantly negative returns. Similarly, Lanoie *et al.* (1997) found that firms that appeared on a second list did receive abnormal returns on the day of the event. These studies indicate that, by allowing investors to benchmark a firm's performance and receive stronger signals about a firm's bad environmental performance, repeated provision of information is effective in generating investor reaction to environmental information.

Muoghalu *et al.* (1990) find that the announcement of the filing of environmental lawsuits under the Resource Conservation and Recovery Act in the U.S. between 1977 and 1986 resulted in significant abnormal losses (-1.228%) in stock market returns for firms on the day of the event but not for extended periods following the event. On the other hand, using data on Canadian-owned firms, Laplante and Lanoie (1994) find that while announcements of incidents and lawsuits did not lead to significant abnormal returns possibly because lawsuits in Canada have historically resulted in low fines, suit settlements with fines imposed on firms did result in abnormal losses for stockholders on the day of the event. White (1995) and Klassen and McLaughlin (1996) examine the impact of information that affects a firm's environmental reputation (determined not only by its environmental performance but also by its management quality) on its stock market return. White (1995) finds that investors could have earned superior returns by investing in firms rated 'green' instead of those rated as 'oatmeal' or 'brown' by the Council of Economic Priorities. Klassen and McLaughlin (1996) show that awards for superior environmental management led to significantly positive stock market returns. Interestingly, environmental information appears to be effective in generating investor reactions even in developing countries. Dasgupta *et al.* (1998) find that the announcement of firm-specific environmental news over the period 1990–94 in Mexico, Chile, Argentina and the Phillipines led to statistically significant increases in market value for firms that had received positive recognition from regulators for superior environmental performance and statistically significant decreases for firms that received government or citizen complaints about their pollution record. These responses were much larger than those reported for U.S. and Canadian firms.

Other studies have examined whether investors value a voluntary initiative undertaken by firms. Under the efficient capital markets hypothesis a firm's market value fully reflects the discounted value of the future profits of the firm after incorporating all available information about it (Fama, 1991). Khanna and Damon (1999) show that participation in the 33/50 program led to an expected decline of 1% in average return on investment but an expected increase of 2% in average excess value per unit sales (defined as (market value-total assets)/sales) over the period 1991–93. This suggests that while the immediate impact of program participation on the profitability of firms was negative, possibly due to the increased expenditures on pollution control, investors expected such firms to be more profitable in the long run. Dowell, Hart and Yeung (2000) examine the impact of environmental management practices of multinational enterprises on their *Tobin's q*[8] for 1994–97. They show that firms adhering to their own stringent internal environmental standards (that exceed any national standards) when operating overseas had higher *Tobin's q* than those using host country standards or U.S. standards.

6.2. *Responsiveness of environmental performance to stakeholder pressure*

The studies above have shown that information provision can lead to a substantial loss in equity value on the day of the announcement of an environmental event or even over a longer duration. The deterrence effect of these penalties on firms depends on the relative magnitudes of the marginal gain in profits by generating that additional pollution (or the avoided costs of abatement) and the marginal loss in equity value due to negative investor reactions. Konar and Cohen (1997) show that the decline in total toxic wastes per dollar revenue in 1992 by the 40 firms that received the largest abnormally negative returns in 1989 was significantly higher than that for an industry-weighted group of 455 firms. They show that of the 40 firms, 32 reduced their TRI releases per unit sales while 8 firms increased their emissions. Khanna *et al.* (1998) conduct a panel data study to examine the impact of abnormal returns on wastes generated disaggregated into on-site releases and off-site transfers for disposal and treatment while controlling for the effects of other firm-specific factors that might influence these releases. They find that among the firms that experienced negative returns, the larger the abnormal losses the greater the reduction in the magnitude of their on-site releases. Abnormal returns, however, led to statistically significant increases in off-site transfers and had an insignificant impact on total toxic wastes generated by firms. This implies that the abnormal losses experienced by firms caused them to substitute off-site transfers for on-site discharges.

Information provision can also lead to community involvement and political action to influence environmental quality that can influence a firm's incentives to undertake pollution reduction. These incentives are likely to be larger in areas where citizens are more likely to engage in collective action because with imperfect monitoring and enforcement, firms may otherwise not internalize the damage arising from their pollutants. Arora and Cason (1999) and Hamilton (1999) analyze empirically whether community characteristics can influence the level of toxic releases reported to the TRI that they are exposed to while Maxwell, Lyon and Hackett (2000) analyze the role of latent political pressure in determining the reduction in toxic releases per unit sales, over the period 1988–92, across states in the U.S. After controlling for differences in levels of toxic releases across neighborhoods due to differences in economic conditions, Arora and Cason (1999) find that the propensity for collective/political action, which is higher in neighborhoods with fewer families with children less than 18, a larger number of residents employed in manufacturing industries and workers that carpool, is a significant determinant of the level of releases in the nonurban areas of southeastern U.S. Hamilton (1999) explains changes in the levels of specific air carcinogens in 1991 relative to its level in 1988 using estimated cancer cases likely to be caused by that air carcinogen, maximum individual lifetime risks and collective action variables. He finds that facilities emitting riskier pollutants and those in areas with the largest voter turnout had the largest reductions in their emissions, possibly because a larger number of expected deaths from cancer may generate greater potential liability payments, stronger pressure from communities, environmental groups and regulators. Maxwell, Lyon and Hackett (2000) find that states with a strong environmental group membership and with fewer plants, that is those with a stronger threat of regulation and fewer free-rider problems, had larger reductions in the toxicity-weighted releases of 33/50 chemicals per unit sales.

A growing number of studies provide evidence that information provision can be effective even in developing countries. A World Bank (1999) study analyzes the impact of PROPER established by the Indonesian environmental agency to publicly disclose a color based rating of firms, as black, red, blue, green or gold, with black indicating non-compliance and gold indicating over compliance, based on their water pollution. Initial ratings showed that two-thirds of the plants failed to comply with regulations. The program led to striking improvements in plants rated as black and red with the number of plants rated as black falling by 50% in the first six months and by 83% in one year. The number of plants in the blue group increased by 54%.

Studies by Wang and Wheeler (1999), by Pargal and Wheeler (1996) and by Blackman and Bannister (1998) show that when formal environmental regulation is weak, community pressure in developing countries such as China, Indonesia and Mexico, respectively, can informally but effectively regulate polluting firms. Pargal and Wheeler (1996) analyze variations (across firms and regions) in water pollution generated by a cross-section of Indonesian factories during a period when there was no effective national program for industrial pollution control. They find strong evidence that community pressure, proxied by per capita income, education and population density, in the vicinity of the plant led to significant reductions in pollution levels. Blackman and Bannister (1998) find that community pressure, proxied by membership in local organizations, was effective in motivating the adoption of a cleaner technology for brickmaking in Mexico, even when the new technology had higher costs. Wang and Wheeler (1999) find that even when a formal regulatory system exists there are differences in the enforcement of a pollution levy across urban areas in China. They find evidence of 'endogenous enforcement', that is, variations in the effective levy rate due to variations in incidence of citizens' complaints (which in turn were affected by local education and per capita income) and ambient air quality after controlling for plant characteristics.

7. Conclusions

Reliance on cooperative voluntary approaches towards environmental protection that involve public participation represent a generational change in environmental policy from the command and control, government-push approach employed traditionally. By reducing the transactions and enforcement costs associated with designing and implementing mandatory regulations, replacing uniform, inflexible standards by flexible, tailored agreements, or allowing firms to replace their emissions tax payments by higher costs of voluntary over-compliance, voluntary approaches have the potential to increase the efficiency and effectiveness of environmental regulations. In addition to promising regulatory cost-savings, such approaches can also induce participation by providing public recognition, reputational effects, lower costs of capital and in some cases information or financial subsidies to induce participation.

The theoretical literature surveyed here shows that the efficiency and effectiveness of voluntary approaches can be enhanced if there are stringent legislative threats. The presence of a threat of mandatory regulations implies the existence of a positive level of voluntary abatement acceptable to both the firm and the regulator when transactions and abatement costs under the voluntary regime are lower. Voluntary approaches may also be more efficient when they replace penalties for non-compliance with government efforts to reduce the costs of compliance for firms and the cost of government effort is lower than that of private effort, as well as in the presence of asymmetric information when regulators lack the information needed to set efficient non-uniform standards. Voluntary agreements are more likely to enhance social welfare if the costs of imposing or enforcing mandatory regulations are high, if the cost of public funds are low (when subsidies need to be provided to induce participation), the costs of voluntary abatement are lower than mandatory abatement and the political will for imposing mandatory regulations are low. The performance of voluntary programs is also likely to improve when firms in the industry are homogeneous, few in number and willing to cooperate with each other.

This literature also highlights several reasons to be cautious about unbridled enthusiasm for voluntary approaches to environmental protection. It demonstrates the potential for firms to be able to preempt regulation with a very modest amount of voluntary abatement that might be less than that would have been imposed by the regulator. This may be acceptable to welfare maximizing regulators either because of savings in regulatory and legislative costs or because high mandatory standards would reduce firm profits and thus social welfare. However, if regulators have political objectives that depart from welfare maximization and if legislators seek to avoid public criticism by shifting the responsibility for environmental protection to the private sector then voluntary agreements that are welfare reducing and provide suboptimal environmental protection may occur. Furthermore, voluntary self-regulation that guides mandatory standard setting by giving firms a first-mover advantage can be welfare reducing.

This literature brings out the complementary role that a credible threat of mandatory regulations can play to a voluntary approach, by reducing the need for subsidies to induce voluntary participation and raising the benefits of over-compliance, without actually being implemented. The threat of regulatory pressure is likely to be particularly important when market-based pressures are weak. However, the government needs to avoid having mandatory regulations appear inevitable, due to strong lobbying by environmental interest groups, since that could reduce any incentives for beneficial self-regulation.

The government can play an important role in providing information in the case of products where knowledge about environmental attributes, such as food safety and nutritional quality, is highly imperfect and consumers cannot practicably assess the quality of the product or learn from experience by consuming the product. Product quality signaling through product labeling and information disclosure requirements encourage market incentives with relatively limited direct government involvement in regulating the firm. The extent to which consumers can provide incentives for firms to self-regulate depend upon consumer preferences for environmental quality, their willingness to internalize the external effects of their consumption decisions, their budget constraints, the quality of information about the environmental consequences of consumption and the toxicity of the pollutant. Firms, in turn, have incentives for self-regulation if they can increase profits by differentiating their products or use their market power to charge premium prices for green products or increase their market value through superior environmental performance. The empirical literature shows that information provision can be effective in generating reactions from stockholders and communities and lead to reductions in toxic releases. Whether information provision is a more efficient strategy to achieve pollution reduction relative to mandatory policies remains to be examined.

Empirical studies surveyed here demonstrate that the participation decision of firms can be explained by their economic self-interest. It quantifies the impact of regulatory threats, reducing costs of compliance, desire for public recognition and enhanced market share, and mitigating adverse stockholders reactions on the motivations for undertaking a variety of voluntary initiatives. However, it provides mixed evidence on the impact of such programs on pollution reduction. Performance oriented programs such as the 33/50 program targeted at specific pollutants, appear to be more successful at achieving pollution abatement than initiatives emphasizing the means (proactive efforts) and not the ends. However, the effort of these studies to measure the impact of these programs has been one-dimensional, focused on toxic releases, due to the availability of data. Better data on the costs of under taking voluntary initiatives relative to mandatory compliance and on their multi-dimensional benefits such as improved worker safety, better community relations and reduced unexpected environmental incidents would improve the assessment of these initiatives.

Notes

1. Information about rankings of firms based on environmental performance can be found at www.scorecard.org; www.cepnyc.org; www.environmentaldefense.org/programs/P-PA/vlc/va_rankings.html Information about information disclosure programs in developing countries can be found at www.worldbank.org/nipr
2. For other surveys of voluntary approaches see Segerson and Li (1999) and Lyon and Maxwell (1999).

3. As an example, Intel Corporation pledged to reduce air emissions to levels below the requirements under the Clean Air Act of 1990 in exchange for greater operational flexibility in the form of a facility wide emission standard and waiving of requirements for new permits for new construction or other modifications (Davies and Mazurek, 1996).
4. http://www.epa.gov/oeca/idea
5. http://www.eren.doe.gov/climatechallenge/factsheet.htm
6. Participants in the WasteWise program, launched in 1994, commit to finding cost-effective opportunities to prevent, reduce and recycle solid waste.
7. They use two alternative measures of improvement in environmental performance. Absolute improvement is defined as the percent change in total toxicity-weighted toxic emissions over a one-year period. Relative improvement measures the change in relative toxic emissions over a one-year period with relative emissions defined as the deviation between observed emissions and predicted emissions, given the facility's size and industry sector.
8. *Tobin's q* is defined as market value per dollar of replacement costs of tangible assets, where market value is the sum of a firm's equity value, book value of long term debt and net current liabilities while replacement costs of tangible assets are proxied by summing the book value of inventory and net value of physical plant and equipment.

References

Akerlof, G. (1970) The market for lemons. *Quarterly Journal of Economics* LXXXIV, 488–500.
Arora, S. and Gangopadhyay, S. (1995) Towards a theoretical model of voluntary overcompliance. *Journal of Economic Behavior Organization*, 2, 289–309.
Arora, S. and T. N., Cason (1996) Why do firms volunteer to exceed environmental regulations? Understanding participation in EPA's 33/50 program. *Land Economics*, 72, 413–432.
—— (1995) An experiment in voluntary environmental regulation: participation in EPA's 33/50 program *Journal of Environmental Economics and Management*, 28, 271–286.
—— (1999) Do community characteristics influence environmental outcomes? Evidence from the Toxic Release Inventory. *Southern Economic Journal*, 65, 4, 691–716.
Arrow, K. (1962) Economic welfare and the allocation of resources for invention. In R. Nelson (ed.), *The Rate and Direction of Innovative Activity*. Princeton: Princeton University Press.
Batie, S. S. (1997) Environmental issues, policy and the food industry. In B. Schroder and T. L. Wallace (eds), *Food Industry and Government Linkages*, Boston: Kluwer Academic Publishers.
Beardsley, D. P. (1996) Incentives for environmental improvement: an assessment of selected innovative programs in the States and Europe. GEMI, Washington D. C., September.
Blackman, A. and Bannister, G. J. (1998) Community pressure and clean technology in the informal sector: an econometric analysis of the adoption of propane by traditional Mexican brickmakers. *Journal of Environmental Economics and Management*, 35, 1, &JTO;1–21.
Blackman, A. and Boyd, J. (1999) The economics of tailored regulation: will site-specific environmental regulations necessarily improve welfare? Discussion Paper 00-03, Resources for the Future, Washington DC.
Blackman, A. and Mazurek, J. (2000) The cost of developing site-specific regulations: evidence from EPA's Project XL', Discussion Paper 99–35, Resources for the Future, Washington D.C.

Borkey, P. and Leveque, F. (1998) Voluntary approaches for environmental protection in the European Union. ENV/EPOC/GEEI(98)29/Final, Organization for Economic Cooperation and Development.

Carraro, C. and Leveque, F. (1999) *Voluntary approaches in environmental policy*, Dordrecht: Kluwer Academic Publishers.

Cavaliere, A. (1999) 'Voluntary agreements and efficiency? The impact of environmental reputation', CAVA Working Paper 99/10/1.

Celdran, A., Clark, H., Hecht, J., Kanamaru, E., Orantes, P. and Santaello Garguno, M. (1996) The participation decision in a voluntary pollution prevention program: The USEPA 33/50 program as a case study. In H. Clark (ed.), Developing the Next Generation of the USEPA's 33/50 Program: A Pollution Prevention Research Project [Report], Duke University Nicholas School of the Environment, Durham, NC.

Cropper, M. L. and Oates, W. E. (1992) Environmental economics: a survey. *Journal of Economic Literature*, XXX, 2, 675–741.

Dasgupta, S., Hettige, H. and Wheeler, D. (2000) What improves environmental compliance? Evidence from Mexican industry', *Journal of Environmental Economics and Management*, 39, 1, 39–66.

Dasgupta, S., Laplante, B. and Mamingi, N. (1998) Capital market responses to environmental performance in developing countries. Policy Research Working Paper 1909, Development Research Group, The World Bank.

Davies, T. and Mazurek, J. (1996) Industry incentives for environmental improvement: Evaluation of U. S. federal initiatives. Global Environmental Management Initiative, Washington D.C.

Dawson, N. L. and Segerson, K. (2000) Voluntary approaches with industries: participation incentives with industry-wide targets. Working Paper, Department of Economics, University of Connecticut.

DeCanio, S. J. and Watkins, W. E. (1998) Investment in energy efficiency: do the characteristics of firms matter? *Review of Economics and Statistics*, 80, 1, 95–107.

Dowell, G., Hart, S. and Yeung, B. (2000) Do corporate global environmental standards create or destroy market value? *Management Science*, 46, 8, 1059–1074.

Esty, D. C. and Chertow, M. R. (1997) Thinking ecologically: an introduction. In M. R. Chertow and D. C. Esty (eds), *Thinking Ecologically: The Next Generation of Environmental Policy*, New Haven: Yale University Press.

Fama, E. F. (1991) Efficient capital markets II. *Journal of Finance*, 46, 1575–1617.

GAO (United States General Accounting Office) (1994a) Toxic substances: EPA needs more reliable source reduction data and progress measures. GAO/RCED-94-93.

GAO (United States General Accounting Office) (1994b) Toxic substances: Status of EPA's efforts to reduce toxic releases. Report to the Chairman, Environment, Energy and Natural Resources Sub-committee, Committee on Government Operations, GAO/RCED-94-207.

Garvie, D. (1997) Self-regulation of pollution: the role of market structure and consumer information. Fondazione Eni Enrico Mattei, Nota di Lavoro 59.97, Milan.

Glachant, M. (1999) The cost efficiency of voluntary agreements for regulating industrial pollution: a Coasean approach. In C. Carraro and F. Leveque (eds), *Voluntary Approaches in Environmental Policy*, Dordrecht: Kluwer Academic Publishing.

Gutfield, R. (1991) Shades of green: eight of 10 Americans are environmentalists, or at least say so. *Wall Street Journal*, August 2.

Hamilton, J. T. (1995) Pollution as news: media and stock market reactions to the toxics release inventory data. *Journal of Environmental Economics and Management*, 28, 98–113.

Hamilton, J. T. (1999) Exercising property rights to pollute: Do cancer risks and politics affect plant emission reductions? *Journal of Risk and Uncertainty*, 18, 2, 105–124

Hansen, L. G. (1999) Environmental regulation through voluntary agreements. In C. Carraro and F. Leveque (eds), *Voluntary Approaches in Environmental Policy*, Dordrecht: Kluwer Academic Publishing.

Hemmelskamp, J. and Brockmann, K. L. (1997) Environmental labels — the German 'Blue Angel'. *Futures*, 29, 1, 67–76.

Henriques, I. and Sadorsky, P. (1996) The determinants of an environmentally responsive firm: an empirical approach. *Journal of Environmental Economics and Management*, 30, 381–395.

Ippolito, P. M. and Mathios, A. D. (1990) Information, advertising and health choices: a study of the cereal market. *Rand Journal of Economics*, 21, 459–80.

Karamanos, P. (2000) Voluntary environmental agreements for the reduction of greenhouse gas emissions: incentives and characteristics of electricity utility participants in the climate challenge program. Working Paper, Sanford Institute of Public Policy, Duke University.

Khanna, M. and Anton, W. R. Q. (2001) Corporate Environmental Management: Regulatory and Market Based Pressures, Working Paper, Department of Agricultural and Consumer Economics, University of Illinois, Urbana-Champaign.

Khanna, M. and Damon, L. (1999) EPA's voluntary 33/50 program: impact on toxic releases and economic performance of firms. *Journal of Environmental Economics and Management*, 37, 1, 1–25.

Khanna, M., Quimio, W. R. H. and Bojilova, D. (1998) Toxics release information: a policy tool for environmental protection. *Journal of Environmental Economics and Management*, 36, 3, 243–266.

King, A. A. and Lenox, M. J. (2000) Industry self-regulation without sanctions: the chemical industry's responsible care program. *Academy of Management Journal*, 43, 4, 698–716.

Klassen, R. and McLaughlin, C. (1996) The impact of environmental management on firm performance. *Management Science*, 42, 1199–1214.

Konar, S. and Cohen, M. A. (1997) Information as regulation: the effect of community-right-to-know laws on toxic emissions. *Journal of Environmental Economics and Management*, 32, 109–124.

Kuhre, W., Lee (1995) *ISO 14001 Certification: Environmental Management Systems*, Upper Saddle River, NJ: Prentice Hall.

Lanoie, P., Laplante, B. and Roy, M. (1997) Can capital markets create incentives for pollution control?' Policy Research Working Paper 1753, Environment, Infrastructure and Agriculture Division, The World Bank.

Laplante, B. and Lanoie, P. (1994) Market response to environmental incidents in Canada. *Southern Economic Journal*, 60, 657–672.

Lutz, S., Lyon, T. P. and Maxwell, J. W. (2000) Quality leadership when regulation standards are forthcoming. *Journal of Industrial Economics*, XLVIII (3), 331–348.

Lyon, T. P. and Maxwell, J. W. (1999) 'Voluntary' approaches to environmental regulation: a survey. In M. Franzini and A. Nicita (eds), *Environmental Economics: Past, Present and Future*, Aldershot, Hampshire: Ashgate Publishing.

Lyon, T. P. and Maxwell, J. W. (2000) Self-regulation, taxation and public voluntary environmental agreements. Working Paper, Department of Business Economics and Public Policy, Indiana University.

Maitland, I. (1985) The limits of self-regulation. *California Management Review*, 27, 3, 132–147.

Maxwell, J. W. and Lyon, T. P. (1999) What causes US voluntary environmental agreements? CAVA Working Paper 99/10/2.

Maxwell, J. W., Lyon, T. P. and Hackett, S. C. (2000) Self-regulation and social welfare: the political economy of corporate environmentalism. *Journal of Law & Economics*, XLIII, 2, 583–618.

Mazurek, J. (1998a) The use of unilateral agreements in the United States: the responsible care initiative. ENV/EPOC/GEEI(98)25/Final, Organization for Economic Cooperation and Development.

Mazurek, J. (1998b) The use of voluntary agreements in the United States: an initial survey.

ENV/EPOC/GEEI(98)27/Final, Organization for Economic Cooperation and Development.

Millock, K. and Salanie, F. (2000) Collective Environmental Agreements: An Analysis of the Problems of Free-Riding and Collusion, FEEM Working Paper 108.2000.

Muoghalu, M. I., Robison, H. D. and Glascock, J. L. (1990) Hazardous waste lawsuits, stockholder returns, and deterrence. *Southern Economic Journal*, 357–370.

NCEE (National Center for Environmental Economics) (2001) The United States experience with economic incentives for protecting the environment. Washington DC, Office of Policy, Economics, and Innovation, U.S. Environmental Protection Agency.

Opschoor, H. (1994) Developments in the use of economic instruments in OECD countries. In G. Klassen and F. R.. Forsund (eds), *Economic Instruments for Air Pollution Control*. Economy and Environment Series, vol. 9, International Institute for Applied Systems Analysis, Laxenberg, Austria; Dordrecht and Boston: Kluwer, 75–106.

Pargal, S. and Wheeler, D. (1996) Informal regulation of industrial pollution in developing countries: evidence from Indonesia. *Journal of Political Economy*, 104, 6, 1314–1327

Reisch, M. (1998) Industry ponders future of responsible care. *Chemical & Engineering News*, May 5, 13.

Ribaudo, M. and Caswell, M. F. (1999) Environmental regulation in agriculture and the adoption of environmental technologies. In F. Casey, A. Schmitz, S. Swinton, and D. Zilberman (eds), *Flexible Incentives for the Adoption of Environmental Technologies in Agriculture*, Norwell, MA: Kluwer Academic Publishing.

Schmelzer, D. (1999) Voluntary agreements in environmental policy. In C. Carraro and F. Leveque (eds), *Voluntary Approaches in Environmental Policy*, Dordrecht: Kluwer Academic Publishing.

Schmidheiny, S. (ed.) (1992) *Changing Course: A Global Business Perspective on Development and the Environment*, Cambridge, M.A.: MIT Press.

Segerson, K. and Miceli, T. J. (1999) Voluntary approaches to environmental protection. In C. Carraro and F. Leveque (eds), *Voluntary Approaches in Environmental Policy*, Dordrecht: Kluwer Academic Publishing.

Segerson, K. and Li, N. (1999) Voluntary approaches to environmental protection. In H. Folmer and T. Tietenberg (eds), *International Yearbook of Environmental and Resource Economics 1999/2000*, Cheltenham, UK: Edward Elgar.

Segerson, K. and Miceli, T. J. (1998) Voluntary environmental agreements: good or bad news for environmental protection? *Journal of Environmental Economics and Management* 36, 109–130.

Segerson, K. (1999) Do voluntary approaches lead to efficient environmental protection?' CAVA Working Paper 99/10/10.

Shapiro, C. (1983) Premium for high quality products as returns to reputations. *Quarterly Journal of Economics* November, 659–679.

Storey, M., Boyd, G. and Dowd, J. (1999) Voluntary agreements with industry. In C. Carraro and F. Leveque (eds), *Voluntary Approaches in Environmental Policy*, Dordrecht: Kluwer Academic Publishing.

Stranlund, J. K. (1995) Public mechanisms to support compliance to an environmental norm. *Journal of Environmental Economics and Management*, 28, 205–222.

Tietenberg, T. (1998) Disclosure strategies for pollution control. *Environmental and Resource Economics*, 11, 3–4, 587–602.

USDOE (United States Department of Energy) (1996) Climate challenge program report (DOE/FE-0355), Office of Energy Efficiency and Renewable Energy, Office of Utility Technology, United States Department of Energy.

USEPA (United States Environmental Protection Agency) (1991) U.S. Environmental Protection Agency pollution prevention strategy. Washington, D.C.

USEPA (United States Environmental Protection Agency) (1995) EPA green lights program snapshot: April 30, 1995. Washington, D.C.

USEPA (United States Environmental Protection Agency) (2000) Taking toxics out of the
    air. Washington, D.C.
van Ravenswaay, E. O. and Blend, J. (1999) Using ecolabeling to encourage adoption of
    innovative environmental technologies in agriculture. In F. Casey, A. Schmitz, S.
    Swinton, and D. Zilberman (eds), *Flexible Incentives for the Adoption of Environmental
    Technologies in Agriculture*, Norwell, MA: Kluwer Academic Publishing.
Videras, J. and A. Alberini, The appeal of voluntary environmental programs: which firms
    participate and why? *Cotemporary Economic Policy* 18, 4, 449–461.
Wang, H. and Wheeler, D. (1999) Endogenous enforcement and effectiveness of China's
    pollution levy system, presented in the workshop 'Market-Based Instruments for
    Environmental Protection' sponsored by the Association of Environmental and
    Resource Economists and Harvard University, Boston.
World Bank (1999) Greening industry: new roles for communities, markets, and
    governments. Policy Research Report, Development Research Group, The World
    Bank.
White, M. (1995) Corporate environmental responsibility and financial performance.
    Working Paper, University of Virginia, Charlottesville, VA.
Wu, J. and Babcock, B. A. (1999) The relative efficiency of voluntary vs. mandatory
    environmental regulations. *Journal of Environmental Economics and Management*, 78,
    4, 935–45.

CHAPTER 4

CARBON TAXES AND CARBON EMISSIONS TRADING

Paul Ekins

SPIRE, Keele University

Terry Barker

DAE, University of Cambridge

Abstract. This paper surveys the literature on, and examples of current implementation of, carbon taxes and carbon emission permits. It sets out the theoretical basis for these instruments, with special reference to the revenue-recycling and tax interaction effects. This theoretical work concludes that instruments which raise revenue which can be recycled so as to reduce pre-existing distortionary taxes are significantly less costly than those which do not. The paper then reviews the sizable literature on the distributional effects of these instruments, especially with regard to industrial competitiveness and regressive effects on low-income groups, evaluating attempts to mitigate these where they are perceived as unacceptable. The paper concludes that such efforts at mitigation, while possible, can substantially reduce the efficiency benefits of the instruments. The projected costs of carbon taxes depend on a wide range of assumptions. This is still a contested area, but the paper concludes that, on a range of plausible assumptions, these costs need not be high. Finally the paper notes that early evaluations of the environmental effectiveness of carbon taxes have been generally positive. This suggests that, if concern about anthropogenic climate change continues to increase, more countries will introduce carbon taxes and emission permits, with the latter increasingly auctioned.

Keywords. Carbon taxes; Carbon trading; Double dividend

1. Introduction and policy context

The Intergovernmental Panel on Climate Change (IPCC) concludes in its Second Assessment Report that 'the balance of evidence suggests that there is a discernible human influence on global climate' (Houghton *et al.*, 1996, p. 5), due to the emission of a number of 'greenhouse gases' into the atmosphere, the most important of which is carbon dioxide (CO_2). The IPCC Third Assessment Report (2001) concludes that 'There is new and stronger evidence that most of the warming observed over the last 50 years is attributable to human activities'. While the impacts of this influence are still uncertain, they include sea level rise, an increase in precipitation intensity, more severe droughts and/or floods in some places, and less severe droughts and/or floods in others, 'a possibility for more extreme rainfall events', and shifts in the competitive balance of species which may include forest die-back (ibid., pp. 6–7). The UK Royal Commission on Environmental Pollution has described climate change as an 'enormous challenge ... threatening generations to come' (RCEP, 2000, p. 9).

182 governments have now signed the UN Framework Convention on Climate Change (UNFCCC), in order to 'prevent dangerous anthropogenic interference with the climate system' (UNFCCC, 1992, Article 2). In 1997 the Kyoto Protocol to the Convention was signed, and mandated that industrial countries should, overall, reduce emissions by about 5% from 1990 levels by the period 2008–2012. Countries accepted different targets of emission reduction such that the overall emission reduction would be reached.

While the Kyoto Protocol still has not been ratified by a sufficient number of countries to enter into force, with the new US President recently declaring his opposition to it, and while some of its key provisions and mechanisms still remain to be adequately defined, many countries are preparing, or have prepared, climate change programmes in order to meet their targets.

An important instrument in many of the programmes is the taxation of energy or, in some cases, the taxation of energy according to its carbon content, which is known as a carbon tax. In addition, a number of countries are preparing schemes for the trading of carbon emission permits. The Kyoto Protocol envisages that such a scheme will in due course be introduced at the international level in order to help countries meet their carbon reduction commitments at least cost.

However, proposals to introduce carbon or energy taxes have met with substantial resistance. As will be seen, carbon taxes have so far only been introduced in a few European countries, at relatively low levels and with exemptions for many energy-intensive industries. There have been major political campaigns against such taxes, especially in Europe when the European Commission was considering a carbon/energy tax in 1993 and 1994 and in the US preceding the Kyoto meeting in December 1997. One effect of the politicization of such taxes has been that governments and interest groups have commissioned research into particular aspects of carbon taxation. Indeed, much of the research reported in the literature has been funded by governments and by the industries likely to be the most affected by the tax, for example the coal and electricity industries. A result of this controversy, therefore, is that the possible impacts of carbon taxation on carbon emissions (and on the economic activities that are responsible for them) have been intensively studied for individual economic sectors and for countries as a whole.

This article first briefly reviews the theories underpinning carbon taxes and carbon emissions trading (Section 2). It then sets out the practical experience with these instruments to date (Section 3). Section 4 discusses the environmental impacts of these instruments which have been estimated or projected, and Section 5 explores their economic and distributional impacts. Section 6 concludes.

2. Carbon taxes and carbon emissions trading: theoretical considerations

The objective of a carbon tax is to slow global warming, usually in the context of agreed targets for limiting or reducing GHG emissions, taking into account the scientific evidence, the risks of inaction and the possibility that some carbon reduction may be achieved at no net cost (policies to achieve which are sometimes referred to as 'no-regrets' policies). Since emissions are expected to be on an indefinite rising trend, any tax would also have to go on rising in order to achieve long-term stabilization and reduction. In this context, a carbon tax appears to have all the hallmarks of good taxation:

- It tackles an accepted economic problem (a damaging externality agreed as such by governments) helping to bring the private costs of emitting CO_2 into line with social costs of global warming.
- Its revenues can be expected to grow with income because energy demand tends to rise with income, and it is not easy to substitute away from fossil fuels in energy supply.
- It should be simple and cheap to administer through use of many existing tax structures for excise duties.
- It is expected to stimulate energy saving, innovation and investment in clean technology, and hence, possibly, economic growth.
- Any regressive side effects (those that disproportionately affect low-income or otherwise disadvantaged groups) are likely to be small enough for compensation to be able to remedy them using a small fraction of the expected revenues.

Both a carbon tax and carbon emissions trading are market-based instruments that depend fundamentally on the efficient working of the market system for their success. This efficiency has many requirements and implications. First, the legal and institutional structure needs to ensure that contracts are

- available,
- freely entered into by the relevant parties and
- enforceable under clear and widely accepted laws and rules.

Thus countries beset by bribery and corruption may not be able to use taxation because the taxes will be evaded or become an excuse for further corruption. Second, prices should reflect costs to some degree, so that the carbon tax will increase the price of carbon-intensive production. Third, buyers and sellers should be well informed as to the costs and availability of alternatives, such that future outcomes (even if not known) should at least be considered. In some cases, especially amongst some socially disadvantaged groups such as the elderly, there may be an unwillingness to consider alternatives, so extra taxation may of itself (and before possible compensation measures are taken into account) have very inequitable effects.

These are some of the issues to be explored in later sections. First, however, it is worth setting out the basic neo-classical theory of environmental, including carbon, taxation.

2.1. *Basic theory of environmental taxes and emissions trading*

Environmental taxes

The theoretical basis for environmental taxes in general, and carbon taxes in particular, is well developed and needs only to be briefly rehearsed here. Thus it is generally agreed among economists that, in a situation where the production or consumption of some good results in a negative external effect (i.e. one that is not reflected in the price of the good in question), then social welfare can be improved by imposing a tax on the good.

There are two basic ways of identifying the level at which the tax should be set. The neo-classical, optimization approach was conceived by Pigou (1932) and formalized by Baumol (1972) (one of many formalizations). The approach seeks to calculate a damage function for different rates of emission of the pollutant, and then seeks to equate the marginal net private benefit (MNPB) of the activity causing the pollution (P) with the marginal external cost (MEC) to which it gives rise. The equality is achieved by imposing a tax equal to the difference between them at the optimal emission level. Figure 2.1 (which is stylised in the sense that it assumes that the curves can be measured and remain stable as prices and outputs change, which may not in practice be the case) sets out this basic theoretical position, in which Q is the no tax pollution level, and Q^* is the optimal pollution level. The optimal tax is then t^*. The theory of environmental taxation has been much developed to take into account market situations other than perfect competition and other considerations (see, for example, Baumol and Oates, 1988), but this is outside the scope of this paper.

While Baumol proved the theoretical validity of the Pigouvian optimising approach to environmental taxation, he despaired of the prospects of making it operational, both because of the difficulty of calculating the marginal damage function and because the presence of multiple local maxima seemed to rule out an iterative approach to the optimal position, concluding: 'All in all we are left with little confidence in the applicability of the Pigouvian approach ... We do not how to calculate the required taxes and subsidies and we do not know how to approximate them by trial and error.' (Baumol, 1972, p. 318).

With regard to carbon taxes, setting aside the issue of ancillary local environmental benefits, Baumol's pessimism about multiple maxima is un-

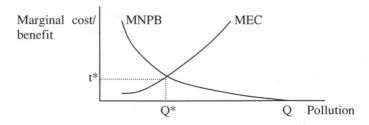

Figure 2.1 The optimising approach to environmental taxation.

founded, because carbon dioxide is a global pollutant: the location of its emission is irrelevant to its impact and there will be no local maxima. However, the problem remains with the calculation of the damage costs related to global warming, given the huge uncertainties about the impacts, and the contested nature of some of the methodologies which are used to value them, especially the non-market impacts such as effects on human health, risk of human mortality and damage to ecosystems. The Policymakers' Summary of IPCC's Working Group III's contribution to the Second Assessment Report, on the Economic and Social Dimensions of Climate Change, admits of its attempts to assess the social costs of climate change that 'The literature on the subject is controversial ... There is no consensus about how to value statistical lives or how to aggregate statistical lives across countries. ... The estimates of non-market damages are highly speculative and not comprehensive.' (Bruce et al., 1996, pp. 9–10).

It is to address such considerations that Baumol and Oates (1971) proposed an alternative approach to implementing environmental taxes, which has come to be called the standards and pricing approach after their article. The approach involves choosing environmental standards on the basis of their desired effects on, for example, human health, or on quality of life more generally, and then using environmental taxes on an iterative basis to bring levels of environmental damage down to the standards. Baumol and Oates showed that such environmental taxation had the property that it would achieve the desired environmental improvement at minimum cost to society at large. This has now become the principal approach to and justification of environmental, including carbon, taxes. Certainly all the carbon taxes that have been implemented to date (see Section 3) have been put in place in order to contribute to defined programmes of CO_2 emission reduction, rather than on the basis of any optimality calculations.

Emissions trading

As noted above, the property of carbon taxes that particularly commends itself both to economists and policy makers on climate change is its ability, in theory, to achieve a given level of emission reduction at least cost to society overall. This comes about because the incentive effects of the tax act to equalise the marginal abatement cost across all emitters.

Precisely the same effect can be achieved in principle through a carbon emissions trading system, whereby emitters have access to emission permits which they can trade among themselves. Experience with emissions trading has until now been largely limited to the US, where sulphur dioxide emissions trading is generally regarded as successful (see Sorrell and Skea, 1999). Yet emissions trading should be even more suited to CO_2, as a uniformly mixed pollutant. It is therefore not surprising that a number of carbon emission trading schemes are now being set up or proposed in different countries (see Section 3).

It has been shown, under a precise set of restrictive assumptions, that there is broad equivalence between an emissions trading scheme, where emission permits are auctioned by the government, and levying a carbon tax at the auction price

(Pezzey, 1992a; Farrow, 1995). The main difference between taxation and trading concerns price/quantity adjustment. With a carbon tax, it is the tax on and hence an increase in the price of carbon that is fixed, and the quantity of carbon emitted as CO_2 that adjusts. With emissions trading, it is the quantity of carbon emitted as CO_2 that is fixed, and the price of the emission permits that adjusts. Weitzman (1974) has shown that (1) it is preferable to fix the price when there is uncertainty over the control cost function, and a possibility that it is very sensitive to greater than optimal carbon emissions reduction, and (2) it is preferable to fix the quantity when there is uncertainty about the damage function, and a possibility that it may be very sensitive to greater than optimal emissions. Using this insight Pizer (1999) has argued that it would be preferable to control carbon emissions using a price, rather than a quantity, instrument, in contrast to the provisions of the Kyoto Protocol, which are for quantity control. Pizer suggests that the problems in negotiating the details of the Protocol derive from the potentially high costs which carbon limits may entail. These costs could themselves be limited by specifying a 'trigger price' for extra emission permits, which would effectively set a maximum cost of abatement (though obviously emissions could then increase). The proposal well illustrates the relation and interaction between prices and quantity limits.

A key decision in emissions trading schemes is how to allocate emission permits. The two most discussed options are their auction by the government (when the scheme resembles or is equivalent to a carbon tax set at the level of the auction price, depending on the auction rules), and their free allocation on the basis of some formula related to current emissions (an allocation mechanism called 'grandfathering'). The two methods of allocation provide the same incentives for emissions reduction at the margin, and, of course, yield the same environmental outcome (because the quantity of permits is unchanged). The difference between them is distributional. Auctions (and carbon taxes) transfer resources from emitters to the government and therefore yield government revenue. Grandfathering of emission permits appears to give assets in the form of tradable property rights to polluters. In any scheme, a proportion of the permits can be auctioned and the rest allocated free of charge: this flexibility gives permit schemes an advantage over corresponding carbon taxation where, conventionally, all revenues are received by governments.

Cramton and Kerr (1998) argue strongly that emission permits should be auctioned by the government rather than grandfathered, on three main grounds: governments can use the revenues to reduce distortionary taxes and therefore increase economic efficiency (this argument is discussed in a wider context below); auctions spread both the costs of carbon control, and the gain of the permit allocation, more equitably through the economy; and auctions remove the need for difficult and inevitably contested decisions over allocation, and give fair access to emission permits to small producers and new entrants. Against these points is the argument that grandfathering better reflects the implicit social contract with current producers, on the basis of which they undertook their investments, that their use of the atmosphere as a carbon sink would be free.

Given the political power of current producers, it is the latter argument which has prevailed in practice, and all proposed carbon emissions trading systems (see Section 3) envisage the grandfathering of permits, initially at least. Over time it may be that an increasing proportion will come to be auctioned.

It is sometimes argued that a permit system is to be preferred to a tax because its outcome is more certain in terms of achieving an emission reduction target. This extra certainty is dependent on the permit regime having clear, enforceable and enforced rules and well-monitored emissions. However, there is no real dichotomy between taxes and permits. An effective scheme to abate carbon emissions would be likely to combine taxes, permits and regulation, with each instrument supporting the others depending on the country, sector and institution concerned. Since carbon abatement does not require a precise abatement by a definite date, the aim of policy must be to achieve significant reductions over a number of years, with policies adjusting to outcomes repeatedly.

2.2. The costs of carbon emissions reduction

2.2.1. The costs of introducing a carbon tax

Economists are generally agreed that, because of the efficiency properties of carbon taxes (and systems of emissions trading using auctioned permits), they will achieve any given level of carbon emissions reduction at a lower cost than regulation. There have been a number of studies which calculate the efficiency advantages of economic instruments over other forms of environmental regulation. OECD 1997 (Table 2, p. 30) cites a range of studies which show that the costs for regulatory instruments of air-pollution control compared to those arising from least-cost instruments can vary by a factor of 1.07 to 22.00. In addition, applying an economic instrument across countries can achieve a given emission reduction at lower cost than applying separate economic instruments within countries, because of the transnational equalisation of the costs of abatement which the common instrument achieves. Thus Bohm (1999, p. 316) finds that a jointly implemented carbon emissions trading system applied across the four Scandinavian countries (Denmark, Finland, Norway, Sweden) saves 48% of the costs of a given level of carbon reduction, even when each country operates its own carbon trading system internally. The reduction in carbon tax rates brought about by coordinating a tax across 11 EU countries has also been studied. Conrad and Schmidt (1998), using a general equilibrium model, GEM-E3, estimate that the coordinated tax rate falls by about 1.5% compared with uncoordinated carbon taxes achieving a 10% reduction in CO_2 emission below baseline levels; and Barker (1999) using a disequilibrium econometric model, E3ME, estimates the fall as 5.2%.

One measure of the cost of reducing carbon emissions is the value of the reduction in output to which it gives rise. In the first instance, this will depend on the opportunities for and economics of abatement. In the extreme, where there are no opportunities to reduce the emissions associated with the output of a product, then they can only be reduced by cutting the output of the product itself. This situation gives rise to the largest cost of emissions reduction.

Although there are fewer opportunities for end-of-pipe reductions of carbon emissions than for some other gases, there will typically be a number of ways of cutting the emissions associated with production, which are cheaper than simply cutting production, and which incur different costs for different levels of emission reduction. Thus the cost of a given level of carbon reduction will, in the first instance, be a combination of the costs of abatement technologies and the value of foregone output. However, in a general equilibrium framework, several other effects can be identified which make the overall cost of reduction much more difficult to compute.

1. The reduction in carbon emissions may be associated with the reductions of other polluting emissions (and will be if it involves reduced use of fossil fuels, which are associated with a number of polluting emissions apart from carbon). These reductions will yield what are called 'secondary' or 'ancillary' benefits of carbon reduction, which should be taken into account when computing its overall economic cost.
2. The output of pollution abatement companies will have increased, which will stimulate the economy.
3. The price of the abating firm's output may have increased, with further knock-on effects through the economy.
4. In response to any increase in the price of the abating firm's output, substitution towards other products will take place.
5. It may be that the productivity of people or other firms will have increased due to the reduction in pollution.
6. On the one hand, the rise in price of the use of the environmental resource may hasten the depreciation of the capital equipment affected. On the other hand, it may be that the shift in relative prices will stimulate research, innovation and investment with a view to economising on the resource, which may be economically beneficial.
7. The tax will yield revenue, which will allow other taxes to be reduced, for the same level of government expenditure, with yet more knock-on effects through the economy. Where the revenues generate economic benefits by permitting distortionary taxes to be reduced, then this benefit, together with the environmental benefit of the tax, is known as a 'double dividend' from the tax.[1]

A number of these points will be discussed further in subsequent sections, together with the numerous results of modelling which have sought to estimate their quantitative importance. The last point, however, merits further theoretical discussion.

As regards the double dividend debate, the first issue to be addressed is that of the economic distortions introduced by taxation. It is a standard result from the neo-classical optimal taxation literature (e.g. Diamond and Mirrlees, 1971; Stiglitz and Dasgupta, 1971) that taxes on economic output or factor inputs are distortionary, thereby reducing output and welfare. According to the static perfect competition model, distortions arise from the taxes changing the prices facing both producers and consumers, so that factors no longer receive their marginal product and the cost of output does not reflect its true economic cost. Some analysts apply such insights to environmental taxes. Thus Gaskins and Weyant (1993, p. 320) write of 'the distortions to the economy caused by the imposition of the carbon tax', and Jorgenson and Wilcoxen (1993a, p. 518) write of the 'introduction of distortions resulting from fossil-fuel taxes'. But the whole point of an environmental tax (at a rate at or below the optimal level) is that it wholly or partially corrects a distortion from a pre-existing environmental externality. The adjustments to the new relative prices, and the resulting shift in resource allocation, are not to be regarded as a 'distortion' due to the tax. Adjustments in the economy to a higher level of allocative efficiency are the effects of *removing* distortions by the internalization of an environmental externality. As Pearce (1991, p. 940) has emphasised: 'While most taxes distort incentives, an environmental tax corrects a distortion, namely the externalities arising from the excessive use of environmental services'.

However, given that the environmental improvement can be envisaged as being brought about through the diversion of economic resources from producing marketed goods or services to the production of unmarketed environmental goods or services, a loss of marketed output is to be expected from such improvement (unless the instrument of improvement permits the reduction of other, pre-existing, economic inefficiencies, as discussed below). Moreover, with regard purely to marketed output (i.e. setting aside the environmental benefits, assuming no correction of an externality), the introduction of a carbon tax will be distortionary, as will any other tax on factor inputs or economic products. In the modelling of an environmental tax, if the base run is considered non-distortionary and at full equilibrium in all markets, then, as Boero *et al.* (1991, p. 34) note, 'any deviation from a "no distortions" base run necessarily involves economic costs'.

However, no economy is at a point of non-distortionary equilibrium. There are distortions due to current taxation patterns, which bear most heavily on labour; and there are distortions due to market or government failure, such as, perhaps, in the market for energy efficiency, or as a result of inefficient government regulation. In addition, economies are not likely to be in equilibrium in all markets: there may be substantial involuntary unemployment in the labour markets; there may be chronic deficits or surpluses in the balance of payments implying disequilibrium in the foreign exchange market. Depending on the type of model used (e.g. general equilibrium or otherwise), the macroeconomic effect of an environmental tax will depend on whether its introduction, or other associated policy, affects these distortions.

It has already been noted that carbon taxes will normally allow a given carbon reduction to be achieved at a lower cost than pure reliance on regulations. It remains to explore their implications for markets other than those of the directly affected goods, for different income groups and for the wider tax system. These implications are significant because the revenues from a carbon tax could be large.

Thus the levels of the carbon taxes proposed as necessary to make substantial reductions in carbon emissions are between $100 and $400 per ton of carbon (see Table 5 from Boero *et al.*, 1991, pp. 87–89). A $250 tax is equivalent to $0.75 per gallon on petrol or $30 per barrel on oil (Cline, 1992, p. 147). Cline (1992, p. 151) also estimates that a $100 per ton global tax rate would raise on the order of $500 billion annually, and about $130 billion from the USA alone. Schelling considers that 'a carbon tax sufficient to make a big dent in the greenhouse problem would have to be roughly equivalent to a dollar per gallon on motor fuel ... (which) would currently yield close to half a trillion dollars a year in revenue.' (Schelling, 1992, p. 11). Barker and Rosendahl (2000, p. 433 and Table 5.3 below) estimate that a carbon tax of 153 euros per ton of carbon will allow western Europe to meet its Kyoto targets, with total revenues by 2010 of 170bn euros.

This revenue can be used in a number of ways:

1. To achieve further environmental benefits (for example, by subsidising energy efficiency measures, or low-carbon technologies). This is discussed in Section 4.
2. To achieve distributional objectives, either in response to the distributional impacts of the carbon tax, or more generally. This is discussed in Section 5.
3. To reduce government borrowing or debt, thereby reducing the level of taxation that will be required in the future.
4. To reduce other inefficiencies in the economy, by enabling, for a given level of government expenditure, other distortionary taxes to be reduced. This has been termed 'revenue-recycling', and the 'dividend' to which it may be able to give rise is the subject of what follows.

2.2.2. *The revenue-recycling dividend*

A revenue-recycling dividend is here defined as an economic (and non-environmental) benefit resulting from the revenue-neutral imposition of a tax (i.e. all the revenue from the tax is returned to taxpayers by cuts in other taxes or lump-sum rebates, rather than saved or spent by the government). Such a dividend can arise if the revenue recycling improves economic distribution (see Section 5), or reduces unemployment or otherwise increases economic efficiency (thereby increasing output).

As noted above, the theoretical possibility for such a dividend depends on the economy being in a non-optimal state to start with: the existing tax structure must be non-optimal in some sense, for example because the tax base is related to employment. Alternatively, there must be existing deficiencies in distribution and market failures in the labour and other markets. Any perception or assumption that the initial condition of the economy is characterized by no externalities, perfectly competitive markets operating in equilibrium, and with taxes imposed on a per capita basis, will *a priori* rule out the existence or possible achievement of a revenue-recycling dividend which increases economic efficiency.

However, with a less ideal initial economic configuration, the existence of such a dividend cannot be ruled out. Figures from the US suggest that distortions from taxation are substantial. Thus Ballard *et al.* calculate the marginal excess burden (MEB) of taxation in the US to be in the range 17 to 56 cents per dollar of extra revenue (Ballard *et al.*, 1985, p. 128). Jorgenson and Yun (1990) find that the MEB of the US tax system as a whole, even after the tax reform of 1986, which was widely held to have reduced the excess burden, is 38 cents per dollar of revenue raised. Some components of the tax system had far higher costs, for example the MEB for individual capital taxes was 95c/$ (Jorgenson and Yun, 1990, p. 20). Jorgenson and Yun (1990, p. 6) acknowledge that their MEB estimates 'are considerably higher than previous estimates. This can be attributed primarily to the greater precision we employ in representing the US tax structure'. Nordhaus (1993, p. 316) notes that 'some have estimated [the marginal deadweight loss of taxes in the US] as high as $0.50 per $1.00 of revenue'.

While there are no comparable figures for Europe, EC 1994 (p. 145) makes the point:

> Marginal costs of taxation increase more than proportionally with the level of taxation. In view of the much higher share of tax revenues in the Community than in the USA (the tax burden in the Community is nearly 50% higher than in the USA and Japan) it would appear that the costs of fiscal systems in terms of forgone GDP and hence employment might be particularly high in the Community. Only if the structure of the Community's fiscal system were much more efficient than in the USA, would this not hold true.

In the absence of grounds for believing European tax systems to be more efficient than that of the US, it seems likely that the distortions from taxation in Europe are at least as great as those in the USA.

The key question then becomes whether the substitution of a non-distortionary environmental tax for a distortionary tax can reduce the distortions from the tax system as a whole, leading to increased efficiency and output. The focus here will be on substituting an environmental tax for a labour tax of two kinds: an income tax on employees and a social security tax levied on employers (the latter substitution is the one implemented in relation to the revenues from the UK's Climate Change Levy, implemented in April 2001). Finally some brief consideration will be given to the so-called erosion and interdependency (or tax interaction) effects, which have been the object of some recent analysis in the literature.

Substituting for a personal income tax

Two immediate first-round effects of substituting an environmental tax for a personal income tax (here considering only labour income) will arise:

S1 The environmental tax will raise the price of the affected items; the reduction in income tax will increase the disposable income of employees.

Insofar as the higher prices are paid by non-employees (unemployed, pensioners, other non-employed, foreigners), and income tax rebates are received by employees, the substitution will raise the real wage. This will increase the labour supply.

S2   The price increases will be concentrated in the goods or activities subject to the tax. Where the tax falls on inputs, producers will tend to substitute away from the taxed input. Where it falls on final demand, consumers will shift demand away from the affected sectors to others that are relatively less environment-intensive and so less affected by the tax. It is of course the intention of the tax to bring about this substitution by both producers and consumers, and it will occur irrespective of how the revenue from the tax is recycled.

Insofar as there is an inverse correlation between labour-intensity and environment-intensity, the demand for labour-intensive goods and services will increase. Barker (1994, pp. 20–21) has shown that such a correlation exists for the production and industrial use of energy (energy-intensive industries tend to use relatively little labour; labour-intensive industries tend to use relatively little energy). A revenue-neutral energy tax would therefore be expected to increase labour demand.

The shift in relative prices would also alter the productivity of the affected capital stock and, perhaps, hasten its depreciation. This adjustment effect could be minimised by introducing the taxation in a gradual, pre-announced way, so that the new relative prices were anticipated and allowed for in investment schedules.

The increase in labour demand as a result of S2 will either reduce unemployment (if it exists) or put to work the increased labour supply induced as a result of S1. Either way employment and output would increase, yielding both an employment and an efficiency dividend. The increased employment and output would result in second-round macroeconomic improvements (lower benefits, higher tax revenues so lower tax rates etc.). The only way these positive benefits would fail to materialize would be if S2's increase in labour demand was far stronger that S1's increase in labour supply in the context of a tight labour market. The increased labour demand would then engender wage inflation with generally negative effects on employment and output.

Substituting for an employers' social security tax (SST)

Consider an average firm using energy E_1 and employing labour L_1, which is subject to a SST of t_L. The firm pays tax of $L_1 t_L$.

Now let a tax t_E be imposed on energy, with full compensation by way of reduction in SST. Then, initially, the firm will pay energy tax of $E_1 t_E$, with a reduction in its SST rate to:

$$t_L - (t_E E_1)/L_1.$$

Now, with energy relatively more expensive and labour relatively cheaper, the firm changes its proportion of inputs, say to L_2 ($> L_1$) and E_2 ($< E_1$).

The tax paid on energy use is now $t_E E_2$. Let the new tax rate on labour, t'_L, be set so that the total tax paid by the firm is unchanged, so:

$$t_L L_1 = t'_L L_2 + t_E E_2$$
$$\Rightarrow t'_L = t_L (L_1/L_2) - t_E E_2/L_2 \qquad (2.1)$$
$$\Rightarrow t'_L < t_L$$

The first term on the right hand side (RHS) of equation 2.1 can be thought of as the result of the substitution effect. The firm's tax rate on labour will be reduced in proportion to its increased employment. The second term is the revenue effect of the energy tax, further reducing the effective tax rate on labour.

The reduction in the effective tax rate on labour will reduce the overall marginal cost of labour to the firm, as long as the wage paid to labour is unchanged. If this is so, then the greater is the fall from t_L to t'_L, the greater is the fall in labour's marginal cost to the firm. The reduced marginal cost of labour will increase labour demand. The reduction in labour costs may also enable firms to cut the price of their output, thereby compensating for any price increases due to the imposition of the environmental tax.

As in the earlier case, if all the SST decrease is passed through to employees as an increase in wages, then evidently the marginal cost of labour to employers will not fall and so labour demand will not rise. Even so, because of the increased cost of energy, a substitution effect still takes place, but less strongly. The situation then becomes identical to where the recycling was achieved by reducing a personal income tax, as in S1 and S2 above.

The effect S1 comes about as a result of a reduction of a distortion in the labour market (employees' disposable income moves closer to their marginal product as paid by their employers), through the simultaneous reduction or removal of a distortion in the market of the taxed good (an externality has been wholly or partially internalised). However, the possibility has been addressed in a number of papers that, through interdependencies in the tax system, or the erosion of the environmental tax base, the reduction of the environmental distortion in the context of a labour market with pre-existing labour taxes could lead to more labour market distortion rather than less. This possibility is considered below.

This discussion of the possible employment effects of introducing a revenue-neutral carbon tax can be summarized as follows. The key question determining the extent to which an efficiency dividend would arise is whether or not the reduction of social security taxes results in higher wages. If it does, then the implications for employment are ambiguous: being negative because of inflation and macroeconomic deterioration, and being positive through the substitution effects in both production and consumption. If it does not, then employment would unambiguously increase, through both the substitution effects and firms' falling labour costs. Although the higher employment would probably mean that overall labour productivity in the economy was lower, it is also likely that output would increase somewhat.

2.3. *Distortions of, and tax interaction effects between, environmental and labour taxes*

It was noted above that, unlike other taxes which tend to introduce distortions, environmental taxes at (or below) their optimal level (partially) correct an economic distortion. As far as the environmental dimension is concerned this argument is uncontroversial.

However, as far as marketed output alone is concerned, and leaving aside issues of unemployment, carbon taxes will only increase output when substituting for other taxes if they have less effect on output than the taxes they replace. Using a general equilibrium model Goulder (1995b) concludes that, leaving aside its environmental benefits, a carbon tax is substantially *more* distorting than personal income, corporate or payroll taxes. He argues that the distortions it introduces arise from its non-uniformity across energy carriers (precisely the characteristic that makes it an efficient environmental tax), the narrowness of the tax base, and the fact that it falls on intermediate inputs as well as final output.

This result has been challenged by INFRAS (1996), who point out that the size of the distortionary effect of a tax depends not only on the tax rate (which, for a given revenue, will tend to be higher and more distortionary the narrower the tax base), but also on the elasticities of demand and supply of the taxed quantity. The net effect of increasing energy and, for example, reducing labour taxes will therefore depend on the relative elasticities of labour and energy. Using the ECOPLAN computable general equilibrium model for Switzerland, INFRAS (1996, p. 141) finds that the so-called distortionary effects of a carbon tax are substantially less than the reduced distortions from lowering employers' labour taxes, yielding a positive effect on output, even before any extra output from reducing unemployment is considered.

In addition to the independent distortionary effects of different taxes, there is the possibility that the taxes interact such that changes in one tax affect the distortions caused by others. This is the effect which has been investigated in a number of recent papers (e.g. Bovenberg and de Mooij, 1994; Goulder, 1995a,b; Parry, 1995, 1997; Bovenberg and Goulder, 1996; Goulder *et al.*, 1997; Parry *et al.*, 1999).

What is known as the tax interaction effect arises when environmental taxes are levied in a context of pre-existing distortionary taxes (the above papers focus predominantly on labour taxes). The interaction of the environmental tax with these pre-existing taxes invalidates the normal result from environmental tax analysis that the tax should be set at a rate equal to the marginal external environmental damage cost at the optimal damage level. In general, the result of the tax interaction effect is that the optimal tax rate is less than the optimal (Pigovian) tax calculated in the absence of pre-existing taxes.

The mathematical analysis which generates this result is formidably complex and cannot be explored here. It is based on the usual assumptions underlying exercises in utility maximisation in perfectly competitive markets (for example, a single representative household, full market clearing in general equilibrium), and this context needs to be borne in mind when interpreting the results or seeking to apply them in practice.

Parry *et al.* (1999), which is representative of the recent literature in this area, explores the implications of the tax interaction effect for two policy instruments: a carbon tax, with revenues recycled by reducing the rate of a pre-existing labour tax; and grandfathered carbon emission permits, which still constrain carbon emissions, but do not generate government revenues.

The paper's analysis generates three main results. It shows the existence of the tax interaction effect, which acts to reduce the optimal carbon tax, as noted above. In the case of the carbon tax the tax interaction effect is offset to some extent by the revenue-recycling effect of using the carbon tax revenues to reduce the labour tax rate. However, the offset is only complete on the first increment of the carbon tax when it is first introduced. At all higher levels the tax interaction effect more than cancels out the gains from revenue recycling, thereby increasing the costs of the carbon tax above what they would have been in the absence of the pre-existing labour tax. In the case of the carbon permits, there is no offsetting revenue-recycling effect, so the negative impact of the tax interaction effect on the costs of carbon control is correspondingly greater.

In a numerical simulation Parry *et al.* (1999) quantify the impact of the tax interaction effect. They find that it is significant. A pre-existing labour tax of 40% increases the cost of the carbon tax by 22% relative to the zero labour tax case. For the carbon permits the cost increase is more than double that of the carbon tax case (for all emission reduction levels up to 25%), reflecting the absence of the revenue-recycling effect (Parry *et al.*, 1999, pp. 69–70).

The general conclusions from this literature are, in line with the arguments above, that the tax interaction effect in actually existing economies (i.e. with significant pre-existing labour taxes) can substantially increase the costs of carbon control, thereby reducing the optimal emission reduction, and that this effect is substantially greater where freely issued permits are the instrument of control, rather than a carbon tax with revenue recycling.

2.4. *Conclusions on the costs of carbon control*

The costs of carbon abatement depend on many factors, which are discussed in a subsequent section. Here the focus has been on theoretical analysis as to whether the costs may be to some extent offset by an instrument which raises government revenue, and returns these to the economy by cutting pre-existing distortionary, especially labour, taxes.

The conclusion of the analysis is unequivocal: revenue-raising instruments such as carbon taxes and auctioned emission permits, with revenue recycling that reduces other taxes, will reduce emissions at lower cost than both regulations and market-based instruments without revenue recycling (such as grandfathered emission permits). The benefits of the revenue-recycling effect will be higher when cuts in employers' payroll taxes increase labour demand, especially where there is unemployment. However, as discussed above, they are also highly significant in the stylised theoretical context that has been used in the analysis of the tax interaction effect. Estimates of the quantitative size of the revenue-recycling effect in other contexts are presented in Section 5 below.

3. Practical experience of carbon taxes and carbon emissions trading

3.1. *Carbon taxes in practice*

Section 2 showed that carbon taxes have a well-established theoretical basis, which suggests that they could be a cost-effective policy instrument for the reduction of CO_2 emissions. As a result there has been much policy interest in carbon taxes, and numerous recommendations from policy analysts that they should form part of any package of measures to address climate change (Pearce, 1991; RCEP, 2000, Recommendation 11, p. 200).

In contrast to this enthusiasm derived from theory, the practical implementation of carbon taxes has been cautious and modest, and is limited to six European countries (see below).

Italy was the most recent country to implement a carbon tax, which was introduced in 1999, and was expected to raise Euros. 1.13bn in that year (ENDS, 1999).

Table 3.1 gives some summary information about the carbon taxes which have been implemented in the five other European countries, together with some comparative information about some other countries' revenues from energy taxation.

Table 3.1 shows revenues from carbon and energy taxes for a number of European countries. Of course, even for those countries without specific carbon taxes, taxes on fossil fuels act as implicit carbon taxes, but they are not efficient, in the sense of equalising the marginal cost of carbon abatement across the tax base, if their purpose is to reduce CO_2 emissions.

Table 3.1 shows that carbon taxes were introduced in the 1990s. Carbon tax revenues compared to energy tax revenues are most significant for Sweden, but even then they comprise only 26%. This reflects the fact that energy taxes were important revenue-raising taxes well before climate change, and therefore CO_2 taxes, became a policy concern. Some of the five countries (for example, Denmark, Netherlands, Sweden) introduced CO_2 taxes as part of a reform of existing energy and other taxes, in order to give greater weight to environmental considerations. Other countries now treat energy taxes *de facto* as environmental taxes, even if they were introduced purely for revenue reasons and have no specific environmental focus.

Table 3.1 also shows that, with the exception of Finland, the countries with CO_2 taxes, compared to the countries without them, derive a relatively large

Table 3.1 Carbon, energy and environmental taxes in some European countries.

Countries with carbon taxes (date of introduction)	Revenues from CO_2 tax (10^6 $PPP)	Revenues from energy taxes (10^6 $PPP)	% CO_2 tax revenues in energy tax revenues	% of energy and environmental taxes in total taxes
Denmark (1993)	457	2905	16	9 (1997)
Finland (1990)	436[1]	2519	17	5 (1995)
Netherlands (1996)	828[2]	6990	12	~ 14 (1997)
Norway (1991)	323[1]	2429	13	10.8 (1993)
Sweden (1991)	1344	5140[3]	26	10.1 (1998)
Other countries				
France	...	21 652	...	5.7 (1995)
Germany	...	31 588	...	6.3 (1995)
Spain	...	8482	...	8.1 (1995)
UK	...	26 223	...	7.9 (1995)

Sources: Baranzini et al., 2000, Table 2, p. 399; EC 1999, various tables
[1] Figure for 1996
[2] Half the total revenue of two energy taxes which are calculated on a 50/50 energy/CO_2 basis
[3] Excludes revenue from an electricity tax

proportion of their taxes from energy and environmental taxes. If this proportion is an indicator of environmental policy concern, then it may be that other countries will introduce carbon taxes if such concern continues to increase.

All the countries which have introduced a carbon tax have also introduced special tax reductions, rebates, or exemptions, in order to address concerns about the effect of the tax on industrial competitiveness (of course, this applies to many countries' treatment of energy taxes as well), as discussed below. These exemptions are complex and discussed in detail in Ekins and Speck (1999a). Some of the principal features of these special arrangements for industrial energy users are:

- In Sweden manufacturing industry only pays 50% of the CO_2 tax rate of around Euros 40/tonne CO_2.
- In Denmark the CO_2 tax rate varies according to whether the use is for space heating, when it is around Euros 80/tonne CO_2 for households and businesses, 'light industrial processes', which pay around Euros 12/tonne CO_2, and 'heavy industrial processes', which only pay around Euros 3/tonne CO_2. Such a differential in tax rates has serious implications for the theoretical efficiency advantages of using carbon taxes to reduce carbon emissions.
- In Norway the CO_2 tax rate varies with the fossil fuel, from about Euros 16/tonne CO_2 for heavy fuel oil, to around Euros 20/tonne CO_2 for coal, to around Euros 44/tonne CO_2 for natural gas. In addition, reduced tax rates apply for some industrial sectors. For example, the pulp and paper industry and the fishmeal industry only pay 50% of the tax on heavy fuel oil.
- The 1992 proposal from the European Commission for a carbon/energy tax provided for the exemption of the six most energy-intensive industrial sectors

(but even so failed to be implemented, at least partly because of strong business opposition, see Ikwue and Skea, 1996).

Such differentials in tax rates have serious implications for the theoretical efficiency advantages, and may be expected to increase the macroeconomic cost, of using carbon taxes to reduce carbon emissions.

Of the five North European countries listed in Table 3.1, Finland, Norway and Sweden allocate the revenues from their carbon taxes to the general government budget. This means that, for a given level of government expenditure and fiscal balance, other taxes are lower than they would otherwise be, but there is no specific offsetting of other taxes against the carbon taxes, as is sometimes the case in what is called 'environmental tax reform'. In Denmark the carbon tax revenues from industry are recycled back to industry through reduced social security contributions and through investment incentives, and in the Netherlands the revenues are recycled back to households and industry through personal and corporate tax relief (EC, 1999).

3.2. Carbon emissions trading in practice

It was noted in Section 1 that it is envisaged that an international carbon emissions trading regime will be put in place under the terms of the Kyoto Protocol. However, by the end of 2000 the details of the scheme had still not been fully worked out and agreed. At that time the only operational carbon emissions trading scheme was the one introduced by Denmark's government for the Danish power sector. This sector currently emits around 40% of Denmark's CO_2 emissions, and the scheme is intended to make a contribution to the 21% emissions reduction (by 2008–2012 from 1990's level) to which Denmark is committed under the Kyoto Protocol. The sector's allocated emission permits are due to be reduced from 23 million tonnes (mt) CO_2 in 2000 to 20 mt in 2003, a cut of 13%, when the scheme will end. The permits will be divided among about 15 companies, which may bank or trade them between themselves. Firms which emit CO_2 in excess of the permits they possess will become liable to an additional carbon tax of Euros 5.4 per tonne CO_2 (ENDS, 1999b; ENDS, 2000; the power sector is currently exempt from Denmark's carbon tax). Analysis of such interactions between carbon taxes and emissions trading schemes would seem to present a useful avenue for future research.

A number of other countries are developing carbon (or greenhouse gas) emissions trading schemes, including Australia, Canada, the US and a number of European countries (including France, Germany, the Netherlands, Norway, Sweden and the UK). In Europe the European Commission issued a Green Paper on greenhouse gas emissions trading in March 2000 (EC, 2000), outlining a scheme that is intended to be introduced in 2005. The scheme is initially intended to cover only CO_2 emissions from 'large fixed point sources' (EC, 2000, p. 10), but could later be extended to other greenhouse gases and sources of emissions.

4. Environmental effectiveness of carbon taxes

The purpose of carbon taxes is to reduce carbon emissions cost-effectively. It has already been noted that they are widely regarded as being (with auctioned tradable permits) the most efficient policy instruments for carbon reduction, meaning that they will achieve a given carbon reduction at less cost than other instruments. This section explores how carbon taxes bring about their reduction effects, the responsiveness of carbon emissions to carbon taxation, and how their environmental effectiveness may be increased.

The reduction of carbon emissions comes about through several possible different effects.

4.1. *Effects of carbon taxes on the demand for carbon-based fuels*

Effects on producers

For producers, carbon dioxide may be related to output (O) through the following decomposition into different ratios:

$$CO_2 = (CO_2/E) * (E/ES) * (ES/I) * (I/O) * O \tag{4.1}$$

where CO_2 is carbon dioxide emissions, E is energy inputs, ES is energy services (useful heat, light, power), I is inputs to production, and * denotes multiplication.

Where the tax falls on the carbon inputs to production, to the extent that producers cannot pass the tax on to consumers it will tend to reduce their profits and output (O), and therefore their CO_2 emissions. To counteract the effect on profits and output, producers will seek to reduce their CO_2 emissions by reducing the other terms in equation (4.1), where it is cost-effective to do so. Thus they will tend to switch to less carbon-intensive fuels (reducing CO_2/E), to use energy more efficiently in current production processes (reducing E/ES), and to reduce their demand for energy services relative to other production inputs (reducing ES/I). They will also seek to develop new technologies for future production processes which reduce all these ratios.

Effects on consumers

For consumers, carbon dioxide may be related to consumer expenditure (CE) through the following decomposition into different ratios:

$$CO_2 = (CO_2/E) * (E/ES) * (ES/EIGS) * (EIGS/CE) * CE \tag{4.2}$$

where the letters are as defined above and EIGS stands for energy-intensive goods and services.

To the extent that producers can pass the tax on production inputs on to consumers, or where the tax falls directly on consumers' consumption of carbon-based fuels, they will seek to switch to less carbon-intensive fuels (reduce CO_2/E), use energy more efficiently (reduce E/ES), and reduce both the proportion of energy services in energy-intensive goods and services (reduce ES/EIGS) and the share of EIGS (including ES) in consumer expenditure on all goods and services (reduce EIGS/CE).

Estimates of the effectiveness of carbon taxes in reducing CO_2 emissions will therefore depend on assumptions about:

- The ease of switching between more and less carbon-intensive fuels (affecting CO_2/E)
- The opportunities for delivering energy services more efficiently (affecting E/ES)
- The growth in demand for energy services, relative either to other production inputs (affecting ES/I), or to other energy-intensive goods and services (affecting $ES/EIGS$)
- The growth in demand for energy-intensive goods and services relative to other goods and services ($EIGS/CE$).

The standard method of estimating energy (and thereby CO_2) elasticities is through the econometric use of time-series or cross-section data. Yet the principal price changes in time-series data have been the sudden price increases in the 1970s, due to OPEC production restrictions, and the equally sudden price reduction in the mid-1980s, when those restrictions proved unsustainable.

Barker *et al.* (1995a, p. 11) note that there are a number of reasons why such price changes are unlikely to reflect satisfactorily the likely responses to a carbon tax that was set to escalate gradually over a number of years:

- Such a tax would be more likely to be perceived as permanent than cartel-induced price increases, increasing the likely behavioural response and giving producers a greater stimulus to develop low-carbon technologies.
- The gradual introduction of the tax would reduce the impacts of the price increase on the economy by allowing the capital stock to be replaced at the end of its useful life rather than inducing premature scrapping.
- Because the tax would be part of a long-term, well understood policy commitment (to mitigate climate change), consumers could also anticipate it in their behaviour, rather than being caught by surprise.
- The revenues from the tax would stay in the domestic economy, rather than accruing to foreign oil producers, giving opportunities to recycle them by reducing distortionary taxes. Even if this were not done, the macroeconomic effects of such taxes would be very different to the OPEC-induced price rises.

All these factors would be likely to increase the price-elasticity of demand in response to a carbon tax relative to those estimated from data from the 1970s and 1980s. In addition, both price and income elasticities will be affected by the degree of market saturation for energy services and energy appliances. For example, domestic warmth will not tend to grow with income, once a desired comfort level has been reached.

The different chapters in Barker *et al.* (1995b) discuss many of these effects in detail. Their overall implication is that many of the published estimates of CO_2

reduction from carbon taxes are likely to be too low (and the costs of a given CO_2 reduction are therefore too high) because these factors are often not taken into account. This also results in a very wide range of published estimates of the effectiveness of a carbon tax, as illustrated by the Energy Modeling Forum (EMF) at Stanford University, which specified standardised scenarios for fourteen widely differing economic models of the US economy. In these models a carbon tax of $80/tonne carbon brought about a change in CO_2 levels with respect to 1990 of between −35% and +20% (Gaskins and Weyant, 1993, p. 319).

Similarly Repetto and Austin (1997, p. 13) have shown that the cost estimates of different models of reducing carbon emissions by 60% from a projected baseline by 2020, reflecting different required levels of a carbon tax, varies from $+7\frac{1}{2}$% to −5% of GDP, depending on the models' treatment of issues including those listed above. The assumptions behind these cost estimates are discussed further in Section 5.3.

4.2. Effects of existing carbon taxes

The problems of estimating the environmental effectiveness of a carbon tax *ex ante* (i.e. in advance of its introduction) are in no way reduced *ex post* (i.e. after the event). This is because *ex post* evaluations have to compare the situation after the event with a baseline of what would have happened without a carbon tax. Constructing such a baseline faces identical problems to estimating the effects of the tax *ex ante*. In addition, carbon (and energy) taxes are often introduced as part of a carbon control policy package, rather than as separate measures. Estimating their effectiveness then requires the impact of the different components of the package to be separated out, which, as OECD 1997 (p. 122) notes, 'can prove completely impossible'.

Notwithstanding these difficulties of evaluation, most of the countries that have introduced carbon taxes have sought to estimate their effectiveness (Ekins and Speck, 1999b for a discussion). Thus the Dutch Green Tax Commission in the Netherlands has calculated that each Euros. 450m raised from its fuel taxes leads to a CO_2 reduction of 1–1.5 mt. Larsen and Nesbakken (1997, p. 287) found that the total effect of the Norwegian CO_2 tax on CO_2 emissions was 3–4% for the period 1991–1993. The Danish Environmental Protection Agency (DEPA) estimated that the Danish CO_2 tax would reduce CO_2 emissions by 1.6% (DEPA, 1999, p. 87). In Sweden a study commissioned by the Swedish Environmental Protection Agency (SEPA) concluded that Swedish CO_2 emissions in 1994 'were just under 5 mt lower than they would have been without the carbon dioxide tax' (SEPA, 1997, pp. 48–49).

4.3. Increasing CO_2 reduction from a carbon tax

It has already been noted that the evaluation of the effects of a carbon tax is incomplete without consideration of the use to which its revenues are put. One possible use of the revenues is the enhancement of the environmental effectiveness of the tax through subsidies, tax expenditures or tax incentives for carbon abatement.

Rajah and Smith (1993) review the issues raised by these kinds of measures. They note that 'first-best policy' would have no role for such measures, but that where considerations of competitiveness or distribution (see Section 5) introduce political constraints on implementing a carbon tax at the desired level, these measures may provide an alternative means of emission reduction. Rajah and Smith explore a number of implications of these measures, noting in particular that they tend to contravene the Polluter Pays Principle, and that their use should therefore be cautious and subject to international monitoring if it is not to risk becoming a trade distortion. However, they conclude that investment subsidies, in particular, may have a role to play as a complement to environmental taxes (Rajah and Smith, 1993, p. 62).

Whatever the soundness of their theoretical basis, tax expenditures and investment incentives for environmental protection are widespread. Rajah and Smith (1993, p. 54) noted that a 1993 OECD study had identified their use in 14 OECD countries, and they play an especially important part, alongside a carbon tax, in the carbon-reduction policy packages of Denmark and the Netherlands (EC, 1999).

5. Economic and distributional impacts of carbon taxes

Implementing a carbon tax will increase the relative price of fossil energy compared to other inputs, an effect which may be enhanced by reducing taxes on these other inputs (e.g. labour, capital). But the change in relative prices could affect economic development in a number of other ways. As discussed in Section 2, one of the most important determinants of the overall impact of a carbon tax will be the use that is made of the revenues. This issue emerges repeatedly in many of the areas of discussion which follow.

5.1. Investment, efficiency and technical change

Increased scrapping

A change in relative prices caused by the imposition of a carbon tax might affect economic development by making existing capital equipment uneconomic, thereby bringing forward its scrapping date. This could be a major potential source of adjustment costs related to the tax. One would expect that the least disruptive imposition of a carbon tax would be one introduced initially at a low level, with modest annual increases over a substantial, pre-announced period of time. This would allow responses to the tax to be synchronised with normal investment schedules.

Ingham and Ulph (1991a) have developed a vintage model of the UK manufacturing sector, which allows firms to change their machines' energy-output ratio, according to relative factor prices, both between different machine vintages and with existing machines. Technical change is thus at least partly endogenised. The model clearly confirms the above intuition. There is a significant increase in the tax rate required to meet, and the associated cost of meeting, a given target if the target date is brought closer or if action is delayed, or if the target entails cutting existing emissions rather than preventing future growth. As Ingham and Ulph (1991a, p. 143) say: 'It is much more expensive to undo the effects of emissions-generating plant already installed, than it is to offset the effects of emissions-generating plant yet to be installed.'

Moreover, the Ingham and Ulph model suggests that the increased scrapping may lead to higher long term growth that outweighs the short term adjustment costs. The authors find that 'in the short run output falls, and this induces considerable scrapping of equipment which leads to lower costs and prices, and output being higher in the longer term than in the case where demand is determined exogenously. In the extreme case, output growth rises from 2 to 4.4%.' (Ingham and Ulph, 1991b, pp. 198–199)

Improvements in energy efficiency

Many analysts have argued that market failures are preventing the implementation of already cost-efficient energy-conservation measures (e.g. Lovins and Lovins, 1991; Jackson and Jacobs, 1991; Jackson, 1995). Jackson (1991) provides evidence that the energy market is far from perfect. He finds that out of 17 technological possibilities for the reduction of CO_2 emissions, eight could be implemented at negative cost on the basis of current prices, saving a total of 165 million tonnes of CO_2 per year by 2005, or 24% of UK 1991 emissions. On this analysis the UK could have exceeded the Toronto target for CO_2 emissions (20% reduction from 1988 levels by 2005) *and* saved money. This is not an unrepresentative result. After reviewing this issue, Cline (1992, p. 227) decides that a reasonable estimate is that the first 22% of carbon emissions from base can be cut back at zero cost. The IPCC survey of this literature (Bruce *et al.*, 1996, pp. 310, 318) finds that zero cost emission reductions by 2025/2030 estimated by various studies ranged from > 61–82% (for the US) and from > 45–60% for other OECD countries.

If it is true that many presently economic opportunities for energy-saving remain unimplemented because of market failures (for example, lack of information, excessive discount rates, landlord/tenant problems etc.), then it might be expected that a continuously increasing energy price, by providing a continuously increasing incentive to correct such failures, would result in substantial investments in energy efficiency and further innovation in this area. Private efforts in this field could be complemented by government initiatives to encourage energy conservation and efficiency. If energy efficiency could thereby be increased at no net cost at the same rate as the price of energy, then the negative effect of the rising price on the competitiveness of even the most energy-intensive sectors would be cancelled out.

Influencing technical change

In addition to encouraging the adoption of existing energy-efficiency technologies, rising energy prices would also give a positive stimulus to the development of new energy-efficiency and non-fossil energy technologies. Such technical change would be what Grubb (1995, p. 305) calls 'induced technology development', which he speculates may be a cause of asymmetrical elasticities of energy demand, for which there is now substantial evidence (in general falls in energy prices have not increased energy demand by as much as the preceding energy price increases reduced it). Grubb concludes: 'If price rises stimulate technical development and in addition governments take further associated action to encourage energy saving, long-term solutions may emerge at relatively lower cost as a result of the accumulation of technical change in the direction of lower CO_2-emitting technologies, infrastructure and behaviour.' (ibid., p. 309).

Technologies do not emerge from on high. They evolve in response to pressures, which may be the competitive forces of the market, or the demands of public policy. Grubb *et al.* (1995, p. 420) point out that the no-regrets potential for increased energy efficiency in the UK in 1980 was identified as about 20%. In 1990 it was again identified as about 20%, despite the fact that the earlier 20% had largely been realized. They comment: 'It seems a curious feature of energy efficiency studies that they seem regularly to identify cost-effective potentials of around 20–30% of current demand, almost irrespective of the potential already exploited. ... The persistence of such results suggests that investing in greater energy efficiency helps itself to stimulate and identify options previously overlooked.'

5.2. *Competitiveness of firms and industrial sectors*

Section 3 noted the reductions in rates of carbon taxes that are levied on manufacturing industries in general, or energy-intensive industries in particular, reductions which are often also applied to other energy taxes. The reason for these reductions is fears of the potential impact of such taxes on industrial competitiveness. The special treatment of Swedish manufacturing industry with respect to the taxation of energy is explicitly due to such fears. It was felt that the tax system prior to the reform of 1993 '... had proved to constrain the competitiveness of the Swedish industry' (TemaNord, 1994, p. 95).

There are no studies explicitly of the *ex post* impact of carbon taxes on industrial competitiveness, partly at least because such taxes have only recently been introduced and have, in any case, been explicitly designed not to have such impacts through the exemptions and lower tax rates that have been applied. However, there have been many studies exploring the impacts on competitiveness of environmental policy in general, which may be considered relevant to the introduction of carbon taxes. There have also been numerous studies which model the potential impacts of carbon and energy taxes on the competitiveness of particular economic sectors and on the economy as a whole. The general and sectoral studies are discussed next below, while those focused on the macroeconomic impacts of carbon taxes are discussed in Section 5.3.

Considerations of competitiveness are important to environmental policy, and carbon taxes, for both economic and environmental reasons:

1. **Economic** — if environmental policy produces negative impacts on competitiveness it will be associated with corporate, sectoral or national economic decline. This is both important in itself, and would make the introduction of environmental policy politically difficult or impossible.
2. **Environmental** — if domestic environmentally or energy intensive industry declines, to be replaced by a growth in such industries in other countries, overall environmental impacts may not change. In respect of a global pollutant such as CO_2, this would mean that the loss of domestic industrial competitiveness will have brought no environmental gain at all.

Competitiveness basically denotes the ability of a firm, economic sector or national economy, or a productive sector, to sell its goods and services in domestic and world markets. There are many possible indicators of competitiveness, some of which become policy targets in their own right and even become taken for competitiveness itself. These indicators include: income per head; balance of trade; exchange rate movements; unit labour costs; generation of employment; labour productivity; market share; profitability; firm growth; and the share of world exports.

At the firm level the logic behind the fear of impacts on competitiveness from environmental taxes is simple and persuasive: taxes on business inputs inevitably add to business costs; where these taxes are imposed in one country only, these extra costs will impair the international competitiveness of the business or sector concerned. However, it may not always be the case that environmental policy imposes costs on firms; even where it does the costs may not be substantial enough to affect competitiveness; or the policy may generate benefits for the firm to set against the costs. In principle, however, it is clear that environmental, including carbon, taxes could affect industrial competitiveness.

It should be clear that effects on competitiveness will only arise if environmental policy in different countries imposes different levels of costs on competing firms. Thus, although the economic effects of environmental policy may be measured in terms of reduced labour productivity, or reduced rates of economic growth, these are only effects on competitiveness if they differentially affect some firms and not their competitors. However, because in practice environmental policy and the regulations to which it gives rise are not greatly harmonised between countries (although such harmonisation is more apparent in groups of countries like the European Union), such measures are often interpreted as indicating effects on competitiveness.

There is now a substantial literature on the effects of past environmental policy, and the possible effects of future environmental policy, on the competitiveness of businesses and countries. Here it is only possible to summarise the main arguments and results of this literature (for a fuller treatment see Ekins and Speck, 1998; other contributions in Barker and Köhler, 1998).

The conventional economic view is that the realisation of environmental benefits through environmental policy is likely to entail economic costs.

One result of these possible cost increases resulting from environmental policy is that affected industries will move to countries which have less stringent or no environmental policies, the so-called 'pollution haven hypothesis', an issue studied by Lucas et al. (1992). They found that the growth rate of the toxic intensity of manufacturing was both higher in the poorest countries and increased through the 1970s and 1980s. The authors consider that this is consistent with the hypothesis that 'stricter regulation of pollution-intensive production in the OECD countries has led to significant locational displacement, with consequent acceleration of industrial pollution intensity in developing countries.' (Lucas et al., 1992, p. 80). This result showing the absolute and relative growth of pollution-intensive industry in poor countries is confirmed by Low and Yeats (1992) through quite different non-econometric analysis of trade statistics. However, while Low and Yeats agree that the result is consistent with the Lucas displacement hypothesis, they stress that there are a number of other possible explanations, including that the strong growth of 'dirty' industries is a normal occurrence at an early stage of development.

Other studies, surveyed by Dean (1992, pp. 16–20), give conflicting results, but overall do not suggest that the forces for displacement are very great. In the same vein, Jenkins (2001) has found that there is no relationship between pollution intensity and foreign ownership in the manufacturing sectors of Malaysia and Indonesia, suggesting that foreign direct investment in such developing countries is not disproportionately driven by the quest for 'pollution havens'. Moreover, if it is true that environmentally intensive sectors are also capital-intensive, as suggested by Nordström and Vaughan (1999, p. 31), comparative advantage theory suggests that these industries would tend to be located in capital-abundant (i.e. industrialised) countries. In fact, they present World Bank data which shows that high-income countries do indeed export more pollution-intensive goods than they import, while the reverse is true for upper-middle-income, lower-middle-income and low-income countries (Nordström and Vaughan, 1999, p. 32).

To set against the reasons for possible increases in cost from environmental policy, there are a number of possible benefits from environmental policy, including cost reduction (from more efficient use of environmental inputs), first-mover advantages and stimulation to innovation, which have become important elements in the debate on this issue. Considerations of this sort have led Porter (1990, pp. 647–648) to hypothesise that environmental regulations may be good for economic competitiveness. This 'win-win' hypothesis of the economic, as well as environmental, benefits of environmental regulation runs clearly counter to economists' normal assumptions of efficient, competitive markets. It has been attacked as being at best a marginal phenomenon with regard to the costs of environmental regulation as whole. Palmer et al. (1995, pp. 127–128) estimate that Porter's 'innovation offsets' amount to only a few percent of the total costs of conforming to environmental regulations, which in the US have been estimated by the EPA at $135 billion in 1992. They contend that the vast majority of these costs conform to the standard economic trade-off model, whereby environmental benefits are gained at the expense of growth and competitiveness.

Analysis by Jenkins (1998) gives marginal support to Palmer *et al.* over Porter. Overall, however, Jenkins' review of the literature suggested that 'there was no strong universal relationship between environmental pressures and competitive performance, either at the firm level or the industry level' (Jenkins, 1998, p. 38). This is very much in line with the OECD's conclusions on the impacts of environmental policy, namely that: 'The trade and investment impacts which have been measured empirically are almost negligible.' (OECD, 1996, p. 45).

However, the past, in terms of the effect of environmental policy on competitiveness, may not be a good guide to the future. The environmental policy measures applied so far have been relatively modest compared to those that are sometimes considered necessary, especially in respect of carbon abatement, and they have not predominantly been in the form of environmental or carbon taxes. These may impose higher costs on seriously affected economic sectors because the firms concerned will need to pay for abatement (up to the efficient level) *and* for residual emissions. While this feature of environmental taxes results in the advantage over regulation that they give an incentive for continual environmental improvement at all levels of use, it also means that affected businesses pay more under an environmental tax regime than under regulations. Therefore the impacts of environmental, including carbon, taxes need to be examined separately from an assessment of the impacts of an environmental policy which has so far relied largely on regulation. Such examinations have been carried out principally through modelling studies.

Modelling the effects of carbon taxes on sectoral competitiveness

The effect of a carbon tax on sectoral competitiveness will be determined by a number of influences, including:

- the carbon intensity of the product.
- the trade intensity of the product (ratio of exports plus imports to production).
- the size of the carbon tax and the manner in which the revenues from it are used.

Because the first two of these influences differ between countries, even the imposition of a carbon tax with an identical use of revenues in all countries would differentially affect their competitiveness. The role of these factors in determining the sectoral impact of a carbon tax was clearly shown by Pezzey (1991), who simulated the introduction of a carbon tax of $100 per tonne carbon in the UK. The results are worth quoting in some detail because they clearly illustrate the essential considerations in evaluating the first order sectoral outcome of a carbon tax with revenue recycling.

Using data for 10 UK manufacturing sectors, Pezzey showed how:

- The first-round impact of a carbon tax resulted in increased costs for all the sectors when the revenues were simply added to the general government budget;
- The tax resulted in increased costs for only the four most relatively carbon-intensive sectors (iron & steel, chemicals, non-ferrous metals, non-metallic minerals) when the revenues were returned to the sectors relative to their output. Six sectors therefore experienced cost reductions due to the carbon tax;
- The cost effects on the four negatively affected sectors were reduced when their trade intensity was taken into account. In particular, the low trade intensity of iron & steel and non-metallic minerals (both sectors comprising heavy, bulky goods including iron and cement) substantially reduced the trade impacts that these sectors suffered from the carbon tax.

It may further be noted that, even if the revenues from the carbon tax are not returned to the affected sectors, they will only experience negative cost impacts from the tax to the extent that they do not reduce their carbon-intensity at a rate equal to the tax being applied. If it is true that there are substantial unexploited opportunities for cost-effective gains in energy efficiency, as discussed above, then competitiveness impacts will be reduced to the extent that these opportunities are realised.

Further analysis by Ekins (2000, pp. 267–268) showed that the four negatively affected sectors accounted for 16% of UK exports, while those that might be expected to be relatively advantaged by such a carbon tax/revenue measure accounted for 55%. On these figures it may well be that the UK's international trading position would be improved by the tax-plus-rebate arrangement. It may also be noted that 57% of UK exports in 1995 were to EU countries, so that if the carbon tax was imposed on an EU-wide basis (as was the proposal from the European Commission in 1992), the trade effects for all sectors would be much attenuated.

The conclusion that environmental taxes need not result in unacceptable effects on industrial competitiveness would appear to be borne out by the experience of Denmark, which has a small, open economy, and which has been a pioneer in the area of environmental taxation. According to its Ministry of Economic Affairs: 'Danish experience through many years is that we have not damaged our competitiveness because of green taxes. In addition, we have developed new exports in the environmental area.' (Kristensen, 1996, p. 126). The study of the Norwegian Green Tax Commission (1996, p. 90) has also endorsed this essential conclusion: 'Reduced competitiveness of an individual industry is not necessarily a problem for the economy as a whole. ... It is hardly possible to avoid loss of competitiveness and trade effects in individual sectors as a result of policy measures if a country has a more ambitious environmental policy than other countries or wishes to be an instigator in environmental policy. On the other hand, competitiveness and profitability will improve in other industries as a result of a revenue neutral tax reform'.

While the Pezzey simulation reported above only takes account of immediate, first-round effects of the relative price-changes, rather than eventual adjustments to equilibrium, the main mechanisms through which imposing environmental taxes influences sectoral competitiveness are clear, as is the difference between the impacts from environmental taxes on sectoral and national competitiveness. The cost increases in the four most affected sectors will impair their position in domestic markets with respect to the products of other sectors. The six sectors whose costs are decreased by the revenue-recycling will be particular beneficiaries from the shift in relative prices.

To gain more detailed insights into the sectoral competitiveness effects of environmental, including carbon, taxes, a disaggregated sectoral economic model incorporating interaction and feedback effects is required. The estimation of the price effects induced by the imposition of an environmental tax is often carried out using a cost driven input-output price model. The impacts on competitiveness are then analysed by the development of the sectoral prices following the introduction of an environmental tax and the respective recycling measures of the generated revenues. The price increase induced by, for example, an energy tax affects not only the economic sectors producing energy products. The prices of all economic sectors are increasing depending on how much energy is required, directly and indirectly via intermediate goods, in the production of the goods. By taking into account indirect and feedback effects from the carbon tax, this goes further than the Pezzey analysis discussed earlier, which only analysed the carbon tax's direct effects.

Using such an approach Barker (1995) has examined the issue of competitiveness using the MDM-E3 model for the UK economy analysing the implications for industrial costs of a $10 per barrel carbon/energy tax in the UK, with compensating cuts in employers' National Insurance Contributions (NIC). The result shows again the importance of how the generated revenues are redistributed: 'If the taxes are not compensated, most industries' prices rise as they face higher energy and labour unit costs. However if NIC contributions are reduced to keep the PSBR ratios at base levels then all industries' costs fall depending on their use of labour — and the most labour-intensive industries will have the largest reduction in costs.' (Barker, 1995, p. 19). For most sectors the effects from the reduction in labour costs more than offset the effects from the increase in energy costs. A very similar result emerged from the study of Germany by the German Institute for Economic Research (DIW, 1994).

Barker (1998) develops the approach further in a more ambitious study of the effects on competitiveness of carbon taxes for the EU Member States. Using the E3ME model, the effects on trade volumes and prices for 11 Member States of a coordinated carbon tax were compared with those for an uncoordinated tax achieving the same 10% reductions in CO_2 emissions below the baseline by 2010. The main conclusions from the study of the effects of carbon taxes imposed unilaterally, with revenues recycled via reductions in employers' social security payments, was that 'the effects on industrial price competitiveness ... are small and mixed ... Nearly all manufacturing sectors have an increase in output ... Any carbon leakage ... is negligible' (p. 1097).

Nevertheless it remains the case that fear of the competitiveness effects of environmental taxes has resulted in most countries that have introduced carbon and energy taxes for environmental reasons giving vulnerable firms or sectors tax exemptions or concessions. Theory suggests that these reduce the economic efficiency of the environmental tax and reduce the economic advantage to be gained from clean production systems. They also slow down the process of structural change in the economy, which would lead to energy- and environment-intensive economic sectors becoming both less intensive, and less important economically relative to less environment-intensive sectors.

The question arises as to how economically costly these exemptions might be. A study by Oliveira-Martins, Burniaux and Martin (1992) showed that, for a given emission-reduction target, the tax exemption of energy-intensive industries in the EU fails to increase the output level of these industries. This outcome arises because the exemptions result in higher tax rates for the rest of the economy, so that the costs of the other sectors are higher and total output falls. A similar result has been reported by Böhringer and Rutherford (1997) in their analysis of the consequences of exempting energy-intensive sectors from a carbon tax. They find that wage subsidies to export- and energy intensive sectors, rather than tax exemptions, retain more jobs and are less costly. The study's general conclusions are: 'Welfare losses associated with exemptions can be substantial even when the share of exempted sectors in overall economic activity and carbon emissions is small. Holding emissions constant, exemptions for some sectors imply increased tax rates for others and higher costs for the economy as a whole' (Böhringer and Rutherford, 1997, p. 201). Rather than exempting energy-intensive sectors from a carbon tax, it would seem preferable either to return the revenues from the tax to the sectors, on some other basis than carbon, or to allow the tax payments to be set against investments in energy efficiency. Both of these measures would cushion the tax's effects while maintaining its incentive for carbon-reduction.

Goulder (2000), based on more detailed work by Bovenberg and Goulder (2001), finds that the potential costs of compensating energy sectors for losses of profits due to an upstream carbon tax or permit system need not be high. Specifically, equity values in these industries can be maintained by grandfathering 10% of the emission permits (auctioning the rest) in the primary energy sectors, and cutting corporate taxes in the downstream energy sectors. These results derive from the fact that these sectors are able to pass on a large part of the costs of the carbon taxes or emission permits to energy consumers. The corporate tax cuts actually improve the efficiency of the economy overall (because corporate taxes are more distorting than the carbon tax), while the grandfathering of the permits only increases the cost of carbon reduction by 7%. Goulder considers that such measures should increase the political feasibility of introducing carbon-control measures of this sort.

Barker and Rosendahl (2000) look at the same issue of maintaining the profits of the energy industries that might otherwise lose out under a carbon tax. They compare 3 scenarios to achieve the Kyoto target of an 8% cut in GHG emissions below 1990/95 levels by 2008–12 for 17 west European countries. The scenarios are: (1) a carbon tax (2) a grandfathered CO_2 emission permit scheme and (3) a mixed multilateral scheme with a permit scheme for the energy sector (energy-intensive industries and electricity generation) combined with a carbon tax for the rest of the EU economy. Permit prices are endogenously determined year by year in the model by market demand and supply, and are the same across the regions.

The mixed scheme has an allocation of permits (between grandfathering and auctioning) designed to maintain the profits of the energy industries at levels close to the baseline. In the scheme, 70% of permits are allocated on a grandfathered basis on 2000 emissions in 2001, 60% in 2002, 2003 and 2004, 55% in 2005 and 50% for all later years. Reductions for CO_2 emissions in terms of permits issued to the year 2010 are calculated to be 25% below those of 1990 levels for the scenario to achieve the Kyoto target. All implied values of grandfathered permits are allowed to increase profits. A carbon tax at the rates in scenario 1 above is introduced for all fuel users not covered by the permit scheme, including transportation and households. All revenues from taxes and auctions are used to reduce regional employers' contributions to social security. The study shows that it may be possible for Europe to achieve Kyoto targets using market-based policies, with negligible effects on GDP and inflation, and without damaging the profitability of energy-producing and using industries (Barker and Rosendahl, 2000, p. 433).

However, other modelling studies have produced a wide range of macro-economic impacts of carbon taxes, analysis of which is the subject of the next section.

5.3. Macroeconomic assessments of carbon taxes and auctioned permits

The objectives of the carbon tax studies

There is an extensive literature on assessing the macroeconomic effects of carbon taxes. The studies are of particular tax proposals, such as the European Commission's carbon/energy tax proposed in 1993, or they are designed for the tax to achieve target reductions in CO_2 or CO_2-equivalent emissions for particular countries or groups of countries. The targets in these studies have changed as the international community has moved towards more detailed and binding agreements:

- Studies of the early 1990s aimed for a 20% reduction in CO_2 emissions below 1988 levels by 2005 (the Toronto target);
- Studies in the mid 1990s aimed at the Rio non-binding target of a return to 1990 levels of CO_2 emissions by 2000;
- Studies in the late 1990s aimed at the Kyoto target for a basket of six GHGs, with a range of targets, intended to become legally enforceable, for Annex B (industrial) countries (US 7%, EU 8%, Japan 6% and all Annex B countries about 5%) for average emissions 2008–12 below 1990 and/or 1995 levels.

The macroeconomic modelling of carbon tax effects

The macroeconomic modelling of the carbon tax has adopted 3 main approaches to the problem (see Barker, 1998 and Zhang and Folmer, 1998).

- *Dynamic optimisation.* Optimising models (e.g. GLOBAL2100 (Manne and Richels, 1992), POLES (Criqui *et al.*, 2000)) show how energy demand can be met at least cost, then impose an additional constraint of a restriction on the CO_2 emissions to yield a shadow cost, which can be interpreted as the implied carbon tax to achieve the reduction. The main problem with such models is common to bottom-up engineering approaches to mitigation, viz. how to deal with new technologies, not already in the process of development and diffusion. This limits them to time horizons in which new, unknown technologies will not substantially affect the outcome. There are other limitations: e.g. there is often a very aggregate treatment of the effects on energy demand of factors other than technology, namely the effects of relative price changes of energy carriers or the effects of real income changes. The models show what the optimised energy structure will be, given a set of technological options and their costs, but have difficulty modelling the institutional introduction of the new technologies and their diffusion over sectors and countries.
- *Computable General Equilibrium (CGE).* CGE models are organised around the assumption that the economy is in a state of equilibrium in all markets, with prices and wages adjusting to match supply and demand. The carbon tax is introduced as an increase in costs and therefore prices, with revenues available for distribution by the government sector (if it is included in the model). The models may be solved with some markets out of equilibrium e.g. the labour market, as in the GEM-E3 application (Conrad and Schmidt, 1998), or to give time paths and adjustment to a series of equilibria, but these aspects of the solution must be imposed by assumption. CGE models are usually calibrated on consensus parameters, rather than estimated on relevant data.
- *Macroeconometric simulation.* Models following this approach are estimated on time-series data, sometimes incorporating a fully specified long-run solution as part of the model structure (Hargreaves, 1992). The carbon tax is modelled alongside other indirect taxes as an increase in the price of energy use according to carbon content. Since the models give short-term solutions out of equilibrium, the economic responses tend to be smaller than those of the CGE models, at least in the first few years following the introduction of a carbon tax.

The effects of a carbon tax on GDP using the CGE and macroeconomic models depends on their treatment of production. Usually an explicit production function is included in the model with energy as a factor of production. In this case, the functional form and the estimated or imposed parameters will determine how output will change when energy prices rise as a result of a carbon tax or the cost of buying carbon permits. The way this is done almost always implies that a carbon tax will have the effect of reducing output and GDP. If the parameters are imposed, as they are with nearly all the models, then the extent of the GDP cost will be a direct result of the size and sign of these parameters. Since there is a wide range of plausible values for the parameters (see Burniaux *et al.*, 1992 for the ranges and a discussion) there is also a wide range of computed effects of the carbon tax on output. In other words, the GDP costs given in the literature are likely to be the direct result of assumptions rather than the outcome of empirical research. The costs are significantly affected by the researchers' judgements of what values to adopt for parameters in the wide range available.

These types of models are often combined together in an integrated assessment framework and Weyant and Hill (1999) provide a helpful way of categorising the models actually used for carbon tax studies. Table 5.1 adapts and extends this categorisation. The models are grouped on 2 dimensions according to their treatment of their energy and economy components. In both dimensions, the more aggregate approaches are given first, so the models further across and down the table are more detailed in their treatment of the energy system and the economy.

The role of assumptions in the modelling

In a comparative study of the results from US models, Repetto and Austin (1997) from the World Resources Institute (WRI) used econometric regression techniques to assess the role of assumptions in determining the projected GDP costs of CO_2 mitigation. Most of the studies used a carbon tax explicitly or as an implicit addition to the price of carbon needed to restrict its use. The WRI study

Table 5.1 Types of model used in the GHG mitigation studies.

		Energy/carbon model		
		Carbon Coefficients	Fuel Supplies & Demands by Sector	Energy Technology Detail
Economy model	Aggregate Production/cost Function	FUND* RICE*		CETA* MERGE3* GRAPE*
	Aggregate Macroeconometric		Oxford*	
	Multisectoral General Equilibrium		MIT-EPPA* WorldScan G-Cubed* GEM-E3 (EU)	ABARE-GTEM* AIM* MS-MRT* SGM*
	Multisectoral Macroeconometric		MDM-E3 (UK) E3ME (EU)	

Note: Most of the models (marked *) are global models described in the EMF-16 study (see Weyant and Hill, 1999). (CPB, 1999) describes WorldScan; (Conrad and Schmidt, 1998) describes GEM-E3; and (Barker, 1995 and 1998) describes MDM-E3 and E3ME.ENDSource: adapted from Weyant and Hill (1999)

covered 162 different predictions from 16 models. The study explains the % change in US GDP in terms of the CO_2 reduction target, the number of years to meet the target, the assumed use of carbon tax revenues (how the revenues are 'recycled' through the economy) and 7 model attributes. It estimates that in the worst case combining these assumptions and attributes, a 30% reduction in US baseline emissions by 2020 would cost about 3% of GDP. The corresponding best case implies an increase of about 2.5% in GDP above the baseline. The total difference of 5.5 percentage points (pp) of GDP in lower costs can be allocated to the recycling assumption (1.2pp) and across the attributes:

- CGE models gave lower costs than macroeconometric models (1.7pp)
- the inclusion of averted non-climate change damages, e.g. air pollution effects (1.1pp)
- whether Joint Implementation and/or international emission permit trading is included (0.7pp)
- the availability of a constant cost backstop technology (0.5pp)
- the inclusion of averted climate change damages in the model (0.2pp)
- whether the model allows for product substitution (0.1pp)
- and how many primary fuel types are included, so as to allow for interfuel substitution (0.0pp).

80% of the variation in GDP is explained by these factors, plus the extent of the CO_2 target reductions. In summary, worst case results come from using a macroeconometric model with lump-sum recycling of revenues, no emission permit trading, no environmental benefits in the model and no backstop technology.

The WRI study is convincing in showing how model approaches and assumptions can and do influence the results. It reveals the influence of the model methodology adopted and the importance of the assumption concerning the recycling of tax revenues. If the published estimates of the macroeconomic effects of carbon taxes are interpreted in the light of these findings, the results of carbon taxes for the US and indeed for the implementation of the Kyoto Protocol may not be as costly as at first sight.

Lump-sum recycling

In the context of CGE modelling, this is the most neutral means of recycling tax revenues because in theory and by assumption it has no behavioural implications in the model, although it can have substantial effects on the distribution of income. The assumption, combined with the usual CGE treatment of the production structure, has the inevitable outcome that any carbon tax will entail GDP costs, and these are therefore to be expected in the empirical studies. The interest is in the magnitude and distribution of these costs. The lump-sum recycling of carbon tax receipts is not very likely and is certainly sub-optimal. Jorgenson and Wilcoxen argue: '(Lump-sum recycling) is probably not the most likely use of the revenue. ... Using the revenue to reduce a distortionary tax would lower the net cost of a carbon tax by removing inefficiency elsewhere in the economy.' (Jorgenson and Wilcoxen, 1993b, p. 20). This is precisely the effect that Jorgenson and Wilcoxen (1993b, Table 5 p. 22) obtain in their model when they do in fact reduce distortionary taxes to offset a carbon tax, finding that a 1.7% GDP loss under lump-sum redistribution is converted to a 0.69% loss and a 1.1% gain by reducing labour and capital taxes respectively. However, the assumption does provide a benchmark to compare effects for different countries and other forms of recycling.

The effects of carbon taxes on GDP: the EMF-16 studies

A series of studies undertaken in a consistent framework of assumptions is reported in an Energy Modeling Forum (EMF) exercise assessing the costs of adopting elements of the Kyoto Protocol. Weyant and Hill (1999) summarise the studies and the results. All the studies use carbon emission permits as the instrument for mitigation and therefore yield implicit carbon tax rates to achieve the targets; all assume lump-sum recycling of revenues; and all set aside the environmental benefits. A consistent range of scenarios is considered by 13 modelling teams, with the emphasis given to how emission permit trading may reduce costs.

Table 5.2 gives the range of results for the carbon tax rates and GDP changes from the EMF-16 studies.

The most striking feature of the extremes presented in Table 5.2 is the wide range of the carbon taxes estimated as needed to reach the Kyoto targets by domestic policies using an efficient economic instrument. Although several of the assumptions are consistent across the studies, there is an extra feature (excluded from the WRI study) that gives rise to differences. The Kyoto target is an absolute one in relation to a 1990 or 1995 base, whereas the WRI study considers CO_2

Table 5.2 Energy Modeling Forum results for the carbon tax and GDP effects in 2010

	Top of range for tax rate in 2010			Bottom of range for tax rate in 2010		
	Carbon tax US$_{90}$ per tC	GDP change %	Model	Carbon tax US$_{90}$ per tC	GDP change %	Model
USA	410	−1.78	Oxford	76	−0.42	G-Cubed
OECD-Europe	966	−2.08	Oxford	159	−0.55	RICE
Japan	1074	−1.88	Oxford	97	−0.57	G-Cubed
Canada, Australia, New Zealand	425	−1.96	ABARE -GTEM	145	−0.96	RICE

Source: Weyant and Hill (1999, pp. xxxi–xxxiv)

emissions relative to a base line over the projection period. This means that the range in the results is partly due to the different regional targets and different rates of growth of CO_2 emissions in the base projection.

The effectiveness of the carbon tax in achieving a given target in different countries depends on the tax and energy systems in place. If energy is already taxed, then a carbon tax will have to be that much higher in order to push up prices by a given proportion. If the existing energy system is such that there are substantial opportunities to switch from carbon-based energy, e.g. substitution possibilities for a switch from relatively high to relatively low carbon fuels, such as from coal to gas, then the tax will be lower. Carbon taxes tend to be estimated at higher levels for Japan and Europe than for the USA, because of the latter's relatively low energy tax rates.

The range of GDP costs is much narrower than that of the carbon tax rates, but a high carbon tax does not necessarily imply high GDP costs. The costs in Japan tend to be lower than in the other regions but there is no strong pattern. However all the GDP effects are negative. It is very likely that this result comes from the assumption in these studies that all the revenues from the carbon tax are returned to the economy by means of lump-sum payments to consumers. This form of recycling implies that the average consumer has a loss in real income from the carbon tax compensated by a gain in wealth from the lump-sum repayment. In most models the loss and the gain, even if they are the same monetary values, have a net effect of reducing expenditure because spending is modelled as being more responsive to a fall in income than to an equivalent rise in wealth.

The results from the Oxford model (Cooper et al., 1999) stand out from the rest in showing very high costs of mitigation. The Oxford study considers the costs of the US reaching its Kyoto target with a carbon tax (whose revenues are recycled lump-sum) but without international permit trading, and holding emissions at their 1990 levels after 2010. It estimates that US GDP is reduced by 4% below the baseline by 2020, e.g. costs rising to 4% of GDP for the US by 2020. This is a striking result especially since the Oxford model deals 'with very important issues not addressed elsewhere in the [Energy Journal] volume', e.g. 'macroeconomic adjustment costs' (Weyant and Hill, 1999, p. xlii). Indeed the study itself asserts that 'unlike CGE models, *the Oxford model has been subject to statistical verification and so is capable of explaining accurately the historical data.*' (Cooper at al. 2000, p. 338, italics in original).

The high costs in the Oxford results appear to be due to three features in the analysis:

- *the choice of assumptions.* The assumptions used in the Oxford study appear to correspond exactly with those identified by Repetto and Austin (1997) as leading to the most pessimistic outcome for GDP costs for the US (see above).
- *the equation used to explain total factor productivity growth.* This appears to be derived from one given by Marion and Svensson (1986, p. 109, footnote 12). It appears to impose high costs of carbon taxation on potential output growth simply by assuming a value for a substitution elasticity picked from

the literature. The equation itself is suspect in terms of its derivation and theoretical validity in this context (see Barker and Ekins, 2001).

● *lump-sum recycling in a macroeconometric model.* If a carbon tax is introduced in such a model, then what happens to the revenues becomes critical to the short-term outcome. This is not so important in CGE models because the solution is one of long-run equilibrium. The huge revenues from the carbon tax in the Oxford model are recycled lump-sum to consumers. If these additions to consumers' income and wealth are largely saved, then the economy will become progressively depressed as the carbon tax rises in order to curb the growth in CO_2 emissions.

The effects of carbon taxes on GDP: other studies with lump-sum recycling

Individual studies for a number of countries considering carbon taxes with lump-sum recycling support the EMF findings. The general results are that reductions in CO_2 emissions of 15% to 25% by 2010 incur GDP or welfare costs of 0.1% to 1.2%.

The problem is that the frame of reference adopted in many of the studies is inappropriate. They start from the position that the economy is in equilibrium at maximum welfare and then measure the loss in welfare from introducing a carbon tax. From this standpoint, a carbon tax is treated as a distortionary tax and is being compared to an ideal instrument, lump-sum payments, which (in theory) are non-distortionary, and is then inevitably judged as being costly. However, as noted earlier, the carbon tax is in essence a means of correcting a distortion arising out of an externality, i.e. the use of the atmosphere to dispose of waste emissions. If the standpoint is changed to one in which a political process has determined a GHG reduction target, as in the draft Kyoto Protocol, then other questions become relevant. What are the least-cost means of achieving the target? If a carbon tax is to be introduced, how should its revenues be recycled to improve economic performance? How does use of economic instruments, such as a carbon tax, compare with regulation to achieve the GHG reduction target?

The effects of carbon taxes on GDP: revenues recycled via reductions in other taxes

Many of the European studies of the effects of carbon taxes have adopted the assumption that the revenues are used to reduce employment taxes. This follows suggestions made by the European Commission for use of revenues in its proposed carbon/energy tax. Many of the studies confirm the WRI study in finding that under this assumption GDP rises above the baseline with a carbon tax (Barker and Kohler, 1998; Capros *et al.*, 1999; Barker, 1999; Bernard and Vielle, 1999; Hourcade *et al.*, 1999). Several studies for Germany adopted the government's 25% reduction target for 2010 and found that an environmental tax reform with a carbon tax replacing some employment taxes led to increases in GDP (Welsch and Hoster, 1995; Schmidt and Conrad, 1996; Boehringer, 1997).

A study for Australia, (McDougall and Dixon, 1996) confirms the magnitude and direction of these results. Studies on mitigation costs for China also suggest that if the tax revenues are recycled, GDP may rise above base. Zhang (1998), with a CGE model, suggests that if carbon taxes are used to reduce some indirect taxes, welfare may improve. Garbaccio et al. (1999, 2000) with another dynamic CGE model for China, but using carbon tax revenues to reduce all other taxes, find that after the first year GDP is always above base.

One study (Håkonsen and Mathiesen, 1997) directly compares lump-sum and employment-tax-reduction as methods of recycling revenues. For a 20% cut in Norwegian CO_2 emissions, an index of welfare is reduced by 1% under lump-sum recycling and 0.3% when social security contributions are used.

The European results differ from most US results when employment taxes are reduced. In the US, this use of revenues does not generally appear to lead to increases in GDP above base (Goulder, 1995b; Jorgenson et al., 1995; Shackleton et al., 1996). An exception is Jorgenson et al. (1999), which finds that if revenues from auctioned permits are recycled via reductions in personal income tax, using a detailed, dynamic, general equilibrium model, then GDP is 0.6% above the baseline by 2020. The general result appears to be partly because the US economy is closer to full employment in the base line and partly because US employment taxes are lower than those in Europe (OECD Jobs Study, 1994).

Another result from the Jorgenson model was that, if the revenues are used to reduce corporate taxes on capital, US GDP is below base by 0.5%. Corporation tax reductions therefore appear to be less beneficial for the US economy than reductions in taxes or capital, which (as noted above, Jorgenson and Wilcoxen, 1993b) lend to increases in GDP.

Outside Europe and the US, Garbaccio et al. (1999, 2000), using a dynamic CGE model for China, consider reductions in CO_2 emissions of 5%, 10%, and 15% below baseline with carbon tax revenues recycled by reducing all other taxes proportionally. In all the scenarios, a very small decline in GDP occurs in the first year of the simulation, but GDP is above base in every year thereafter.

The magnitude of the double dividend for the European countries is lower in studies that use CGEs compared with the results from studies that use macroeconometric models. Barker (1999) directly compares sets of results from GEM-E3 (a CGE model) and E3ME (an econometric model) and concludes that the econometric model tends to have stronger effects for a very similar set of assumptions. Linking this finding with the Repetto and Austin (1997) result suggests that the key difference between the two modelling approaches in the carbon tax literature is that the CGE models, without adjustment for short-term interactions, tend to have smaller feedbacks affecting GDP when the tax is introduced. Therefore the CGE responses are smaller both if GDP is projected to fall and if it is projected to rise.

A recent comprehensive study of the effects of achieving the Kyoto targets for the EU is that by Barker and Rosendahl (2000). The macroeconomic results of 3 scenarios are shown in Table 5.3.

Table 5.3 Macrovariables in EURO-19 for 2010 in the three mitigation scenarios.

	Base	Carbon Tax	Permits + profits	Mixed policies
Tax rate euro(2000) per tonne carbon	0	153.1	0	153.1
Tax revenue (billion euro)	0	170.1	0	108.4
Permit price euro(2000) per tonne carbon	0	0	135.2	147.8
Permit revenue billion euro	0	0	0	30.7
GDP %pa 2000–10	2.6	2.7	2.6	2.6
GDP% difference from 2010 base	0	0.8	−0.3	0.5
GDP cost euro(2000) per tonne carbon equivalent	0	−1008.5	355.7	−698.6
Ancillary benefits difference as % of GDP	0	0.11	0.10	0.10
Ancillary benefits euro(2000) per tonne carbon equivalent	0	137.5	126.3	133.0
Employment 2010 million	162.2	163.9	162.1	163.5
Employment % difference from 2010 base	0	1.1	−0.1	0.8
Consumer prices %pa 2000–10	2.4	2.4	2.5	2.4
Consumer prices % difference from 2010 base	0	0.2	1.4	0.4
Trade balance Percentage point difference from base	0	0.2	0	−0.1
Government financial balance percentage point difference from base	0	−1.2	0.2	−0.7
Energy profits billion (1990)euros difference from base	0	−19.2	20.1	0.8

Source: (Barker and Rosendahl, 2000)

According to the E3ME model, the tax rates or permit prices in 2010 lie between 135 and 154 euro (2000) per tonne carbon. Moreover, consistent with other simulations of the Energy Modelling Forum (see e.g. Weyant, 1999), the net impact on GDP is quite small, less than 1% from base in all scenarios. Indeed, in two of the three scenarios the GDP effect is positive. The effects are very small with inflation higher in all the scenarios, with the fully grandfathered permit scheme implying the highest price rises. Two scenarios increase employment by about 1% above base, whereas the second scenario, that is grandfathered permits with higher profits, shows more or less no change in employment. Introducing carbon taxes with revenue recycling seems to be the best policy choice measured in GDP and employment effects. In contrast, the permit scheme scenario with higher profits seems to be the least advantageous.

The European studies also give examples of reductions projected in GDP for small economies taking unilateral action (Proost and van Regemorter, 1995 (Belgium); Andersen et al., 1998 (Denmark); Barker, 1999 (the Netherlands)).

In summary, the literature points to the following factors giving rise to differences in estimated GDP costs:

- the extent of the required reduction in GHG emissions
- the cost and availability of less carbon-intensive technologies and products compared to the reference case
- the responsiveness of the production structure and final demand to increases in real energy prices
- the time period available for adjustment to higher real prices
- the use of revenues from carbon taxes, with the opportunities for negative costs, i.e. increases in GDP, depending on the existing tax structure
- the coverage of the emission permit trading scheme, with a wider scheme covering more countries, leading to lower costs.

In addition, there are environmental benefits from reductions in emissions associated with CO_2 emissions.

5.4. *Distributional implications of carbon taxes*

The different impact of carbon taxes, and environmental taxes in general, on the competitiveness of different sectors is an example of the distributional effects of the policy instruments. In this case, the differential impact is in accordance with the polluter pays principle, such that relatively carbon-intensive sectors experience a higher burden from the tax than sectors using relatively less carbon. However, a carbon tax may have other distributional effects which are unintended, and may be undesirable. The effects may be on different regions or income groups within a country, or, in the case of a global tax regime, between different countries. These effects are the focus of this section.

In principle it would be desirable to analyse the net distributional effects of the full range of costs and benefits deriving from the carbon tax. Relevant considerations include:

1. The increased costs to consumers of purchasing those goods to which the carbon tax has been directly applied.
2. The increased costs to consumers of purchasing those goods and services which were produced using a taxed input (both these costs being computed after taking into account the responses of producers and consumers to the incentive effects of the tax).
3. The benefits deriving from reduced carbon emissions, and from reductions in other polluting emissions, as a result of the carbon tax.
4. The distributional situation following the allocation of the revenues from the carbon tax (which may, of course, be made specifically to counteract the distributional effects, as was the case in the preceding discussion on competitiveness).

There is also the issue of the baseline against which the costs and benefits should be evaluated. In particular, should it be the status quo of no action on carbon emissions, or should it be relative to other actions on carbon emissions that yield the same reduction? This point is particularly important because of carbon taxes' efficiency property of being able to achieve a given carbon reduction at least overall social cost.

In practice, this full distributional analysis has proved too complex, and the majority of the studies do not address all these elements, as will be seen, and take the 'no action' situation as their baseline. The third point is largely outside the scope of this paper altogether. However, it is important to bear all these points in mind when overall conclusions about a carbon tax's distributional impacts are being drawn.

The is little doubt with regard to the first of the cost categories above that carbon taxes levied on domestic fuel tend to be regressive. In Poterba (1991, Table 3.5, p. 79), household fuel accounted for 7.6% of total expenditure for the lowest expenditure decile, but only 4.0% for the highest expenditure decile. For Europe, in Smith (1992, p. 253), fuel expenditures relative to total expenditures for the lowest expenditure quartile were 1.2% higher than for the highest quartile in Italy, 1.9% in Spain, 2.7% in Netherlands, 3.4% in France, 3.5% in Germany, and 5.8% in Ireland. In the UK the difference in expenditure share between the highest and lowest decile was more than 10% (Smith, 1992, p. 252). In addition, Johnstone and Alavalapati (1998, p. 9) calculated that in the UK the poorest income quartile uses relatively more carbon-intensive coal, and less low-carbon gas, than the richest quartile, so that they would be relatively hard hit by a carbon tax for this reason as well.

The expenditure distribution of transport fuel is very different, accounting for the lowest share of total expenditures in the lowest-expenditure quartile in the six European countries in Smith (1992). In terms of the direct effects on households, therefore, a carbon tax might be expected to be regressive in respect of domestic fuel and progressive in respect of transport fuel.

In modelling studies where these effects of the tax on household and transport fuels are combined with consideration of the second of the four considerations listed above (the effects of the tax on the prices of other goods and services), the review in Bruce et al. (1996, p. 420) shows the overall effect to be generally mildly regressive for OECD countries, a finding also in line with that of Barker and Köhler (1998) for the Member States of the EU. The regressivity is significantly less if expenditure rather than income shares are used in the analysis (Poterba, 1991). Poterba (1991, p. 82) also notes that the effects of a carbon tax on asset markets (especially the stocks of energy-intensive and fossil fuel industries) would be likely to reduce the tax's regressivity. For developing countries, OECD 1995 (p. 25) reports a single study for Pakistan (Shah and Larsen, 1992), which suggests that regressivity may be less important in such countries than in the OECD.

With regard to the inter-country distribution of costs from a global system of carbon taxes, Whalley and Wigle (1991) show this, not surprisingly, to be very dependent on the nature of the tax. A system of national production taxes would cause revenues to flow from oil consumers to oil producers, benefiting oil exporters. A system of national consumption taxes would relatively benefit oil-consuming countries at the expense of producers. A comparison of models reported in Dean (1994), in which the same percentage emission reduction was imposed in five world regions (US, Other OECD, China, ex-USSR, Rest of World) found no clear pattern except that the Rest of World region generally experiences the highest relative costs. This outcome should be considered in conjunction with evidence (for example, Fankhauser, 1995, Table 3.16, p. 55), that developing countries are expected to bear the highest relative costs from climate change, and therefore have the most relatively to gain from carbon abatement.

The fourth important consideration in respect of the distributional impact of a carbon tax is what is done with the revenues. The basic position may be simply expressed. High-income groups or countries use more energy than low-income groups or countries, and will therefore contribute more in absolute terms to carbon tax revenues. It is therefore always possible in theory to remove any regressive effects, if desired, by distributing the revenues such as to benefit adversely affected groups.

Between countries this is clearly shown in Whalley and Wigle (1991, Table 7.6, p. 250). Under a system of national production taxes, developing countries have the highest relative cost, at 7.1% of GDP. With the redistribution of the revenues from a global production tax on the basis of regional population, developing countries receive a benefit of 1.8% of GDP, with all other regions experiencing a net cost.

For households, one way of effecting such a redistribution is through the so-called 'eco-bonus', whereby tax revenues are distributed to households on an equal per household basis. This would clearly make low-income households better off than they were before, more than compensating them for any regressive effects experienced from the tax itself. Such a redistribution is carried out in Switzerland with the revenues from the taxes on light fuel oil, sulphur and volatile organic compounds (VOCs), through a per capita reduction in medical insurance (EC, 1999). Equivalent in its distributional effect to an eco-bonus is the granting of a tax-free allowance of energy use to all households, as practised by the Netherlands (see below).

Alternatively governments may wish to target the redistribution of tax revenues on adversely affected groups, through the welfare or benefit system or in some other way (although it should be noted that it may be administratively difficult to reach all those in these groups). For the UK Symons et al. (1994) show that, for the two lowest decile expenditure groups, benefits reform can change an 18% and 15% reduction in disposable expenditure from a carbon tax (with no revenue recycling) into a 54% and 25% increase for the same groups. In practice governments are likely to seek to distribute only part of the tax revenues in this way.

The most sophisticated rebate system aimed at avoiding regressive effects from energy taxation is that associated with the small energy users' tax in the Netherlands. This combines a tax-free allowance for electricity and natural gas with personal income tax reductions for individuals, and reductions in social security contributions and other tax reductions for businesses (EC, 1999). Calculations prior to the introduction of the tax showed that such measures were able to offset potentially regressive effects completely and also to prevent large transfers between tax-paying groups.

It is therefore clear that, while a carbon tax could have a regressive effect on low-income households (or countries), it does not need to do so. The overall desirability of a carbon tax, as well as its likely political and ethical acceptability, depend on regressive effects being avoided.

5.5. *The costs of climate stability*

The objective of the UN Framework Convention on Climate Change is to prevent dangerous anthropogenic interference with the global climate. Climate scientists have not yet converted this objective into a maximum atmospheric concentration of CO_2 (and other greenhouse gases), but have projected a number of different carbon emissions scenarios which result in different atmospheric concentrations. The pre-industrial concentration was about 280ppmv (parts per million by volume), and in 1994 was 358ppmv. The lowest of the IPCC's projections involved stabilisation of the carbon concentration at 450ppmv, concerning which the IPCC estimated: 'For stabilisation at 450ppmv (parts per million by volume) in the 1994 calculations fossil emissions had to be returned to about a third of today's levels (i.e. to about 2GtC/year) by the year 2200.' (Houghton *et al.*, 1996, p. 80) It is therefore worth enquiring what the costs of such carbon reduction might be.

In the study cited above, Repetto and Austin (1997) find that, with their most unfavourable assumptions, a 50% reduction in US baseline emissions by 2020 (the kind of cut that would be necessary to get on the IPCC 450ppmv trajectory) was projected to cost about 6% of GDP. With favourable assumptions there would be a modest increase in GDP relative to the baseline.

For another estimate, the EMF modelling exercise discussed earlier (Gaskins and Weyant, 1993) found that the average GDP loss from a 50% emissions cut by 2050 was about 3% of GDP. However, this does not take account of the factors reviewed above which could substantially reduce this cost:

- the 35% to over 100% that can be offset by recycling the revenues in such a way that distorting taxes are reduced;
- the > 45% (minimum) reduction in emissions (by 2025/2030) by implementing energy efficiency technologies.:
- in addition, 4–18% of global CO_2 emissions could be cut with increases in output by phasing out fossil fuel subsidies (Bruce *et al.*, 1996, p. 73);
- and it is now well established that the ancillary benefits of CO_2 abatement (the reduction in air pollutants apart from CO_2) substantially reduce the gross costs of such abatement; Ekins (1996) has calculated that, even if only the ancillary benefits from SO_2-reduction are considered, 25–50% of the CO_2 abatement brought about by a $100/tC carbon tax would be achieved at negative net cost.

Combining these offsets and no-regrets options makes it seem unlikely that the EMF 50% reduction would cost anything at all.

Looking beyond 2050, whether further reductions in emissions will incur more costs depends most importantly on whether backstop energy technologies will have been developed which are competitive with the by-then substantially depleted fossil fuels. Nordhaus, in his DICE model, rather pessimistically assumes that they will not, and projects several scenarios with rising costs of abatement through to the next century. These suggest that, by 2100, the climate stabilisation scenario (which restricts the global average temperature rise to 1.5 °C above the level in 1900) would cost about 8% of per capita consumption, reducing it from about $9,500 in the no-controls case to $8,750. This scenario involves substantially earlier stabilisation than the IPCC 450ppmv case (which was by 2200), and therefore much more ambitious emission reduction up to 2100. Nordhaus (1994, Figure 5.2, p. 87) has CO_2-equivalent emissions falling practically to zero by 2035 and staying below about 1.5GtC (compared to current levels of about 7GtC) per annum thereafter.

The cost estimate of 8% of global consumption by 2100, as with the EMF estimates, does not contain the offsets from revenue-recycling, energy efficiency or removing subsidies, nor any considerations of risk aversion or secondary benefits. It is also pessimistic about the possibility of stimulating the development of a backstop technology, such as solar power. Taking such considerations into account would reduce the cost of climate stabilisation very substantially.

6. Conclusions

This paper has shown that there is now a very large literature on carbon taxes and carbon emission permits, which this paper has, despite its length, only been able to survey in general terms. Nevertheless a number of conclusions about these instruments have now clearly emerged from the literature. These may be summarised as follows.

First there is general agreement that market-based instruments of carbon control will achieve a given level of emissions reduction at lower cost than regulations. Among market-based instruments, those that raise revenue, and recycle it through the economy by reducing pre-existing distortionary taxes, will have lower costs than those that do not raise revenue. This conclusion clearly favours carbon taxes and auctioned emission permits (with revenue recycling as described) over grandfathered emission permits.

Notwithstanding the perceived advantages of carbon taxes and auctioned emission permits, they have to date only been introduced in relatively few countries, and then at relatively low levels. This is largely because the distributional effects of the instruments have made them politically problematic. These distributional effects have also received considerable attention in the literature.

The most important of the distributional effects is that on industrial competitiveness, such that energy-intensive sectors, which are often perceived as industrially important, emerge as significant losers. The result of this has been that carbon taxes have been introduced with substantial exemptions for these sectors, and grandfathered permits have been favoured over auctioned permits. While this may have allayed concerns over the competitiveness of the relevant sectors, the literature clearly shows that these choices have significant economic costs for society as a whole.

Other potential distributional effects of concern, especially from a carbon tax, are those on low-income groups. It is clear that revenues from the tax can be devoted to removing regressive effects, although this may be institutionally complex to achieve. It also means, of course, that revenues used for this purpose cannot be used to gain the benefits of the revenue-recycling effect by reducing the rates of distortionary taxes.

There is a very wide range of projections of the costs of imposing a carbon tax. The paper has showed how these projections depend on a number of crucial assumptions about the rate of development of non-carbon fuels, the flexibility of the economy, the way the revenues are used and other factors. It is this paper's conclusion that, with realistic assumptions on these matters, the costs of attaining the Kyoto targets, in particular, need not be high. However, this is still a matter of some controversy.

It is still early days to come to firm conclusions about the environmental effectiveness of carbon taxes, but studies of their effects where they have been introduced have broadly concluded that they have achieved the projected level of carbon reduction. Their effectiveness can be enhanced by dedicating some of the carbon tax revenues to stimulating further carbon control measures, though this means that fewer revenues are then available to reduce other tax rates or compensate for regressive distributional effects. Such trade offs are, of course, common in complex areas of policy.

The overall conclusion of this paper is that, assuming that concern over anthropogenic climate change continues to increase, the advantages of carbon taxes and auctioned permits over other means of carbon abatement will lead them to be progressively introduced for this purpose. However, the distributional concerns will mean that their introduction is slower, and departs further from the first-best means of their implementation, than would otherwise be the case.

Notes

1. There has been an extensive controversy on the nature and existence in theory and practice of the double dividend, since the concept was first clearly set out by Pearce (1991). Much of the theoretical literature is confusing and misleading in that it sets aside the essential character of the carbon tax as an environmental tax. In particular the distinction between the 'weak' and the 'strong' form of the double dividend brought about by spending revenues from a carbon tax, introduced by Goulder (1995a), is not helpful as explained by Bohm (1997, p. 114). More recently, Sanstad and Wolff (2000) have elucidated some of the more refined theoretical niceties in the debate and have

explored why one empirical model might yield a higher double dividend for the US than another.

References

Andersen, F. M., Jacobsen, H. K., Morthorst, P. E., Olsen, A., Rasmussen, M., Thomsen, T. and Trier, P. (1998) EMMA: En energi- og miljørelateret satellitmodel til ADAM (EMMA an energy an environmental related satellite model to ADAM). *Nationaløkonomisk Tidsskrift*, 136, 3, 333–349.

Ballard, C. L., Shoven, J-B. and Whalley, J. (1985) General equilibrium computations of the marginal welfare costs of taxes in the United States. *American Economic Review*, 75, 1, March, 128–138.

Baranzini, A., Goldemberg, J. and Speck, S. (2000) A future for carbon taxes. *Ecological Economics*, 32, 395–412.

Barker, T. (1995) Taxing pollution instead of employment: greenhouse gas abatement through fiscal policy in the UK. *Energy and Environment*, 6, 1, 1–28.

Barker, T. (1998) The effects on competitiveness of coordinated *versus* unilateral fiscal policies reducing GHG emissions in the EU: an assessment of a 10% reduction by 2010 using the E3ME model. *Energy Policy*, 26, 14, 1083–1098.

Barker, T. (1999) Achieving a 10% cut in Europe's CO_2 emissions using additional excise duties: coordinated, uncoordinated and unilateral action using the econometric model E3ME. *Economic Systems Research*, 11, 4, 401–421.

Barker, T. and Ekins, P. (2001) How high are the costs of Kyoto for the US Economy?, mimeo, Department of Applied Economics, University of Cambridge, Cambridge.

Barker, T. and Rosendahl, K. E. (2000) Ancillary benefits of GHG mitigation in Europe: SO_2, NOx and PM10 reductions from policies to meet Kyoto targets using the E3ME model and EXTERNE valuations, Ancillary Benefits and Costs of Greenhouse Gas Mitigation, Proceedings of an IPCC Co-Sponsored Workshop, March 2000, OECD, Paris.

Barker, T., Ekins, P. and Johnstone, N. (1995a) Introduction. In Barker, T., Ekins, P. and Johnstone, N. (eds), 1995b *Global Warming and Energy Demand* (pp. 1–16). Routledge, London/New York.

Barker, T., Ekins, P. and Johnstone, N. eds (1995b) *Global Warming and Energy Demand*. Routledge, London/New York.

Barker, T. and Köhler, J. (1998) *International Competitiveness and Environmental Policies*. Edward Elgar, Cheltenham.

Baumol, W. (1972) On taxation and the control of externalities. *American Economic Review*, 62, 3, 307–321.

Baumol, W. and Oates, W. (1971) The use of standards and prices for the protection of the environment. *Swedish Journal of Economics*, March, 73, 42–54.

Baumol, W. and Oates, W. (1988) (2nd edition) *The Theory of Environmental Policy*. Cambridge University Press, Cambridge.

Bernard, A. L. and Vielle, M. (1999) Rapport à la Mission Interministérielle sur l'Effet de Serre relatif aux évaluation du Protocole de Kyoto effectuées avec le modèle GEMINI-E3. Ministère de l'équipement des transports et du logement. Commissariat à l'énergie atomique.

Boehringer, C. (1997) NEWAGE — Modellinstrumentarium zur gesamtwirtschaftlichen Analyse von Energie- und Umweltpolitiken. In S. Molt and Fahl U. (eds), *Energiemodelle in der Bundesrepublik Deutschland — Stand der Entwicklung*. Juelich, p. 99–122.

Boero, G., Clarke, R. and Winters, L. (1991) *The Macroeconomic Consequences of Controlling Greenhouse Gases: a Survey*. Department of the Environment, HMSO, London.

Bohm, P. (1997) Environmental taxation and the double dividend: fact or fallacy? In Tim O'Riordan (ed.), *Ecotaxation* (pp. 106–124). Earthscan Publications, London.

Bohm, P. (1999) An emission quota trade experiment among four Nordic countries. In S. Sorrell and J. Skea (eds), *Pollution for Sale: Emissions Trading and Joint Implementation* (pp. 299–321). Edward Elgar, Cheltenham.

Böhringer, C. and Rutherford, T. F. (1997) Carbon taxes with exemptions in an open economy: a general equilibrium analysis of the German tax initiative. *Journal of Environmental Economics and Management*, 32, 189–203.

Bovenberg, A. L. and de Mooij, R. A. (1994) Environmental levies and distortionary taxation. *American Economic Review*, 94, 4, September, 1085–1089.

Bovenberg, L. and Goulder, L. (1996) Optimal environmental taxation in the presence of other taxes: general equilibrium analyses. *American Economic Review*, 86, 985–1000.

Bovenberg, L. and Goulder, L. (2000) Neutralizing the adverse industry impacts of CO_2 abatement policies: what does it cost? In C. Carraro and G. Metcalf (eds), *Behavioral and Distributional Impacts of Environmental Policies*. University of Chicago Press, Chicago.

Brendemoen, A. and Vennemo, H. (1994) A climate treaty and the norwegian economy: a CGE assessment. *The Energy Journal*, 15, 1, 77–93.

Bruce, J., Lee, H. and Haites, E. eds (1996) *Climate Change 1995: Economic and Social Dimensions of Climate Change*. Contribution of Working Group III to the Second Assessment Report of the Intergovernmental Panel on Climate Change (IPCC), Cambridge University Press, Cambridge.

Burniaux, J. M., Martin, J. P., Nicoletti, G. and Oliveira-Martins, J. (1992) *GREEN- A Multi-Region Dynamic General Equilibrium Model for Quantifying the Costs of Curbing CO_2 Emissions: A Technical Manual*. Working Paper 116. Economics and Statistics Department, OECD, Paris.

CPB Netherlands Bureau for Economic Policy Analysis (1999) *WorldScan: the Core version*. CPB, The Netherlands.

Cline, W. R. (1992) *The Economics of Global Warming*. Institute for International Economics, Washington DC.

Cooper, A., Livermore, S., Rossi, V., Walker, J. and Wilson A. (1999) Economic impacts of reducing carbon emissions: The Oxford model. *The Energy Journal*, Special Issue, 335–65.

Conrad, K. and Schmidt, F. N. (1998) Economic impacts of an uncoordinated versus a coordinated carbon dioxide policy in the European Union: An applied general equilibrium analysis. *Economic Systems Research*, 10, 2, 161–182.

Cramton, P. and Kerr, S. (1998) Tradable permit auctions: how and why to auction not grandfather. Discussion Paper 98–34, Resources for the Future, Washington DC, *http://www.rff.org/environment/climate.htm*.

Criqui, P., Kouvaritakis, N. and Schrattenholzer, L. (2000) The impacts of carbon constraints on power generation and renewable energy technologies. In L. Bernstein and J. Pan, *Sectoral Economic Costs and Benefits of GHG Mitigation: Proceedings of an IPCC Expert Meeting*, 14–15 February 2000, Technical Support Unit, IPCC Working Group III, RIVM, The Netherlands.

Dean, A. (1994) Costs of cutting CO_2 emissions: evidence from 'top-down' models. In OECD (Organisation for Economic Cooperation and Development) 1995 *The Economics of Climate Change: Proceedings of an OECD/IEA Conference*, OECD, Paris.

Dean, J. (1992) Trade and the environment: a survey of the literature. In P. Low (ed.) *International Trade and the Environment* (pp. 15–28). World Bank Discussion Paper 159, World Bank, Washington D.C.

DEPA (Danish Environmental Protection Agency) (1999) *Economic Instruments in Environmental Protection in Denmark*, DEPA/Ministry of Environment and Energy, Copenhagen.

Diamond, P. and Mirrlees, J. (1971) Optimal taxation and public production, I: production efficiency and II: tax rules. *American Economic Review*, 61, 8–27, 261–278.

DIW (1994) *Wirtschaftliche Auswirkungen einer ökologischen Steuerreform*, Berlin.

EC (European Commission) (1994) Taxation, employment and environment: fiscal reform for reducing unemployment. Study 3, *European Economy*, 56, 137–177, Directorate-General for Economic and Financial Affairs, European Commission, Brussels.

EC (European Commission) (1999) *Database on Environmental Taxes in the European Union Member States, plus Norway and Switzerland, Evaluation of Environmental Effects of Environmental Taxes*, European Communities, Office for Official Publications of the European Communities, Luxembourg.

EC (European Commission) (2000) Green Paper on greenhouse gas emissions trading within the European Union, EC, Brussels, http://europa.eu.int/comm/environment/docum/0087_en.htm.

Ekins, P. (1996) How large a carbon tax is justified by the secondary benefits of CO_2 abatement? *Resource and Energy Economics*, 18, 2, 161–187.

Ekins, P. (2000) *Economic Growth and Environmental Sustainability: the Prospects for Green Growth*. Routledge, London/New York.

Ekins, P. and Speck, S. (1998) The impacts of environmental policy on competitiveness: theory and evidence. In T. Barker and J. Köhler (1998) *International Competitiveness and Environmental Policies* (pp. 33–69). Edward Elgar, Cheltenham.

Ekins, P. and Speck, S. (1999a) Competitiveness and exemptions from environmental taxes in Europe. *Environmental and Resource Economics*, 13, 4, 369–395.

Ekins, P. and Speck, S. (1999b) Evaluation of environmental effects of environmental taxes. In EC 1999 *Database on Environmental Taxes in the European Union Member States, plus Norway and Switzerland, Evaluation of Environmental Effects of Environmental Taxes* (pp. 1–23). European Communities, Office for Official Publications of the European Communities, Luxembourg.

ENDS (1999a) Carbon tax boosts Italian fossil fuel prices. *ENDS Daily* email information service, January 19, ENDS, London.

ENDS (1999b) Go-ahead for Danish power sector CO_2 quotas. *ENDS Daily* email information service, May 28, ENDS, London.

ENDS (2000) EU backs first Kyoto trading scheme. *ENDS Daily* email information service, March 29, ENDS, London.

Fankhauser, S. (1995) *Valuing Climate Change: the Economics of the Greenhouse*. Earthscan, London.

Farrow, S. (1995) The dual political economy of taxes and tradable permits. *Economic Letters*, 49, 217–220.

Frandsen, S. E., Hansen, J. V. and Trier, P. (1995) *GESMEC — En generel ligevægtsmodel for Danmark. Dokumentation og anvendelser (GESMEC — An applied general equilibrium model for Denmark — Documentation and applications)*. The Secretariat of the Economic Council, Copenhagen.

Garbaccio, R. F., Ho, M. S. and Jorgenson, D. W. (1999) Controlling carbon emissions in China. *Environment and Development Economics*, 4, 4, 493–518.

Garbaccio, R. F., Ho, M. S. and Jorgenson, D. W. (2000) The health benefits of controlling carbon emissions in China. *Ancillary Benefits and Costs of Greenhouse Gas Mitigation*. OECD, Paris.

Gaskins, D. W. and Weyant, J. P. (1993) Model comparisons of the costs of reducing CO_2 emissions. *American Economic Review (AEA Papers and Proceedings)*, 83, 2, May, 318–323.

Gørtz, M., Hansen J. V. and Larsen M. (1999) CO_2-skatter, dobbelt-dividende og konkurrence i energisektoren: Anvendelser af den danske AGL-model ECOSMEC (CO_2 taxes, double dividend and competition in the energy sector: Applications of the Danish CGE model ECOSMEC)', Arbejdpapir 1999:1, Danish Economic Council.

Goulder, L. H. (1995a) Environmental taxation and the double dividend: a reader's guide. *International Tax and Public Finance*, 2, 157–183.

Goulder, L. H. (1995b) Effects of carbon taxes in an economy with prior tax distortions: an intertemporal general equilibrium analysis. *Journal of Environmental Economics and Management*, 29, 271–297.

Goulder, L. (2000) Confronting the adverse industry impacts of CO_2 abatement policies: what does it cost?. Climate Issues Brief No.23, September, Resources for the Future, Washington DC, *http://www.rff.org/environment/climate.htm*.

Goulder, L., Parry, I. and Burtraw, D. (1997) Revenue-raising versus other approaches to environmental protection: the critical significance of pre-existing tax distortions. *RAND Journal of Economics*, 28, 4, Winter, 708–731.

Grubb, M. (1995) Asymmetrical price elasticities of energy demand. In T. Barker, P. Ekins N. Johnstone (eds), 1995 *Global Warming and Energy Demand* (pp. 305–310). Routledge, London/New York.

Grubb, M., Chapuis, T. and Ha Duong, M. (1995) The economics of changing course: implications of adaptability and inertia for optimal climate policy. *Energy Policy*, 23, 4/5, 417–432.

Hargreaves, C. (1992) *Macroeconomic Modelling of the Long Run*. Edward Elgar, Cheltenham.

Håkonsen, L. and Mathiesen, L. (1997) CO_2-stabilization may be a 'no-regrets' policy. *Environmental and Resource Economics*, 9, 2, 171–98.

Houghton, J., Meira Filho, L., Callander, B., Harris, N., Kattenburg, A. and Maskell, K. eds (1996) *Climate Change 1995: the Science of Climate Change*, contribution of Working Group 1 to the Second Assessment Report of the Intergovernmental Panel on Climate Change (IPCC), Cambridge University Press, Cambridge.

Ikwue, A. and Skea, J. (1996) The energy sector response to European combustion emission regulations. In F. Lévêque 1996 *Environmental Policy in Europe: Industry, Competition and the Policy Process* (pp. 75–111). Edward Elgar, Cheltenham, UK.

INFRAS (1996) *Economic Impact Analysis of Ecotax Proposals: Comparative Analysis of Modelling Results*, Final Report of a project conducted in co-operation with the 3rd Framework Programme of DGXII of the European Commission, INFRAS, Zurich.

Ingham, A. and Ulph, A. (1991) Market-based instruments for reducing CO_2 emissions: the case of UK manufacturing. *Energy Policy*, 19, 3, March, 138–148.

Ingham, A., Maw, J. and Ulph, A. (1992) Energy conservation in UK manufacturing: a vintage model approach. In D. Hawdon (ed.) 1992 *Energy Demand: Evidence and Expectations*, Surrey University Press, Guildford, 115–141.

Jackson, T. (1991) Least-cost greenhouse planning. *Energy Policy*, January/February, 35–46.

Jackson, T. (1995) Price elasticity and market structure — overcoming obstacles to ensure energy efficiency. In T. Barker, P. Ekins and N. Johnstone (eds), *Global Warming and Energy Elasticities* (pp. 254–266). Routledge, London.

Jackson, T. and Jacobs, M. (1991) Carbon taxes and the assumptions of environmental economics. In T. Barker (ed.), *Green Futures for Economic Growth* (pp. 49–67). Cambridge Econometrics, Cambridge.

Jenkins, R. (1998) Environmental regulation and international competitiveness: a review of literature and some european evidence. UNU/INTECH Discussion Paper #9801, January, UNU/INTECH, Maastricht.

Jenkins, R. (2001) Trade, investment and industrial pollution: lessons from South-East Asia. In N. Adger, M. Kelly and N. Hun Ninh (eds), 2001 *Living with Environmental Change*. Routledge, London/New York.

Jensen, J. and Rasmussen, T. N. (1998) Allocation of CO_2 emission permits: a general equilibrium analysis of policy instruments. The MobiDK Project, The Ministry of Business and Industry, Copenhagen.

Jerkkola, J., Kinnunen, J. and Pohjola, J. (1993) A CGE model for Finnish environmental and energy policy analysis: effects of stabilizing CO_2 emissions. *Discussion paper No. 5, Helsinki School of Economics*. Helsinki.

Johnsen, T. A., Larsen, B. M. and Mysen, H. T. (1996) Economic impacts of a CO_2 tax. In K. H. Alfsen, T. Bye and E. Holmøy (eds), *MSG-EE: An Applied General Equilibrium Model for Energy and Environmental Analyses*. Social and Economic Studies 96, Statistics Norway.

Johnstone, N. and Alavalapati, J. (1998) The distributional effects of environmental tax reform. Discussion Paper 98–01, IIED (International Institute for Environment and Development), London.

Jorgenson, D. W., Goettle, R. J., Gaynor, D., Wilcoxen, P. J. and Slesnick, D. T. (1995) Social cost energy pricing, tax recycling and economic change. Final Report submitted to the US EPA, EPA contract No. 68-W2-0018.

Jorgenson, D. W., Goettle, R. J., Slesnick, D. T. and Wilcoxen, P. J. (1999) Carbon mitigation, permit trading and revenue recycling. *Harvard-Japan Project on Energy and the Environment 1998–99*, March 1999.

Jorgenson, D. and Wilcoxen, P. (1993a) Reducing U.S. carbon dioxide emissions: an assessment of different instruments. *Journal of Policy Modeling*, 15, 5&6, 491–520.

Jorgenson, D. and Wilcoxen, P. (1993b) Reducing US carbon emissions: an econometric general equilibrium assessment. *Resource and Energy Economics*, 15, 1, March, 7–25.

Jorgenson, D. and Yun, K-Y. (1990) The excess burden of taxation in the US. Harvard Institute of Economic Research Discussion Paper 1528, November, Harvard University, Cambridge MA.

Kristensen, J. P. (1996) Environmental taxes, tax reform and the internal market — some Danish experiences and possible community initiatives. In *Environmental Taxes and Charges: NATIONAL Experiences and Plans* (pp. 121–136). European Foundation for the Improvement of Living and Working Conditions, Dublin, and Office for Official Publications of the European Communities, Luxembourg.

Larsen, B. N. and Nesbakken, R. (1997) Norwegian Emissions of CO2 1987–1994. *Environmental and Resource Economics*, 9, 275–290.

Lovins, A. B. and Lovins, H. L. (1991) Least cost climatic stabilization. *Annual Review of Energy and Environment*, 16, 433–531.

Low, P. and Yeats, A. (1992) Do 'dirty' industries migrate? In P. Low (ed.) *International Trade and the Environment* (pp. 89–103). World Bank Discussion Paper No.159, World Bank, Washington DC.

Lucas, R., Wheeler, D. and Hettige, H. (1992) Economic development, environmental regulation and the international migration of toxic industrial pollution: 1960–88. In P. Low (ed.) 1992 *International Trade and the Environment* (pp. 67–86). World Bank Discussion Paper 159, World Bank, Washington DC.

Manne, A. (1993) International trade: the impacts of unilateral carbon emissions limits. Paper presented at the OECD International Conference on the Economics of Climate Change, Paris, June 14–16.

Manne, A. and Richels, R. (1992) *Buying greenhouse insurance: the economic costss of CO2 emission limits*. MIT Press, Cambridge, Mass.

Marion, N. and Svensson, L. (1986) The terms of trade between oil importers. *Journal of International Economics*, 20, 99–113.

McDougall, R. A. and Dixon, P. (1996) Analysing the economy-wide effects of an energy tax: results for Australia from the ORANI-E model. In W. J. Bouma, G. I. Pearman and M. R. Manning (ed.), *Greenhouse: Coping with Climate Change* (pp. 607–619). Wellington New Zealand.

Nilsson, C. (1999) Unilateral versus multilateral carbon dioxide tax implementations — a numerical analysis with the European model — GEM-E3. Preliminary version, National Institute of Economic Research, Stockholm.

Nordhaus, W. D. (1993) Optimal greenhouse gas reductions and tax policy in the 'DICE' model. *American Economic Review* (AEA Papers and Proceedings), 83, 2, May, 313–317.

Nordhaus, W. D. (1994) *Managing the Global Commons: the Economics of Climate Change*. MIT Press, Cambridge MA.

Nordström, H. and Vaughan, S. (1999) Trade and Environment. Special Studies 4, World Trade Organisation (WTO), Geneva.

Norwegian Green Tax Commission (1996) *Policies For A Better Environment and High Employment*, 1996, Oslo.

OECD (Organisation for Economic Cooperation and Development) (1994) *The OECD Jobs Study — Evidence and Explanations*. OECD, Paris.

OECD (Organisation for Economic Cooperation and Development) (1995) *Climate Change, Economic Instruments and Income Distribution*. OECD, Paris.

OECD (Organisation for Economic Cooperation and Development) (1996) *Implementation Strategies for Environmental Taxes*. OECD, Paris.

OECD (Organisation for Economic Cooperation and Development) (1997) *Evaluating Economic Instruments for Environmental Policy*. OECD, Paris.

Oliveira-Martins, J., Burniaux, J.-M. and Martin J. P. (1992) Trade and the effectiveness of unilateral CO_2-abatement policies: evidence from GREEN. *OECD Economic Studies*, 19, 123–140, OECD, Paris.

Palmer, K., Oates, W. and Portney, P. (1995) Tightening environmental standards: the benefit-cost or the no-cost paradigm? *Journal of Economic Perspectives*, 9, 4, Fall, 119–132.

Parry, I. (1995) Pollution taxes and revenue recycling. *Journal of Environmental Economics and Management*, 29, S64–S77.

Parry, I. (1997) Environmental taxes and quotas in the presence of distorting taxes in factor markets. *Resource and Energy Economics*, 19, 203–220.

Parry, I., Williams, R. and Goulder, L. (1999) When can carbon abatement policies increase welfare? The fundamental role of distorted factor markets. *Journal of Environmental Economics and Management*, 37, 52–84.

Pearce, D. (1991) The role of carbon taxes in adjusting to global warming. *Economic Journal*, 101, 938–948.

Pezzey, J. (1992a) The symmetry between controlling pollution by price and controlling it by quantity. *Canadian Journal of Economics*, 25, 4, 983–991.

Pezzey, J. (1992b) Analysis of unilateral CO_2 control in the european community and OECD. *The Energy Journal*, 13, 159–171.

Pigou, A. C. (1932) *The Economics of Welfare*, 4th edition (1st edition 1920), Macmillan, London.

Pizer, W. (1999) Choosing price or quantity controls for greenhouse gases. Climate Issues Brief No.17, Resources for the Future, Washington DC, *http://www.rff.org/environment/climate.htm*.

Porter, M. (1990) *The Competitive Advantage of Nations*. Free Press, New York.

Poterba, J. (1991) Tax policy to combat global warming. In R. Dornbusch and J. Poterba (eds), 1991 *Global Warming: Economic Policy Responses* (pp. 71–98). MIT Press, Cambridge MA.

Proost, S. and Van Regemorter, D. (1995) The double dividend and the role of inequality aversion and macroeconomic regimes. *International Taxes and Public Finances*, 2, 217–219, Kluwer Academic Publishers.

RCEP (Royal Commission on Environmental Pollution) (2000) *Energy — the Changing Climate*, 22nd Report of the Royal Commission of Environmental Pollution, The Stationery Office, London.

Repetto, R. and Austin, D. (1997) *The Costs of Climate Protection: a Guide for the Perplexed*, World Resources Institute, Washington D.C.

Rutherford, T. (1992) The welfare effects of fossil carbon restrictions: results from a recursively dynamic trade model. OECD Dept. of Economic Statistics, Resource Allocation Division, Working Paper No.112, OECD/GD (91), Paris.

Sanstad, A. and Wolff, G. (2000) *Tax Shifting and the Likelihood of Double Dividends: Theoretical and Computational Issues*, Redefining Progress, *www.rprogress.org*.

Schelling, T. (1992) Some economics of global warming. *American Economic Review*, 82, 1, March 1992, 1–14.

Schmidt, T. and Conrad, K. (1995) National economics impacts of an EU environmental policy — an applied general equilibrium analysis. ZEW Discussion Paper No. 95–22, Mannheim.

SEPA (Swedish Environmental Protection Agency) (1997) *Environmental Taxes in Sweden — Economic Instruments of Environmental Policy*, Report 4745, Stockholm.

Shackleton, R., Shelby, M., Cristofaro, A., Brinner, R., Yanchar J., Goulder, L., Jorgenson D., Wilcoxen, P. and Pauly, P. (1996) The efficiency value of carbon tax revenues. In D. Gaskins and J. Weyant (eds), *Reducing Global Carbon Dioxide Emissions: Costs and Policy Options*. Stanford University Energy Modeling Forum, Stanford, CA.

Shah, A. and Larsen, B. (1992) Carbon taxes, the greenhouse effect, and developing countries. Background Paper No.6, for the *1992 World Development Report*, World Bank, Washington DC.

Smith, S. (1992) The distributional consequences of taxes on energy and the carbon content of fuels. *European Economy* (pp. 241–268). Special Edition on The Economics of Limiting CO_2 Emissions, Commission of the European Communities.

Sorrell, S. and Skea, J. eds (1999) *Pollution for Sale: Emissions Trading and Joint Implementation*, Edward Elgar, Cheltenham.

Stiglitz, J. and Dasgupta, P. (1971) Differential taxation, public goods, and economic efficiency. *Review of Economic Studies*, 38, 2, 151–174.

Symons, E. Proops, J. and Gay, P. (1994) Carbon taxes, consumer demand and carbon dioxide emissions: a simulation analysis for the UK. *Fiscal Studies*, 15, 2, 19–43.

TemaNord (1994) *The Use of Economic Instruments in Nordic Environmental Policy*. TemaNord 1994:561, Copenhagen.

UNFCCC (UN Framework Convention on Climate Change) (1992) the full text of the Convention is available on *http://www.unfccc.int/resource/conv/index.html*, UNFCCC, Bonn.

Weitzmann, M. (1974) Prices vs. Quantities. *Review of Economic Studies*, 41, 477–491.

Welsch, H. and Hoster, F. (1995) A general equilibrium analysis of European carbon/energy taxation — model structure and macroeconomic results. *Zeitschrift fuer Wirtschafts- und Sozialwissenschaften* (ZWS), 115, 1995, 275–303.

Weyant, J. P. and Hill J. N. (1999) Introduction and overview. pp. vi to 1xliv in *The Costs of the Kyoto Protocol: A Multi-Model Evaluation*, Special Issue of the *Energy Journal*. John Weyant (ed.).

Whalley, J. and Wigle, R. (1991) The international incidence of carbon taxes. In R. Dornbusch and J. Poterba (eds), 1991 *Global Warming: Economic Policy Responses* (pp. 233–263). MIT Press, Cambridge MA.

Zhang, Z.X (1998) Macro-economic and sectoral effects of carbon taxes: a general equilibrium analysis for China. *Economic Systems Research*, 10 (2) 135–160.

Zhang, Z.X and Folmer, H. (1998) Economic modelling approaches to cost estimates for the control of carbon dioxide emissions. *Energy Economics*, 20, 1, 101–120.

CHAPTER 5

THE DESIGN OF STABLE INTERNATIONAL ENVIRONMENTAL AGREEMENTS: ECONOMIC THEORY AND POLITICAL ECONOMY

Ulrich J. Wagner

Kiel Institute of World Economics

Abstract. International environmental agreements typically strive for the solution of a common property resource dilemma. Since the sovereignty of states precludes external enforcement, international environmental agreements must be self-enforcing. Game theoretical models explain why rewards and punishments imposed through the environmental externality generally fail to enforce full cooperation. Therefore, environmental treaties incorporate provisions that enhance the incentives for participation such as transfers, sanctions and linkage to other negotiation topics in international politics. Moreover, interaction with markets and governments as well as the rules and procedures adopted in the negotiation process influence the design and the effectiveness of an international environmental agreement.

Keywords. International environmental agreements; Game theory; Political economy.

1. International environmental agreements and economics

International environmental agreements (IEAs) typically strive for the solution of a common property resource dilemma. The fundamental difficulty with maintaining international common property resources resides in the fact that the user countries treat its services as free while they are in reality scarce. As a consequence, each country that uses the resource imposes a negative externality on the other countries using the resource. Transboundary pollution of the air or rivers is one example. Overuse of openly accessible natural resources such as fishing grounds and the rain forests is another.

The common property resource framework is one way of looking at international environmental protection. An alternative approach casts the issue as the provision of a public good. This accounts for the fact that the benefits from environmental protection are realized by all countries using the resource. By contrast, the associated cost is incurred by the very country which takes action to protect the environment.

The implications are well-known: On the one hand, non-rivalry results in voluntary provision levels which are not efficient. When acting on its own, a country does not take into account the external benefits it creates for the other countries. On the other hand, non-excludeability provides incentives to free ride. Every country may be tempted to leave care of the global environment to the other countries and to enjoy the benefits of an improvement in environmental quality without contributing to its cost. This points to the scope for strategic behavior in international environmental policy.

At the national level a common property dilemma can be resolved by intervention of the government (Demsetz 1967). Yet at the international scale the 'interventionist' solution is not feasible because there is no supra-national authority that could coerce countries to provide an efficient level of environmental protection. On the contrary, countries are sovereign. Sovereignty implies that the only way out of an international common property dilemma is agreement (Barrett 1990).

Over the past decade economists have tried to shed some light on the formation of IEAs. In summarizing their findings, this paper introduces the reader to an economic theory of international environmental cooperation.

The following section discusses game theoretical models that reveal the incentives and disincentives for participation in an IEA when countries have a single environmental choice variable. Section 3 extends the analysis to allow for additional instruments that stabilize an IEA and explains how interaction with markets and governments affect treaty design. The concluding section gives a brief summary and evaluation of the results and points out directions of future research.

2. International environmental agreements as games

2.1. *A non-cooperative game of emission abatement*

A game theoretical framework easily reveals the dilemma inherent in the provision of environmental protection. Consider the one-shot game $\Gamma = (\mathbf{N}, \mathbf{A}, \mathbf{\Pi})$ of emission abatement where $\mathbf{N} = \{1, ..., N\}$ is the set of N countries, $\mathbf{A} = \times_{i \in \mathbf{N}} A_i$ is the strategy space given by the Cartesian product of all pure strategy sets $A_i \subset \mathbb{R}_0^+$, $i \in \mathbf{N}$, and $\mathbf{\Pi}$ is the payoff space.

All countries emit a harmful pollutant which is regarded as a pure public bad. The strategic choice variable $q_i \in A_i$ of country i is the level of emission abatement it undertakes to reduce emissions. Upon realizing a policy level q_i country i incurs a cost given by a non-negative function $C_i(q_i)$. The cost is 'private' or 'national'. By contrast, the benefits from environmental protection accrue from *aggregate* protection $Q = \sum q_i$. Country i's benefit function $B_i(Q)$ is concave and increasing in Q. The payoff Π_i is determined by country i's net benefits from abatement

$$\Pi_i(q_i, q_{-i}) = B_i(Q) - C_i(q_i) \tag{1}$$

where $q_{-i} = Q - q_i$. Assume that $\Pi_i(q_i, q_{-i})$ is a continuous, twice differentiable function that is strictly concave in q_i. What is more, the structure of the game is common knowledge, meaning that all players have complete information about **N**, **A** and **Π** and all players know that all players have complete information and so on.

The optimal unilateral policy level in country i is given by

$$R_i(q_{-i}) = \arg\max_{q_i \in A_i} \Pi_i(q_i, q_{-i}). \tag{2}$$

Equation (2) defines country i's best-reply function with regard to the other countries' policies. A fixed point $(q_1^u, ..., q_N^u)$ of the best-reply correspondence $R = \times_{i \in \mathbf{N}} R_i(q_{-i})$ is a Nash equilibrium of the game. Given that all other countries choose their optimal policy levels $q_j^u, j \in \mathbf{N}\backslash\{i\}$, country i can do no better than to play q_i^u, too.

If a benevolent supra-national authority were to choose abatement levels in all countries it would assign efficient levels according to

$$q_i^c = \arg\max_{q_i \in A_i} \sum_{j=1}^{N} \Pi_j(q_j, q_{-j}) \qquad i \in \mathbf{N}. \tag{3}$$

This is a representation of the well-known Samuelson condition for the efficient provision of a public good and shows that benefits in all countries are counted. For symmetric countries we drop subscripts i and rearrange to obtain the more common first-order condition

$$NB'(Nq^c) = C'(q^c) \tag{4}$$

which contrasts with the selfish provision equilibrium satisfying

$$B'(Nq^u) \leqslant C'(q^u). \tag{5}$$

The dilemma of environmental protection arises from two factors. First, as depicted in Figure 1, the non-cooperative protection levels typically fall short of the efficient ones. Second, every country faces an incentive to free ride. This follows immediately from the non-positive slope of the reaction functions in the neighborhood of a Nash equilibrium in the interior of **A**, given by

$$-R_i'(q_{-i}) = -\frac{\partial q_i}{\partial q_{-i}} = \frac{-B_i''(Q)}{C_i''(q_i) - B_i''(Q)} \in [0; 1] \qquad i \in \mathbf{N}. \tag{6}$$

Depending on the economics of a specific environmental problem — that is, the benefits and costs associated with its mitigation — we shall distinguish between two types of free riding (Carraro 2000). When the benefits of abatement are linear then $R_i'(q_{-i}) = 0$ and (2) solves for a constant $\bar{q}_i$, regardless of q_{-i}. Hence, playing $\bar{q}_i$ is a *dominant strategy* for country i and its reaction curve is orthogonal to the aggregate reaction curve of the other countries. We thus speak of *orthogonal free riding*.

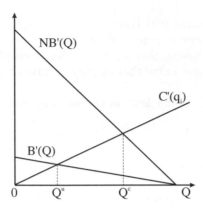

Figure 1. Non-cooperative vs. cooperative abatement levels.
Source: modified from Barrett (1994b, p. 881)

By contrast, for $B_i''(Q) < 0$, (6) tells us that i's optimal response towards an increase in q_{-i} is to reduce its own abatement so that reaction curves are downward sloping. This phenomenon is called *non-orthogonal free riding*. In the limiting case in which marginal abatement cost is constant, country i will vary q_i so as to exactly offset any change in q_{-i}.

Figures 2(a) and 2(b) depict the reaction curves for both types of free riding, assuming that (5) has an interior solution. The figures well illustrate the fundamental difference between the two types of free riding. An empirical estimation of such reaction curves, however, is difficult even when the costs and benefits of mitigating a given international environmental problem are known with certainty. This is because environmental policy may entail adjustments in the

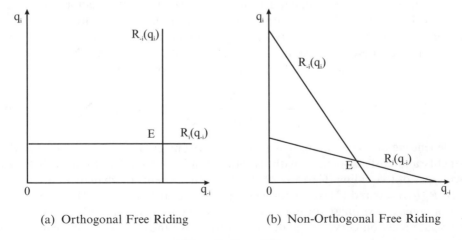

(a) Orthogonal Free Riding   (b) Non-Orthogonal Free Riding

Figure 2. Free riding.

international division of labor which in turn give incentives for non-orthogonal free riding. This point will be illustrated below in more depth.

2.2. Do we need an environmental leader?

In the public debate on international environmental policy it has been argued, in particular by environmentalist groups, that a country should take action *unilaterally* and undertake abatement in excess of its non-cooperative level. The objective of this policy is to reduce total emissions on the one hand and to influence other countries' behavior on the other hand, so as to initiate a process of gradual improvements in environmental quality (Siebert 1998).

Hoel (1991) investigates whether altruistic unilateral efforts will be matched by selfish countries. Starting with the assumption that free riding is non-orthogonal, Hoel analyzes the comparative statics of the abatement game to evaluate the effect of a single environmental leader pursuing a policy in excess of the non-cooperative level. He finds that aggregate net benefits may improve marginally, but the conditions under which this holds true are far from being general. Depending on the distribution of marginal benefits across countries, such behavior can also result in aggregate net benefits *below* the non-cooperative level.

In a similar model framework with linear abatement cost Buchholz, Haslbeck and Sandler (1998) inquire into the magnitude of non-orthogonal free riding when either a single country or a relatively small coalition of countries increase their emission abatement levels. Such efforts will be entirely offset by free riders unless they are driven into a corner solution or else the sensitivity of marginal benefits with regard to the aggregate level of abatement is very low.

While these papers suggest that the case for unilateral action is rather weak, changes in the assumptions made on the economics of environmental protection may lead to different theoretical results. In fact, unilateral environmental policy can substantially improve environmental quality if it produces reinforcement effects in other economies, as proposed by Heal (1993). Reinforcement effects occur when marginal benefits are multiplicative rather than additive or when cost functions are interdependent across countries. Then it is true that

$$\frac{\partial^2 [B_i(q_i, q_{-i}) - C_i(q_i, q_{-i})]}{\partial q_i \partial q_{-i}} > 0. \tag{7}$$

This might be the case if a higher abatement level in the leader country results from the development of a new abatement technology. To the extent that technological spillovers to other countries drive their marginal cost below marginal benefits, these countries are given an incentive to further curb their emissions: abatement becomes a strategic complement (Barrett 1998b).

It is important to note that the results reported here critically depend on the Nash conjecture and on the static model framework. Hence, the effects of unilateral action remain ambiguous. However, an efficient solution to international environmental problems can always be implemented if all countries are willing to cooperate. Since countries are sovereign and their individual incentives work in the opposite direction, this begs the question of how a cooperative outcome can be enforced.

2.3. *Altruism versus self-interest: which game is played?*

The way we have set out the international abatement game is equivalent to the N-player prisoners' dilemma (Dasgupta 1982). Full cooperation is not a likely outcome if countries are selfish and behave non-cooperatively. The opposite approach is to presuppose that free riding does not occur: then countries play a *cooperative* game.

The literature on IEAs has taken both roads and can thus be subdivided into a cooperative and a non-cooperative strand (Tulkens 1998). Cooperative analyses of IEAs typically assume that an efficient policy target is sustained in a full cooperative outcome. Their main concern is with burden-sharing rules that exhibit desirable properties like efficiency, equity, and uniqueness. By contrast, in the non-cooperative literature free riding and non-compliance are considered the major constraints on international cooperation for the environment. This strand thus focuses on strategies aimed to solve these problems.

As is well-known, a common property dilemma at the national level can be resolved by the intervention of the municipal government (Demsetz 1967). Consequently, it makes sense to apply cooperative game theoretical solutions to environmental problems that occur within the borders of a country. What precludes the 'interventionist' solution in the context of transboundary environmental problems is the fact that there is no supra-national authority that could coerce countries to pursue cooperative environmental policies. To the contrary, countries are sovereign: Under the rules of international law, a state can always withdraw from a multilateral treaty, and this freedom is something it cannot forfeit (Barrett 1990).

It is for this reason that a state cannot commit to adhering to a cooperative policy if doing so runs counter to its self-interest. Such commitment plainly lacks credibility when a selfish policy makes the country better off. Yet applying cooperative game theory to international environmental problems presupposes commitment. Hence, this misses the fact that the setting for negotiations among sovereign states necessarily is a non-cooperative environment.

As an illustration, consider the pledges to unilaterally reduce CO_2 emissions made by a number of predominantly European OECD countries before the United Nations Conference on Environment and Development in Rio 1992. These countries announced reduction targets for CO_2 emissions ranging from moderate growth or stabilization to substantial cut backs by up to 30% from late 1980s' levels to be reached by 2005. Recent developments have revealed that such announcements were cheap talk. Plainly, 'if a country learned later that its interests would be badly served by meeting its target, then there would be nothing to stop it from failing to meet it' (Barrett 1998c, p. 25). The lesson from this is straightforward: sovereignty precludes commitment.

Non-cooperative game theory — to the extent that it properly accounts for the characteristic dilemma situation — provides us with a cutting edge for analyzing international environmental cooperation. For this reason, the remainder of this paper focuses on advances in the non-cooperative theory of IEAs.[1]

2.4. *The scope for international environmental cooperation*

In spite of the theoretical assertion that full cooperation is not sustained as an equilibrium in the abatement dilemma, we observe that the number of multilateral environmental agreements in the world is close to 200 (Barrett 2000). Probably the most prominent treaties are the 1987 Montreal Protocol on Substances that Deplete the Ozone Layer and the United Nations Framework Convention on Climate Change which was established during the Rio Earth Summit in 1992 and supplemented by the so-called Kyoto Protocol in 1997.

While both treaties aim at the mitigation of a global environmental problem, the outcomes of the negotiations differ substantially. The Montreal Protocol and its amendments have succeeded in reducing the emissions of ozone depleting substances tremendously since its enforcement in 1987. By contrast, alarmingly little has been achieved so far in terms of an effective reduction of greenhouse gas emissions.[2]

The Montreal Protocol is special in that estimates of the costs and benefits suggest that the phase out of ozone depleting chlorofluorcarbons (CFCs) by developed countries was not so much a manifestation of collective action. In the first place the phase out was advantageous to national interests in developed countries, whereas developing countries' net benefits tended to be negative (Barrett 1999c, USEPA 1988). In an econometric study, Murdoch and Sandler (1997) could not reject the hypothesis that global reductions of CFCs in the late 1980s were consistent with Nash behavior. Nevertheless, (non-orthogonal) free riding by large developing countries such as India could have been very detrimental to the signatories (Benedick 1998). Hence the treaty's merit is that it encouraged participation by developing countries despite their foregoing free riding gains.

While the economics of climate change — though subject to tremendous uncertainty — are believed to be consistent with the dilemma outlined above, the close to full participation in the Framework Convention apparently contradicts the free rider hypothesis. However, 'targets and timetables' for the reduction of CO_2 emissions were laid down only in the Kyoto Protocol which requires Annex I countries — OECD countries plus economies in transition — to reduce emissions by up to 8% of 1990 levels until 2012. In no way does the current status of ratification of the Protocol nurture the hopes that it will ever become legally binding on its signatories.

The Kyoto Protocol demonstrates that sovereign countries actually make use of their free riding option in the sense that they do not opt into an agreement and comply with it unless doing so is their best alternative. The non-cooperative theory of IEAs thus requires that agreements be *self-enforcing* (Barrett 1990). In spite of the intrinsic differences regarding the particular scientific and economic aspects of different environmental problems, the theory identifies two general conditions for self-enforceability.

Starting with the weaker requirement, it is immediately seen that a country has no incentive to join an agreement which drives its net benefits below the non-cooperative level. Hence, a necessary condition for accession is that the agreement is *profitable*. Following Carraro and Siniscalco (1998) a coalition K formed by k countries is profitable if

$$\Pi_i(q_i, q_{-i}) \geqslant \Pi_i\left(q_i^u, \sum_{j \neq i} q_j^u\right) \quad \forall i \in K. \tag{8}$$

The LHS gives the payoff country i receives as a signatory to a (possibly incomplete) agreement, while the RHS is the payoff i gets in the Nash equilibrium of the abatement game. In the terminology of game theory, the profitability condition is sufficient to ensure that accession to the agreement is *individually rational* for a country.

Does the profitability condition (8) frustrate cooperation of all N countries? In a dilemma game the difference between aggregate net benefits in the full cooperative outcome and aggregate benefits in the Nash equilibrium — henceforth referred to as the 'gains to cooperation' — must be positive. Therefore, the profitability condition is always satisfied for identical countries choosing identical abatement levels $q^c > q^u$.

It is possible, however, that the profitability condition constrains participation in a coalition of strongly asymmetric countries. This is because countries with favorably low marginal abatement cost are assigned higher-than-average abatement levels in order to minimize total cost of achieving a given abatement level. Hence, these countries possibly lose from accession. For instance, simulations by Eyckmans, Proost and Schokkaert (1993) show that China, the former USSR and Eastern Europe would be worse off in a cost-efficient climate change agreement.

In a non-cooperative environment, the profitability condition (8) does not entirely capture the restrictions on cooperation imposed by the selfish behavior of countries. After all, there is no reason to believe that a country is eager to join an agreement once that cooperation is profitable. In effect, free riding could be even more profitable.

Therefore, a second condition for self-enforceability must be imposed. It requires that the agreement not be vulnerable to free riding and deviant behavior by individual countries or sub-coalitions of countries. In what follows, such an agreement will be referred to as 'stable': participation is the *best* alternative for its member states. Note that stability is a sufficient condition for profitability because an agreement which is not profitable clearly lacks stability.

2.5. *Self-enforcing cooperation in the participation game*

The simple abatement game corresponds to the *status quo ante* to negotiations. As noted earlier, cooperation in this game is not stable because free riding incentives prevail. Therefore, an IEA must change the rules of the game so as to render accession self-enforcing for all countries. Such enforcement strategies employ both 'sticks' and 'carrots'.

Barrett (1991b, 1994b) and many others assume that signatories to an agreement reward acceding parties by increasing their level of abatement themselves. Conversely, upon withdrawal of a party the remaining signatories punish the deviant country by reducing their abatement levels. This IEA, the so-called participation game, is modeled as the formation of a stable coalition that proceeds in three stages: First, all countries decide whether to join the agreement or not. Next, signatories cooperatively choose their abatement levels. Non-signatories follow in the last stage and simultaneously choose their optimal abatement levels, taking the decision of the other countries as given.

For an outline of the solution to the participation game it is assumed that countries are symmetric with regard to their costs and benefits from abatement. Subscripts n and s denote variables associated with non-signatories and signatories, respectively. To determine the subgame perfect equilibrium the game must be solved backwards.

In the last stage, each non-signatory chooses its best response q_n to the signatories' joint abatement level kq_s. Assuming that its choice does not influence that of the other non-signatories, a representative non-signatory country abates to the level

$$q_n = \arg\max_{q_i \in A_i} B\left(q_i + kq_s + \sum_{j \in \overline{K} \setminus \{i\}} q_j \right) - C(q_i) \tag{9}$$

where $\overline{K}$ denotes the set of non-signatories. Notice that moving first gives signatories a strategic advantage over non-signatories. Upon choosing an abatement level that maximizes the net benefits of a representative signatory they anticipate the non-signatories' reaction. Hence, it is optimal for signatories to abate to the level

$$q_s = \arg\max_{q_i \in A_i} B[kq_i + (N - k)q_n(kq_i)] - C(q_i) \tag{10}$$

where $q_n(kq_s)$ is the anticipated stage-three reaction of a representative non-signatory towards a given q_s.

For the solution of the first stage it is assumed that only one agreement forms and non-signatories do not form coalitions. Denote by

$$\Pi_l(k) = B(kq_s + (N - k)q_n) - C(q_l) \qquad l = s, n \tag{11}$$

the payoffs to signatories and non-signatories, respectively, when the agreement comprises k countries. Then the equilibrium number of signatories k^* must satisfy the following stability conditions

$$\Pi_s(k^*) \geqslant \Pi_n(k^* - 1) \qquad \text{and} \qquad (12a)$$

$$\Pi_n(k^*) \geqslant \Pi_s(k^* + 1). \qquad (12b)$$

According to this definition, an IEA is *internally stable* if no signatory country wishes to withdraw unilaterally from the agreement. This is true if (12a) holds. Conversely, an IEA is *externally stable* if no non-signatory can do better by unilaterally acceding to the IEA, hence, (12b) is satisfied.[3]

Two factors render the IEA self-enforcing. First, since q_s in (10) is increasing in the number of signatories k, the mechanism of punishments and rewards gives an incentive for accession and works in favor of a larger coalition. Second, given the assumption that signatories comply with the agreement, the rewards and punishments are credible. This is because they result from joint maximization of net benefits — in subgame perfect equilibrium signatories cannot do better collectively by choosing other policy levels.

The number of signatories in the participation game critically depends on the costs and benefits of environmental protection and so the participation game is compatible with three types of games: the prisoners' dilemma, the coordination game, and the game of chicken.

In a worst case scenario, the punishments and rewards are too weak to encourage accession to the treaty. The IEA is not capable of deterring free riding incentives and so the characteristic dilemma of international environmental protection remains unchanged. A precondition for this phenomenon is that free riding is non-orthogonal (Barrett 1995).

By contrast, the participation game may also be represented as a coordination game — a game with at least two Pareto-ranked equilibria in which players are faced with the problem of moving from an inferior equilibrium towards a better equilibrium. Cost interdependencies or linkage to other issues can transform the participation game into a coordination game. Since diplomats meet face-to-face in multilateral negotiations, they are free to employ coordination devices such as a minimum participation clause that provides for the selection of the 'good' equilibrium in which each country is better off. Minimum participation clauses and issue linkage will be discussed in more detail below.

Finally, the participation game may result in an incomplete agreement with $1 < k^* < N$ signatories. This situation bears likeness to the game of chicken inasmuch as a subset of countries opt into the agreement whereas the others stay outside. The chicken game is consistent with a variety of net benefit functions that give rise to both types of free riding. For orthogonal free riding, Barrett (1994b) finds that the number of signatories cannot exceed three regardless of the total number of countries N involved in the negotiations. For the case in which free riding is non-orthogonal numerical simulations demonstrate an unfortunate trade-off: When the potential gains to cooperation are high participation in the IEA falls well short of the total number of countries, and vice versa.

The participation game can be augmented in several ways to allow for asymmetries between countries. Hoel (1992) assumes that countries have different constant marginal benefits from abatement while cost remains identical. Signatories choose a uniform abatement level that reflects the preferences of the median country (Bowen 1943, Black 1948). In equilibrium an agreement comprises at most three countries. Bauer (1992) models asymmetries in such a way that larger countries have both higher benefits and lower cost of abatement. With free riding being orthogonal, only the two largest countries form an agreement at the equilibrium.

Barrett (1997a) conducts numerical simulations for more general forms of asymmetries. The simulations confirm the equilibrium size of $k^* = 3$ when free riding is orthogonal, indicating that this result is not sensitive to the symmetry assumption and robust with regard to parameter changes. When free riding is non-orthogonal, a self-enforcing IEA exists and may comprise up to the total number of countries for the range of parameters considered. However, cooperation results more in a redistribution of abatement across countries than in an increased aggregate level of environmental protection (Barrett 1997a). What is more, if aggregate net benefits are redistributed by assigning each signatory its Shapley value then global net benefits increase but still the IEA remains incomplete.[4] This result underlines the importance of the stability constraint in international environmental treaty-making: An equitable burden-sharing rule does not enforce cooperation on its own since free riding may still be more advantageous for some countries.

2.6. *Non-compliance and free riding*

In the participation game signatories always comply with their contractual obligations. While backward induction ensures that *accession* is subgame perfect for a signatory, IEAs usually become legally binding on its members for many years. As such, signatories do face incentives to deviate from the contract.

This does not dismiss the suitability of the model, since an observation common to the majority of IEAs in place is that non-compliance is extremely rare. Chayes and Chayes (1995) conclude that non-compliance is not the problem theory makes out of it which explains why many agreements lack credible sanctions to punish non-compliance. Downs, Rocke and Barsoom (1996) take the opposite position, claiming that the high rate of compliance results from the fact that countries prefer 'shallow' cooperation to 'deep' cooperation, so as to circumvent the costs of incorporating effective enforcement mechanisms into an agreement.

Barrett (1998c) shows that free rider deterrence and compliance enforcement are related problems which can be solved jointly. Starting with the assumption that signatories can impose a credible punishment to deter free riding he argues as follows:

> The worst harm that a signatory could do by not complying would be for it to
> choose an emission profile that matched what it would do if it withdrew from

the agreement. Hence, if every signatory is deterred from withdrawing, each also is deterred from not complying. The binding constraint on international cooperation is free rider deterrence, not compliance enforcement. Once free riding can be deterred, compliance can be enforced free of charge. (Barrett 1998c, p. 35)

Barrett's line of reasoning derives from a model framework other than the participation game. A formal corroboration of his assertion requires that we recast the issue of international cooperation for the environment in a dynamic game.

2.7. *The supergame of environmental protection*

One way of looking at IEAs in a dynamic framework is by assuming that the one-shot abatement game $\Gamma = (\mathbf{N}, \mathbf{A}, \mathbf{\Pi})$ outlined above is repeated *ad infinitum*. The theory of infinitely repeated games provides powerful tools for the analysis of dynamic strategic interaction, and large support can be found for its application in the context of IEAs.

First, states interact repeatedly in various policy domains and a static 'equilibrium' is hard to observe. Rather, violations of the contract or exogenous changes entail renegotiations or new contracts. Renegotiation is actually part of an IEA that stipulates regular meetings of the Conference of Parties or a similar decision-making body.

Moreover, inertia in world politics creates a reaction time lag. For example, when a signatory fails to comply with its obligations, the aggrieved countries probably cannot immediately act upon it. Retaliation might thus become effective only in future periods for institutional or technological reasons. Delayed punishments are properly modeled in supergames with discounting.

Finally, some IEAs aim at the mitigation of long-run environmental problems, such as global warming, that cover very long time spans. When intergenerational trade-offs are involved and uncertainty about the end of the negotiations prevails, the discount factor in supergames reflects both a country's ethical conception of intergenerational equity and the probability for that state to disappear from the political landscape.[5]

In what follows we consider the supergame $\Gamma_\delta = [\mathbf{N}, \mathbf{S}, \mathbf{u}(\delta)]$ which is the infinite repetition of the abatement game Γ. Let $\mathbf{A}$ be the space of feasible actions q_i, $i \in \mathbf{N}$ at every stage of the game. Then $\mathbf{q}(t) = (q_1(t), ..., q_N(t))$ is the vector of actions played in period t. A pure strategy s_i for player i maps to every possible history of actions a period-t action $q_i(t)$ for all $t = 0, 1, ...$. S_i denotes the strategy set of player i and then $\mathbf{S} = \times_{i=1}^{N} S_i$ is the strategy space. An N-tuple of strategies is referred to as a strategy profile $s = (s_1, ..., s_N)$.

The profile s is a Nash equilibrium in Γ_δ if s_i is a best response to $s_{-i} = s \backslash \{s_i\}$ for all $i \in \mathbf{N}$. Moreover, s is a subgame perfect equilibrium if the subgame strategies $\mathbf{q}(t \mid s)$ induced by s are a Nash equilibrium in every subgame t. The sequence of action profiles $\{\mathbf{q}(t+1 \mid s), \mathbf{q}(t+2 \mid s), ...\}$ induced by an equilibrium s is a continuation equilibrium of s in period t. Accordingly, the (normalized) continuation payoff of a given strategy profile s in period t is given by

$$u_i(t \mid s, \delta) = (1 - \delta) \sum_{\tau = t}^{\infty} \delta^{\tau - t} \Pi(q_i(\tau \mid s), q_{-i}(\tau \mid s)). \qquad (13)$$

This is the average per-period payoff along the equilibrium path induced by s when players have a common discount factor δ. Finally, $\mathbf{u}(\delta)$ denotes the vector of normalized continuation payoffs.

Reciprocity

The supergame framework gives rise to strategies based on reciprocity that exploit the sequential nature of the game to enforce cooperation: If a player defects at any stage of play the other players fight back in the following periods. If the retaliation is sufficiently strong to offset the gain from cheating, and if the threat to carry it out is credible, then no player has an incentive to deviate from the cooperative abatement level.

To see this, suppose that a country defects once and then reverts to cooperation, which gives it the maximum gain from cheating for one period. In the subsequent period, the aggrieved countries may regard the defection as a bygone and continue to cooperate. However, if the deviation goes unpunished then free riding cannot be deterred and cooperation is bound to break down.

To deter free riding in the given model framework, the compliant countries must punish the defection by lowering their own levels of abatement. In so doing, these countries realize lower net benefits than under full cooperation. Nevertheless, it is rational to carry out the self-harming punishment provided that it induces the deviant country to revert to the cooperative abatement level. This is because the long run gains from full cooperation outweigh the loss from punishing the deviation. This is precisely what makes a punishment credible. A credible punishment discourages cheating *ex ante* by virtue of the inevitability by which it is going to be carried out.

Renegotiation-proofness

The requirement that punishments be credible is not innocuous: It dismisses a well-known strategy of reciprocity, the trigger strategy. This strategy stipulates that all countries start out cooperating. When a unilateral deviation occurs all countries revert to their non-cooperative abatement levels for all subsequent periods.

The trigger strategy is codified in Article 60 of the Vienna Convention on the Law of Treaties, according to which 'a material breach of a multilateral treaty by one of the parties entitles the other parties by unanimous agreement to suspend the operation of the treaty in whole or in part or to terminate it'. A similar provision is laid down in the Convention on Conservation of North Pacific Fur Seals of 1957, an IEA which limits the hunting of seals in the open sea (Barrett 1991a). Article 12 of this treaty stipulates that any of the four parties (Canada,

Japan, U.S.A., U.S.S.R.) can give notice of its intention to terminate the treaty after a violation has occurred. The termination becomes effective provided signatories cannot agree upon remedial measures.

The termination of a treaty is equivalent to the punishment phase of the trigger strategy, which is severe enough to sustain full cooperation as a subgame perfect equilibrium in dilemma supergames (Friedman 1971, Fudenberg and Maskin 1986). But the punishment clashes with collective rationality since it is too relentless, too unforgiving. Why should countries damage themselves by reverting to Nash abatement levels forever? They are free to jointly renegotiate away from the punishment towards the full cooperative outcome upon which they cannot improve collectively.[6] In fact, the 1957 Fur Seal Treaty was the result of renegotiations over its predecessor of 1911. This treaty was nullified in 1941 after Japan had given notice of its intention to withdraw from it (Barrett 1999b).

This brings us back to the credibility issue. Suppose that the countries called upon to punish a deviation by country j prefer to renege on that punishment because resuming cooperation makes all N countries better off. Since j anticipates that the punishment is not *renegotiation-proof*, the threat to impose it is not credible and thus cannot deter j from free riding.

Farrell and Maskin (1989) have defined renegotiation-proof equilibrium for two-player games. Following their definition, a subgame perfect equilibrium s is (weakly) renegotiation-proof if there do not exist continuation equilibria s^1, s^2 of s such that s^1 strictly Pareto-dominates s^2. Likewise, we say that payoffs in $\mathbf{u}(s, \delta)$ induced by a (weakly) renegotiation-proof strategy profile s are (weakly) renegotiation-proof.

In a symmetric prisoners' dilemma, the punishment equilibrium s^p stipulated by the trigger strategy is strictly dominated by the cooperative equilibrium s^c so that we have $\mathbf{u}(s^c, \delta) > \mathbf{u}(s^p, \delta)$. This means that all players are strictly better off in the cooperative phase and hence those called upon to punish a deviation would rather renegotiate away from s^p towards s^c. This is why the trigger strategy is not renegotiation-proof.

A way to eliminate the incentives to renegotiate arising in the punishment phase is by requiring that a deviant country j make amends for the deviation before cooperation is resumed (Farrell and Maskin 1989, van Damme 1989). To illustrate this, assume that there are N identical countries and their common discount factor δ is close to unity. Countries start out in the cooperative phase and provide abatement levels q^w which give them a per-period payoff Π^w each. Following a deviation by country j, the aggrieved countries provide a joint abatement level $q^j_{-j} < (N-1)q^w$ below the cooperative one so as to rule out j's gain from cheating. Then country j has no *ex ante* incentive to deviate in the cooperative phase if

$$\max_{q_j \in A_j} \Pi_j(q_j, q^j_{-j}) \leqslant \Pi^w \tag{14}$$

holds.

To demonstrate its willingness to resume cooperation, country j must cooperate in its own punishment by choosing an abatement level satisfying $q_j^j \geq q^w$. This is because j's reparation must be high enough to make the punishing countries at least as well off as in the cooperative outcome. Otherwise, all countries would have an incentive to jointly renege on the punishment. Therefore, it must also be true that

$$\Pi_i(q_j^j, q_{-j}^j) \geq \Pi^w \quad \forall i, j \in \mathbf{N}, \ i \neq j. \tag{15}$$

Inequalities (14) and (15) characterize the set of feasible (weakly) renegotiation-proof payoffs. Barrett (1999a) refers to a (weakly) renegotiation-proof treaty as 'weakly collectively rational' if it gives countries the maximum payoff satisfying (14) and (15).

It bears noting that the efficient payoff Π^c of the stage game need not be sustained in a weakly collectively rational equilibrium of the N-player supergame. This depends on the economics of the environmental problem at hand, on the number of countries, on the countries' discount factors, on the punishment imposed as well as on feasibility constraints the choice of the reparation q_j^j is subject to (Barrett 1994a, 1999a, Finus and Rundshagen 1998).

With respect to the size of an agreement that sustains the efficient abatement levels q^c, the supergame framework yields similar results as the participation game. Barrett (1994b, 1999a) finds that the full cooperative outcome $\Pi^w = \Pi^c$ can be sustained in a renegotiation-proof agreement comprising at most three countries when free riding is orthogonal. In the presence of non-orthogonal free riding Barrett's simulations confirm the paradoxical result derived in the participation game: Participation in a renegotiation-proof IEA is close to full when the gains to cooperation are relatively small. Conversely, if full cooperation significantly improves upon the non-cooperative outcome then a self-enforcing agreement either remains incomplete or else cannot assign first-best policy targets to its members even though participation is full.

Consensus treaties

Given that full cooperation is not enforceable, diplomats have more options than negotiating either partial cooperation or no agreement at all. Instead, they may agree to provide the maximal abatement level that preserves self-enforceability for all N countries. Formally, the treaty adopts a weakly collectively rational strategy that gives all N countries a payoff $\Pi^w < \Pi^c$ satisfying (14) and (15). Barrett (1999a) refers to this type of treaty as a consensus treaty. A consensus treaty is a self-enforcing agreement with full *participation*, but signatories choose abatement levels that fall short of the full *cooperative* levels q^c.

The merit of consensus treaties resides in the fact that there is no *individual* free riding as is the case when the agreement remains incomplete. Instead, the parties to a consensus treaty take a *collective* free ride. Therefore, the observation that participation in many international environmental agreements is close to full must not hide the fact that 'free riding has different guises' (Barrett 1999a, p. 23). Notice that this model provides a rationale for Downs, Rocke and Barsoom's conjecture that countries prefer low obligations while also explaining the Chayes' (1995) observation that actual treaties incorporate few enforcement mechanisms. The synthesis of these approaches is that reciprocity does enforce a certain level of international cooperation, but this level falls well short of the efficient one.

If full cooperation cannot be enforced, do signatories prefer a consensus treaty to an incomplete agreement? The literature is indecisive on this point. If the number of countries is sufficiently large, symmetric countries prefer a broad but shallow agreement which amounts to free riding collectively (Barrett 1999a). By contrast, asymmetric countries would rather opt for the incomplete agreement (Finus and Rundshagen 1998).

Finally, a fundamental result of the supergame framework is that the scope for cooperation narrows if countries have a high time preference. This is intuitive because impatient countries care very little about future punishments and thus cannot easily be prevented from free riding.

3. Enforcement strategies and political economy

The studies reviewed so far arrive at the conclusion that a self-enforcing IEA may remain incomplete if strategic interaction is limited to the environmental policy variable. These models give insight into how the economics of a particular environmental problem basically influence the countries' incentives to participate in its mitigation. However, the game of international environmental cooperation certainly is more complex and players control more than just one strategic choice variable. It is also important to take account of interference and reinforcement effects arising from the interaction of IEAs with markets and governments. This section recasts the analysis in a richer game theoretic environment and looks at political economy issues that affect the design of a stable IEA.

3.1. *Minimum participation*

Many IEAs contain a minimum participation clause which stipulates that the treaty does not enter into force unless it is ratified by at least a critical number of countries. Sometimes additional criteria are specified. For example, the obligations laid down in the Kyoto Protocol become binding only after being ratified by not less than 55 countries, including Annex I countries that account for at least 55% of Annex I CO_2 emissions in 1990.

From a theoretical point-of-view the role of these clauses is contentious. Some authors believe that a clause prescribing a minimum participation number k^+ is always capable of enforcing cooperation provided that participation is profitable. They argue that setting $k^+ = N$ sustains full cooperation because, if a country fails to sign the agreement, all countries revert to the non-cooperative equilibrium which makes them worse off (Nash reversion). This threat to enforce participation is relied upon in the cooperative strand of the literature, as e.g. in Chander and Tulkens (1995, 1997).

When there is uncertainty about the benefits of abatement, a minimum participation level of $k^+ = N$ may no longer be optimal in this framework (Black, Levi and de Meza 1993). While the gains to cooperation are increasing in k^+ due to less free riding, the *expected value* of these gains may decrease as k^+ approaches N. This is because the probability that no country fails to ratify the treaty tends to be very low, and so setting $k^+ = N$ is likely to prevent the agreement from ever entering into force. Simulations in Black *et al.* (1993) demonstrate that maximization of the expected gains may require a minimum level significantly below full cooperation. This result is consistent with the fact that minimum participation levels in actual IEAs stipulate far less than full cooperation, especially so when a large number of parties is involved. However, the analysis does not reveal how this level could be determined endogenously.

A more fundamental objection has been raised with respect to the threat of Nash reversion which is supposed to sustain cooperation of a minimum coalition (Barrett 1995). Assume that $1 < k^* < N$ is the only stable agreement satisfying the stability conditions (12) whereas the treaty stipulates a minimum participation level of $k^+ = N$. Can this provision sustain the full cooperative outcome? In a non-cooperative environment the answer must be no. Free riding incentives are strongest in the full cooperative outcome and this is why ratification is not rational for the Nth country. On the other hand, cooperation does not completely unravel when the minimum participation is not achieved. This is because exactly k^* countries will renegotiate to form a self-enforcing agreement, and the remaining $N - k^*$ countries benefit from free riding on this treaty. Hence, given the existence of a non-trivial self-enforcing coalition, enforcement cannot be based on a minimum participation clause (Barrett 1998b).

Nevertheless a minimum participation clause can serve as an important coordination device when full cooperation is sustained as an equilibrium but its selection is at risk due to the existence of an inferior equilibrium. That is, diplomats play a coordination game and the minimum participation rule can provide for the selection of the good equilibrium. As long as ratification falls short of the minimum participation level, the bad equilibrium will be reached and hence no country loses by ratifying the agreement. If the minimum participation requirement is matched, however, the Pareto-superior outcome is sustained as a subgame perfect equilibrium, and so the clause makes ratification a weakly dominant strategy (Barrett 1998b).

3.2. Transfers

Another striking feature of environmental treaties at both the national and the international scale is that they incorporate provisions for transferring resources among signatories and/or from signatories to acceding parties. Transfers are given either cash or in kind.

Monetary side payments form an integral constituent of numerous international agreements in various domains of world politics. One can distinguish between direct bilateral payments as, for example, in the North Pacific Fur Seal Treaty and indirect payments made via multilateral environmental funds, like, for example, the Global Environmental Facility maintained by the World Bank and the Multilateral Fund established in the 1990 London Amendments to the Montreal Protocol. In-kind transfers include direct investments, technical assistance and financial aid for projects controlled by the donor.

IEAs incorporate transfers for different reasons. As was mentioned earlier, an appropriate transfer scheme among asymmetric countries makes sure that participation in a cost-effective IEA is profitable for each party. Apart from that, signatories can use transfers to induce non-signatories to accede to an initially incomplete agreement. That is, non-signatories are compensated for the 'incremental cost' they incur upon acceding to the treaty and complying with its obligations. Since this incremental cost amounts to the foregone gain from free riding, such transfers serve as a free rider deterrent.

Theoretical research has dealt with two issues in this context. One is the question whether transfers to non-signatories can broaden an initially stable but incomplete agreement. The other relates to the risk that either party of the transfer agreement does not comply with its obligations.

Enlargement

Several papers examine the enlargement issue in the participation game framework. When the game is played by identical countries the stability conditions (12) preclude enlargement of an originally stable coalition of k^* countries by self-financed transfers. Self-financed transfers would help enlarge a self-enforcing agreement only if a group of countries were committed to taking over the burden (Carraro and Siniscalco 1993). Heister, Mohr, Stähler, Stoll and Wolfrum (1997) argue that this assumption is justified only if the countries in the donor coalition succeed in establishing stable cooperation among themselves. In fact, since the setting of international environmental negotiations is essentially non-cooperative, negotiators cannot expect to take the second step — enlargement — before having mastered the first: stabilization.

It is intuitive that transfers become more important as we allow for asymmetries between countries. Barrett (1998a) distinguishes between two types of players — rich and poor countries — and augments a linear version of the participation game by including side payments. Costs and benefits are such that the poor countries prefer to stay outside the agreement regardless of the number of signatories. Therefore, in the absence of transfers only a subset of rich countries join a self-enforcing agreement. By contrast, when rich signatories compensate poor non-parties for the incremental cost of complying with the agreement then all poor countries accept transfers and participation by rich countries is higher than before. The model shows that *strong* asymmetries can substitute for the commitment assumption made by Carraro and Siniscalco (1993). Furthermore, it illustrates how side payments in the Montreal Protocol encouraged accession by developing countries and transition economies. These countries joined the Protocol only after it had been amended to compensate them for the incremental cost of participating through a Multilateral Fund and the Global Environmental Facility.

It is essential, however, that care be taken not to offer transfers to countries which would have joined the agreement anyway. Clearly, the prospect of receiving a transfer when staying outside the agreement gives a country a further disincentive to accede in the first place. The success of transfers thus depends on which countries are entitled to receive them.

Hoel and Schneider (1997) demonstrate this in the framework of a participation game where countries differ with respect to a 'non-compliance cost' they incur as non-signatories. This cost is supposed to arise from various exogenous factors like, for example, social norms or trade sanctions (Elster 1989, Heister 1993, Barrett 1997b). Hoel and Schneider show that side payments result in a lower participation rate. This is because non-signatories are rewarded with a transfer that enhances the *ex ante* incentive to free ride. In equilibrium signatories choose lower policy levels than in the benchmark scenario whereas non-signatories are paid for choosing higher ones. Hence, the effect on aggregate environmental protection is ambiguous. From a number of simulations, Hoel and Schneider conclude that the effect of side payments on the aggregate level of environmental protection is likely to be negative, too.

A fundamental reason for this result is that the non-compliance cost works in favor of a larger coalition than in the participation game without transfers. In fact, the cost is more stabilizing than the side payments. From this we might conclude that 'sticks' are better suited than 'carrots' to broaden an IEA. This conclusion, however, is shaky. Taking the non-compliance cost to be exogenous misses the fact that sanctions are generally costly for those countries called upon to impose them. Sanctions may thus lack credibility, which in turn renders them ineffective. I shall come back to this point below.

Compliance

A payment that compensates for the incremental cost of participating in an IEA is a form of agreement between donor and recipient. As such, it is subject to the risk of non-compliance just like the actual treaty it is part of. Whenever a side payment is made prior to the fulfillment of the associated obligations, the recipient's best reply is to accept the money and to free ride anyway. Conversely, if the recipient moves first and undertakes irreversible investment in abatement technology the donor country has an incentive to refuse to give the negotiated support.

Misappropriate use of transfers is easiest when transfers are given in cash. Clearly, money adds to the recipient country's welfare without restricting its strategy space. Donors may earmark payments but international law does not provide them with an effective means to control the purpose to which their money is put, once that it has reached its destination. Governmental development aid is probably the best example (Heister 1997).

To enforce compliance with a transfer agreement, the donor can make payments as a perpetual rent. Unlike a single payment, regular payments provide the donor country with a strategic choice variable. This renders the transfer contract a supergame: Donor and recipient interact repeatedly by choosing between a cooperative and a non-cooperative move in every subgame. Consequently, the donor can behave strategically to induce the recipient to fulfill the obligations tied to the side payment. As in the actual agreement, strategies of reciprocity are capable of sustaining a favorable equilibrium.

Heister (1997) casts the transfer agreement in a supergame where compliance is enforced by means of strategies of reciprocity. These strategies are tailored in such a way that defecting does not give a recipient country a higher continuation payoff than complying with its obligations. Moreover, when the recipient cheats donors do not renege on the punishment they agreed upon in the first place. A renegotiation-proof punishment consists of suspending side payments while the recipient reverts to a cooperative policy level or undertakes abatement beyond that level for a pre-specified number of periods.

Heister shows that an incentive compatible transfer not only covers the incremental cost but is augmented by a 'sovereignty rent' which counterbalances the incentive to misappropriate the transfer. The higher is the recipient's time preference the higher must be the sovereignty rent to enforce compliance. The logic behind this is that an impatient country cares less about future payoffs than a patient one. Therefore, when punished by a suspension of payments in future periods, the impatient country must be given a higher sovereignty rent than the patient country for both countries to suffer the same loss in present value.

Another way to mitigate the sovereignty risk associated with welfare transfers is by making transfers in kind (Heister et al. 1997). In general, in-kind transfers are less flexible than cash transfers because resale to other countries or reallocation to other sectors of the recipient's economy is associated with a cost. This is advantageous for the donor because it reduces the incentive to put transfers to purposes other than they were earmarked for. When the cost of retrading or reallocating an in-kind transfer covers its total value the incentive to do so completely vanishes. It is for this reason that the sovereignty rent is decreasing in the cost of reallocation and nil when the transfer is sunk (Wagner 2000). This suggests that a donor country would rather give side payments in kind than in cash to compensate the recipient for a given incremental cost (Stähler 1995).

However, it sometimes proves impossible to transfer only the incremental cost of complying with the agreement. For example, if a transfer consists of direct investment in clean technology, its full cost generally exceeds the incremental cost the recipient country actually incurs (Heister 1997). Hence, an in-kind transfer is unnecessarily high and entails a welfare loss on the donor side unless the recipient pays back the difference.

In addition to a positive cost of reallocation, there is yet another factor that can render payments in kind a superior strategy. In fact, the donor might transfer irreversible technology that guarantees a certain minimum abatement level for the time it is being used. Unlike a monetary payment, the transfer of irreversible technology produces a ratchet effect on the recipient country's emissions and thereby credibly restrains its free riding option (Heister *et al.* 1997). The compliance risk is reduced for either side of the treaty. Therefore, it may be rational for donors to transfer irreversible technology even though it is more expensive than a cash payment (Stähler 1996).

Finally, if payments are administered by a multilateral fund with various contributors, the risk of non-compliance extends to the coalition of donors. For example, the Convention on Biological Diversity stipulates that developed countries should provide funds to developing countries to cover the incremental cost of biodiversity conservation. Economically, the contribution of financial resources to a multilateral fund is equivalent to the provision of a public good. Hence, the game played by donors can be modeled in a similar way as the abatement supergame, and strategies of reciprocity can be employed to enforce compliance. The results obtained in such a framework thus do not differ much from those reported above (Barrett 1994a).

3.3 *Leakage*

So far our concern has been with multilateral agreements that concern a single environmental issue. This implies the presumption that IEAs are stand-alone contracts which are isolated from other spheres of the world economy and international politics. In the real world, however, environmental policy is only one out of a variety of domains in international relations. The different issues interact with each other in a complex manner, ranging from interference to mutual reinforcement.

For instance, IEAs interact with markets. Suppose an agreement prescribes a standard for pollution emissions by a specific sector of production. Then comparative advantage in the pollution-intensive industries may shift to non-signatories because pollution abatement is costly. Under a free trade regime, pollution-intensive industries in non-signatory countries become more competitive and boost output and emissions. This phenomenon is called *trade leakage*. While signatories clean up the environment non-signatory countries turn into so-called 'pollution havens'.

A consequence of leakage is that global emissions fall by less than the original reduction undertaken by the signatory states. This implies that leakage reduces the signatories' net benefits from pollution abatement. Worse, trade leakage enhances the *ex ante* incentives to free ride: If the positive spillovers from abatement in the signatory states plus the gain in world market share is large enough then being a 'pollution haven' is more attractive than being a signatory (Barrett 1997b).

Trade leakage in developing countries was a cause for concern in the Montreal Protocol (Benedick 1998). With regard to a climate change treaty it is feared that trade leakage is worsened by adjustment effects in the energy market (Pezzey 1992, Hoel 1994). Suppose, for example, that Annex I countries reach the Kyoto emission targets. Factor substitution in energy-intensive sectors may result in a shrinking demand for fossil fuels in Annex I countries. This in turn would cause world market prices for fossil fuels to fall. As a consequence, energy consumption in non-Annex I countries would probably go up and thereby cause a further increase in global emissions (Barrett 1998c).

A measure of carbon leakage is the so-called leakage rate which denotes the increase in carbon emissions in non-Annex I countries per ton of carbon reduced in Annex I countries. Estimates for the leakage rate in the Kyoto Protocol are obtained from simulation studies based on computable general equilibrium models. The majority of them predict a positive leakage rate with estimates ranging from 5% up to 35% (Paltsev 2000, Springer 2001).

Yet not all economists believe in the relevance of such numbers. Grubb (2000a) objects that 'these models do not take account of the implications of induced technical change and its international diffusion, which is a positive factor tending to offset the negative aspects [of] leakage' (p. 30). In a recent paper Copeland and Taylor (2000) emphasize the ambiguous workings of the income effect that arises from the very terms of trade improvement that also causes trade leakage. They argue that this 'bootstrap' effect limits or even reverts trade leakage when environmental quality is a normal good.

I shall not go further into the debate on leakage here but maintain the focus on stabilization of IEAs. The reader should bear in mind, however, that stabilizing an IEA ultimately resolves the leakage problem when all countries join the agreement.

3.4. *Issue linkage*

As the previous discussion has shown, *automatic* links such as trade leakage alter the incentives to join an IEA. On the other hand, the diversity in international politics gives rise to *strategic* issue linkage. This means that negotiators deliberately link two or more issues to each other in a single agreement so as to render cooperation attractive to as many parties as possible (Tollison and Willett 1979, Raiffa 1982, Sebenius 1983). For example, it has been argued that participation of developing countries in the Rio Earth Summit in 1992 was close to full solely because the topics of global environmental protection and economic development were linked to each other (Heister, Klepper and Stähler 1992).

Strategic linkage in multilateral environmental negotiations may substitute for side payments to enforce compliance. But unlike side payments, making concessions in other policy domains is not associated with a bad reputation (Mäler 1990) or a 'psychic cost of being labeled a weak negotiator' (Folmer, v. Mouche and Ragland 1993, p. 325). It thus cannot be surprising that countries seem to prefer this instrument to making side payments. Cesar and de Zeeuw (1996) explain this observation by the reluctance of countries to reveal their precise willingness to pay.

Conversely, sanctions can be regarded as the suspension of strategic links. For example, signatories to an IEA may restrict trade with non-signatories in order to deter free riding (Heister 1993, Barrett 1997b). Strategic linkage of trade and environment has the advantage that the automatic links mentioned above are explicitly accounted for. This is important if the success of an agreement is at risk due to trade leakage. Moreover, the gains from free trade are a club good, so that any country can be excluded from its benefits by means of appropriate trade sanctions. If the threat to impose them is credible, trade sanctions can effectively deter free riding without necessarily being carried out.

Barrett (1997b) demonstrates this point by linking the participation game to a model of international trade with imperfect competition in segmented markets. He shows that signatories to an agreement can deter free riding by threatening to restrict trade with non-signatories. The trade ban plugs the trade leak. Hence, a non-signatory is faced with a smaller market and thus reduces output and emissions. This in turn improves environmental quality and raises firm profits in the signatory countries. To the extent that these positive effects compensate for the deadweight loss arising from a smaller number of suppliers the threat to impose trade sanctions is credible. It transforms the participation game into a coordination game where a minimum participation clause provides for the selection of the favorable equilibrium.

Barrett argues that trade sanctions in the Montreal Protocol have worked this way to encourage accession of developing countries. As a matter of fact, participation in this treaty is close to full and sanctions were never carried out. This is consistent with the game theoretical logic that credible punishments need not be carried out in equilibrium. Moreover, it helps explain the remarkable observation that no country has officially objected to the sanctions although they violate the non-discrimination principle of the GATT/WTO.

The clashing of trade sanctions with multilateral trading rules demonstrates that, despite its virtuous effects, strategic issue linkage can also backfire. As Cesar and de Zeeuw (1996) put it, 'linkage may create too many hostages' (p. 160). They allude to the fact that linked negotiations on several issues might become too complex, drive up decision costs and increase the risk of unintentionally harmful consequences (Sebenius 1983).

Carraro and Siniscalco (1997) and Botteon and Carraro (1996) suggest that technological cooperation can be a suitable linkage issue to stabilize an IEA. They link a game of R&D cooperation among oligopolist firms to the participation game. R&D is supposed to lower both per unit cost of output and its associated emissions. As in the trade game, the threat to exclude non-signatories from R&D cooperation drives all countries into the agreement. However, the credibility of this threat is undermined if signatories do not have effective technical means to prevent technology spillovers.

Unlike the assumptions in Carraro and Siniscalco (1997) but nevertheless likely, R&D spillovers might reduce the cost of abatement. This effect raises non-cooperative abatement levels in the non-signatory states *ceteris paribus*, which is why signatories would have no incentive to exclude them from cooperative R&D. In other words, R&D spillovers are an important transmission channel for cost interdepencies (Heal 1993) that eventually render abatement a strategic complement. Then exclusion from R&D is not credible, either.

Technically speaking, strategic linkage corresponds to an extension of the strategy space that is aimed to increase the number of equilibria which sustain full cooperation. We have just seen that this can be achieved by linking the participation game to the provision of a club good (Carraro and Siniscalco 1998). Issue linkage in a supergame framework, on the other hand, increases the scope for reciprocity by allowing for asymmetric retaliation. A drawback is that linkage quickly inflates mathematical complexity in that model framework.

For a simple illustration, suppose N players interact repeatedly in two games, game A and game B. We say that games A and B are interconnected if players are free to choose strategies that condition their actions in game A on past moves of the other players in game B, and vice versa (Folmer et al. 1993). Deviant behavior in game A may thus be punished by retaliation in game A, in game B, or in both games.

Interconnected supergames have favorable, non-trivial equilibria when countries are asymmetric. Folmer et al. (1993) give an example where two countries are asymmetrically affected in a game of transboundary pollution and a trade game. If countries negotiate these issues separately they can only reach an agreement by means of side payments which reduce welfare due to a 'psychic cost'. By contrast, when both issues are negotiated jointly the downstream country can make trade concessions to the upstream country conditional on pollution reductions in that country. This way an agreement is reached without side payments because the favorable outcome can be sustained by a so-called multi-trigger strategy that punishes a deviation in either of the games by indefinite reversion to the Nash equilibria in both games.

As was pointed out earlier, a drawback of the (multi-)trigger strategy is its lack of credibility. Cesar and de Zeeuw (1996) ensure the credibility of punishments by employing renegotiation-proof strategies in a game of linked negotiations. They look at a two-player prisoners' dilemma D with strongly asymmetric payoffs: In the cooperative outcome, player one is driven below her minimax payoff whereas player two's payoff is so high that this outcome nevertheless maximizes joint payoffs. When the game D is repeated ad infinitum the cooperative outcome cannot be sustained because it gives player one a payoff that is not individually rational (Fudenberg and Maskin 1986). Given that players cannot modify the payoff matrix through side payments, the only way to reach the Pareto efficient outcome is by linking the asymmetric prisoners' dilemma to its mirror image game D'. Since asymmetries exactly offset, linkage transforms the interconnected game into a symmetric prisoners dilemma where both players realize individually rational payoffs in the cooperative outcome. In this game full cooperation can be sustained in a renegotiation-proof equilibrium when players threaten to punish a deviation in both issues (van Damme 1989). Cesar and de Zeeuw invoke this result to demonstrate that linkage of two roughly offsetting issues in an IEA is beneficial to either party and can substitute for unpopular side payments.

Finally, mention should be made of theoretical research that inquires into the linkage of IEAs to international debt. In a deterministic model of international debt and intertemporal trade in emission permits, Mohr (1995) assumes that private lenders and public environmental agencies in the creditor country commit to jointly punish non-compliance with either the environmental treaty or the debt contract. Analogous to multi-trigger strategies, such a cross-default scheme provides for the stability of both contracts. Moreover, the threat to jointly punish any violation is credible because the cross-default contract is enforceable through domestic jurisdiction in the creditor country. Mohr and Thomas (1998) show that risk pooling in a cross-default contract may mitigate the sovereignty problem facing the parties to the cross-default contract. They also derive conditions under which the cross-default contract sets the stage for welfare-enhancing debt-for-nature-swaps.

3.5. Negotiating an agreement

To gain a deeper understanding of the design of IEAs it is also enlightening to take a closer look at the actual negotiation process. Countries face incentives for strategic behavior even before treaties are formalized. These concern the choice of a specific policy target as well as the rules and mechanisms guiding the negotiations.

The choice of policy targets

When it comes to setting explicit emission targets, many IEAs on pollution control prescribe uniform quota reductions that apply to the emission level in a base year. Uniform percentage reductions hardly coincide with cost-effective solutions, but it has been argued that they represent 'focal points' in the bargaining process (Barrett 1992, Schelling 1960). The choice of a base year in the past removes the incentive facing a country to increase emissions in the run-up to the negotiations with the objective of reducing its expected burden.

Another adverse incentive emerges when the IEA stipulates 'targets and timetables' for pollution control, that is, when it is known from the beginning that emission caps are not permanent. This gives rise to strategic underinvestment in abatement technology because extensive investments that substantially lower variable abatement cost will compromise a country's bargaining position in future negotiation rounds. Clearly, the country is likely to be assigned a higher abatement target (Barrett 1998c). By contrast, a cost-inferior technology lowers its best-reply level of abatement — its threat point — in subsequent negotiations. In a simple two-stage game Buchholz and Konrad (1994) demonstrate that these incentives may ultimately cause a race to the bottom.

Establishing permanent emission caps, on the other hand, is not a reliable remedy to the problem because the parties to a treaty are free to renegotiate them at any time. As a result the sheer belief that tight emission caps will be reneged upon in the near future induces a country to underinvest in abatement technology. Worse, such beliefs might prove self-fulfilling (Barrett 1998c).

Empirical evidence lends some support to the hypothesized positive relationship between past reductions and future targets. For example, the Oslo Protocol of

1994 assigned higher reduction targets for sulphur emissons to countries that had already achieved higher current cutbacks (Murdoch, Sandler and Sargent 1997). The amendments to the Montreal Protocol followed a similar pattern and culminated in a complete phase out. These developments hardly characterize a race to the bottom. On the other hand, as noted earlier, they do not necessarily correspond to the full cooperative outcome of an abatement game either. To the extent that further cutbacks can be explained by GDP growth in a statistically significant magnitude they may instead reflect Nash behavior (Murdoch and Sandler 1997, Murdoch *et al.* 1997).

The negotiation process

The large number of countries involved in many IEAs entails the necessity of organizing the negotiation process so as to keep transaction cost reasonably low. This requires that the process follow certain rules and adopt mechanisms that facilitate bargaining. These rules and mechanisms, however, can be expected to affect the outcomes we observe.

For example, the Intergovernmental Negotiation Committee (INC) that drafted the Framework Convention on Climate Change was subdivided into separate negotiating groups. Although the INC rules allowed for decisions to be taken by vote negotiators chose to negotiate by consensus (Barrett 1998b).

Moreover, the INC worked with a single negotiating text. A single negotiating text is a customary starting point in large-scale negotiations because it is more efficient than having multiple texts in circulation. By agreeing in advance and submitting a basic negotiating text, blocs of nations might attempt to get an advantage in framing the approach to subsequent discussions (Benedick 2000).

Sometimes a deadline is imposed to accelerate negotiations when a final text has to be drafted. For example, the United Nations General Assembly demanded that the Framework Convention be ready for signing in Rio 1992. We ignore what the INC would have negotiated without this deadline, but we know that self-imposed deadlines are not credible. Countries are free to renegotiate at any time and they are willing to do so if there are mutual gains to realize. A recent example for this is the sixth session of the Conference of Parties to the Framework Convention. As no agreement could be reached on key political issues of the Kyoto Protocol, negotiators suspended talks and scheduled a 'resumed sixth session of the Conference of Parties'[7] six months later.

On the other hand, it can be argued that symbolic deadlines raise expectations of the public and thereby exert political pressure on negotiators. I shall discuss such domestic influences now in further detail.

3.6 Ratification

The literature on IEAs predominantly treats states as monoliths, in the sense that the game of international negotiations is played by benevolent planners. Yet in reality the outcome of the negotiations also reflects the dependence of policymakers upon *domestic* pressure groups among which they seek support to maintain themselves in office. Putnam (1988) concludes that international negotiations is a game played at two levels — at the international scale *and* at the domestic level.

Domestic pressure manifests itself in the requirement that a state's national parliament ratify an IEA before it becomes legally binding for that state. In taking up Putnam's notion of two level games, Barrett (1998b) gives an outline of a ratification game in two stages. In the first stage diplomats negotiate a tentative agreement which in stage two comes before national parliaments for ratification. Solving this game backwards for the subgame perfect equilibrium establishes the equivalence to Putnam's stylized chief negotiator who 'has no independent policy preferences, but seeks simply to achieve an agreement that will be attractive to his constituents' (Putnam 1988, p. 435–6).

The logic of two level games is illustrated by the U.S. Senate's 95–0 vote on the Byrd–Hagel resolution which stated that the Senate would not ratify a global CO_2-treaty that would exempt developing countries from emission reductions. The timing of the resolution — five months before the Kyoto negotiations — suggests that it was intended to alter the stance of the Clinton Administration in the negotiations (Barrett 1998b). Since the resolution was common knowledge it could also have influenced behavior of other countries involved in the negotiations and of course it might have been intended to do so.

Not much of the theoretical work on IEAs has allowed for negotiations at two levels. Currarini and Tulkens (1998) construct a *cooperative* negotiation game in which a country only ratifies the agreement if a majority of domestic voters does not have a preferred proposal. Meyne (1997) models the stage-two game at the national level by assigning probabilities for an agreement to be ratified. Since the game is solved backwards, a country's expected gain from joining the agreement depends on the probability that it is ratified. If integrated into the participation game framework, ratification probabilities enter the stability conditions (12) and so become decisive for the size of a stable agreement. However, the model does not determine ratification probabilities endogenously.

Econometric studies give some evidence for the two level logic, though necessarily at a more aggregate level. Congleton (1992) finds that the political regime prevailing in a country had a significant impact on the stringency of environmental regulation for ozone depleting substances in the mid-1980s. His cross-sectional regression analysis lends support to the hypothesis that democratic countries imposed significantly higher environmental standards than authoritarian regimes. Congleton explains this by the presumably shorter time horizon and the lower degree of risk aversion of an authoritarian leader as compared to the median voter who is taken to be his democratic counterpart.

Fredriksson and Gaston (1999) confirm the importance of civil liberties in the context of the ratification of the UN Framework Convention for Climate Change. A hazard rate analysis leads them to the conclusion that countries with a higher degree of political freedoms and civil liberties — as measured by an index by Gastil (1987) — were quicker to ratify the Convention than those with less liberal societies.

Rothfels (1997) assumes that national governments maximize a weighted average of pressure groups' utilities and econometrically estimates their influence on the voluntary CO_2 reduction targets some OECD countries brought to the bargaining table in Rio 1992. Her results suggest that both a higher donation to GREENPEACE per unit of GDP — as a proxy for pressure by environmentalists — as well as higher share of non-CO_2-intensive sectors in GDP had a significantly positive effect on reduction targets.

It must be emphasized, however, that the emission targets explained by these variables correspond to voluntary announcements made in the run-up to Rio. The reduction targets agreed upon in Kyoto were much more modest, and most OECD countries are well on track to miss even these. Therefore, Rothfels's regression model rather explains why governments engage in cheap talk before it comes to lay down obligations in an IEA.

3.7. Dynamic treaties

The theory of infinitely repeated games we have used above highlights the fact that international cooperation for the environment is better represented as a process than an as outcome. In effect, countries are involved in 'continuous dealings' (Congleton 1995) but in reality this process depends much more on history than is allowed for in a supergame.

Modern IEAs develop over time and the development follows typical patterns: countries first agree on an umbrella convention which provides for the establishment of institutions such as the Conference of Parties as a supreme body entitled to negotiate all subsequent protocols and amendments, a secretariat that is in charge of the administration, and subsidiary bodies for scientific advice and implementation. As a rule precise environmental regulations are put into writing only at later meetings of the Conference of Parties when protocols or amendments are negotiated.

Note that a party to the umbrella convention is not obliged to ratify all subsequent protocols. Murdoch et al. (1997) argue that this freedom of choice enhanced effectiveness of the Convention on Long-Range Transboundary Pollution because emission targets for sulphur and nitrogen oxide were prescribed in separate protocols. This allowed for more of a differential treatment of the parties to the convention, for patterns of emissions varied substantially across member states.

Congleton (1995) integrates these features of the treaty-making process in his transaction cost theory of IEAs. He distinguishes between symbolic, procedural and substantive treaties, and contends that treaty-making proceeds in stages following this order. Before taking a further step towards a substantive agreement, a country rationally weighs the associated expected benefits and opportunity cost. The deepening of a treaty results in a higher probability for a substantive treaty to eventually be reached but, on the other hand, simultaneously increases transaction cost. This is because a more substantial environmental standard takes longer to be negotiated and agreed upon than just a symbolic recognition of potential mutual gains from cooperation. The process may also get stuck before a substantive agreement is reached, which helps explain why symbolic and procedural treaties are more common to observe.

Heister *et al.* (1997) point out that dynamic treaties tie its parties into a repeated bargaining process that allows for revision and readjustments of a treaty when the basic conditions change. These authors conclude that if adjustments are not arbitrary but follow pre-specified rules and conditions then a dynamic regime with institutionalized forms of discussion and negotiation is well suited to stabilize an IEA.

4. Conclusions

Free riding incentives jeopardize cooperation in a multilateral agreement aimed to maintain an internationally shared common property resource. Since the sovereignty of states precludes external enforcement, IEAs must be designed in such a way that participation is self-enforcing.

When strategic interaction is limited to a single environmental choice variable such as abatement, the member states of a self-enforcing agreement punish non-cooperative behavior by reducing their abatement levels and demand that a deviant country make amends before cooperation is resumed. The theory shows that this reciprocal mechanism is too weak to enforce a full cooperative solution when it is most needed. In addition, punishments via the environmental externality are in reality restricted by technological and political factors. Hence, IEAs need to employ further stabilizing instruments.

Many international treaties provide for transfer payments in cash or in kind to induce free riders to accede. This instrument may substantially broaden an agreement but it also has limitations. First, the prospect of receiving a payment gives a disincentive for accession in the first place. Second, the transfer agreement must be self-enforcing as well. Third, transfers possibly affect the donor's reputation in future negotiations.

Rather than to transfer resources, negotiators will thus be willing to make concessions in other domains of international politics. If concessions in the linked issue are conditional on participation in the IEA they act like a side payment to enforce compliance. Conversely, their withdrawal is an effective sanction to punish non-compliance. Trade sanctions may stabilize an agreement, but in general this instrument is incompatible with multilateral trading rules. Besides trade, economists analyzed the special cases of linkage to R&D cooperation and to international debt.

More subtle linkages in international politics are manifested in a country's reputation. Failure to cooperate in a given issue automatically reduces a country's credibility when other issues are on the agenda. Similarly, one might ask to what extent social norms matter in environmental diplomacy. These phenomena are not yet well understood and future research on the formation of IEAs ought to address them.

Furthermore, we have seen that every stage of the negotiation process gives rise to strategic behavior. The rules and procedures adopted in this process are thus relevant for the outcomes we observe. Also strategic interaction between negotiators and domestic groups must be taken into account. Empirical research highlights the importance of domestic factors influencing international environmental negotiations but the theoretical literature has largely disregarded this point so far.

Finally, the notion of dynamic treaties stresses the aspect of historical dependence in environmental treaty-making. A dynamic IEA is characterized by the succession of treaties all of which employ stabilizing instruments to establish a temporary equilibrium. This repeated bargaining results in a more process-oriented stability of IEAs. However, a coherent theory of dynamic treaties has yet to be developed.

In sum, the theory of international environmental cooperation that economists have developed over the past decade explains how and to what extent the design of environmental treaties can give incentives for participation. If future research proceeds at this pace and mends the shortcomings mentioned in the preceding paragraphs, we can expect the theory to further improve our understanding of how the international community can take collective action for the mitigation of challenging environmental problems today and in the future.

Acknowledgements

I would like to thank my supervisor Frank Stähler for his open-minded and encouraging support. I am grateful to Scott Barrett for the excellent environmental economics course he taught in the Kiel Institute's Advanced Studies Program in December 1999 and for very fruitful discussions. I am indebted to Christiane Kasten, Nick Hanley and Gernot Klepper who carefully read through previous versions of the paper, pointed out mistakes to me and made suggestions which lead to significant improvements of the paper. All remaining mistakes are mine.

Notes

1. A survey on applications of cooperative solution concepts to transboundary pollution problems is in Missfeldt (1999).
2. Of course, this point is controversial. Grubb (2000b) points out that the Kyoto Protocol '— the culmination of several years of intensive negotiation ... — represents a huge advance that economists should welcome' (p. 234). By contrast, Nordhaus and Boyer (1998) give the key-note for a 'requiem for the Kyoto Protocol' which reflects the believe held by some economists that the Protocol will prove a 'dead duck' (Nordhaus 1998).
3. The stability concept at hand originated in the literature on price collusion and stable cartels in oligopolistic markets and is due to d'Aspremont, Jacquemin, Gabszewicz and Weymark (1983). If one allows for more than a single coalition the definition generalizes to the notion of coalition-proof Nash equilibrium (CPNE) defined by Bernheim, Peleg and Whinston (1987). Bloch (1997) applies CPNE to the participation game and Bauer (1992) uses an alternative equilibrium concept that allows for the formation of multiple coalitions. Neither of these concepts sustains the full cooperative outcome, but the global provision of abatement is higher than with a single agreement.
4. The Shapley value (Shapley 1953) maps the worth of a coalition to a unique payoff

allocation rule that satisfies the axioms of the Nash bargaining solution (Nash 1950, Nash 1953). In particular, this allocation is symmetric with respect to a permutation, lies in the core of the game, and satisfies individual rationality, see e.g. Myerson (1991).

5. Another approach to modeling strategic interaction in the emission of stock pollutants such as greenhouse gases is by employing differential game theory that allows for stock-dependent strategies. Solving these mathematically complex models, however, requires that very restrictive assumptions be made which cannot be given a meaningful interpretation in the context of IEAs. Moreover, the supergame framework is justified because countries usually do not negotiate abatement *trajectories* but — as is the case in the Kyoto Protocol — specify abatement *levels* that they renegotiate at a future meeting (Chander, Tulkens, van Ypersele and Willems 1999). A standard text on differential games is Basar and Olsder (1982), de Zeeuw (1998) gives an introduction to applications in environmental economics and Missfeldt (1999) summarizes some of the main results of this literature.

6. As players start out in the 'good' equilibrium they do behave in a collectively rational manner. In the punishment phase, however, they abandon collective rationality and repeat the 'bad' equilibrium *ad infinitum*. Mohr (1988) argues that such a change in rationality clashes with the theory of infinitely repeated games in that it implicitly modifies the *structure* of the game.

7. Press release of November 25, 2000, published on the COP-6 web site, see *http://cop6.unfccc.int/pdf/pressreloutcome1.pdf*.

References

Barrett, S. (1990) The problem of global environmental protection. *Oxford Review of Economic Policy*, 6, 1, 68–79.

—— (1991a) Economic analysis of international environmental agreements: Lessons for a global warming treaty. In OECD (ed.), *Responding to Climate Change: Selected Economic Issues*, OECD, Paris, chapter 3, 109–145.

—— (1991b) The paradox of international environmental agreements. *Mimeo*. London: London Business School.

—— (1992) *Convention on Climate Change: Economic Aspects of Negotiations*. Paris: OECD.

—— (1994a) The biodiversity supergame. *Environmental and Resource Economics*, 4, 1, 111–122.

—— (1994b) Self-enforcing international environmental agreements. *Oxford Economic Papers*, 46, (Special Issue), 878–894.

—— (1995) Toward a theory of international environmental cooperation. *Nota di lavoro 60.95*. Milano: Fondazione Eni Enrico Mattei.

—— (1997a) Heterogeneous international environmental agreements. In C. Carraro (ed.), *International Environmental Negotiations. Strategic Policy Issues*, (chapter 2, pp. 9–25) Cheltenham, UK: Edward Elgar.

—— (1997b) The strategy of trade sanctions in international environmental agreements. *Resource and Energy Economics*, 19, 4, 345–361.

—— (1998a) International cooperation for sale, *Mimeo*. Washington, DC: SAIS, Johns Hopkins University.

—— (1998b) On the theory and diplomacy of environmental treaty-making. *Environmental and Resource Economics*, 11, 3–4, 317–333.

—— (1998c) Political economy of the Kyoto Protocol. *Oxford Review of Economic Policy*, 14, 4, 20–39.

—— (1999a) Consensus treaties. *Mimeo*. Washington, DC: SAIS, Johns Hopkins University.

—— (1999b) Environment & Statecraft. *Preliminary Draft.*

—— (1999c) Montreal versus Kyoto — International cooperation and the global environment. In I. Kaul, I. Grunberg and M. A. Stern (eds), *Global Public Goods. International Cooperation in the 21st Century* (pp. 192–219). New York: Oxford University Press.

—— (2000) International environmental agreements: Feasibility, efficiency, stability. In H. Siebert (ed.), *The Economics of International Environmental Problems* (pp. 111–124). Tübingen: Mohr.

Basar, T. and Olsder, G. J. (1982) *Dynamic Noncooperative Game Theory.* London: Academic Press.

Bauer, A. (1992) International cooperation over environmental goods. *Münchener Wirtschaftswissenschaftliche Beiträge 92–17.* Munich: Volkswirtschaftliche Fakultät der Ludwing-Maximilians-Universität.

Benedick, R. E. (1998) *Ozone Diplomacy: New Directions in Safeguarding the Planet,* enlarged edn. Cambridge, MA: Harvard University Press.

—— (2000) Diplomatic and institutional aspects of environmental treaties. In H. Siebert (ed.), *The Economics of International Environmental Problems* pp. 207–222. Tübingen: Mohr.

Bernheim, B. D., Peleg, B. and Whinston, M. D. (1987) Coalition-proof Nash equilibria I. Concepts. *Journal of Economic Theory,* 42, 1, 1–12.

Black, D. (1948) On the rationale of group decision making. *Journal of Political Economy,* 56, 23–34.

Black, J., Levi, M. D. and de Meza, D. (1993) Creating a good atmosphere: Minimum participation for tackling the 'greenhouse effect'. *Economica,* 60, 239, 281–93.

Bloch, F. (1997) Non-cooperative models of coalition formation in games with spillovers. In C. Carraro (ed.), *International Environmental Negotiations. Strategic Policy Issues* pp. 311–352. Cheltenham, UK: Edward Elgar.

Botteon, M. and Carraro, C. (1996) Strategies for environmental negotiations: Issue linkage with heterogeneous countries. *Nota di lavoro 81.96.* Milano: Fondazione Eni Enrico Mattei.

Bowen, H. R. (1943) The interpretation of voting in the allocation of economic resources. *Quarterly Journal of Economics,* 58, 27–48.

Buchholz, W., Haslbeck, C. and Sandler, T. (1998) When does partial cooperation pay? *Finanzarchiv,* 55, 1, 1–20.

Buchholz, W. and Konrad, K. A. (1994) Global environmental problems and the strategic choice of technology. *Journal of Economics,* 60, 3, 299–321.

Carraro, C. (2000) Roads towards international environmental agreements. In H. Siebert (ed.), *The Economics of International Environmental Problems* (pp. 169–202). Tübingen: Mohr.

Carraro, C. and Siniscalco, D. (1993) Strategies for the international protection of the environment. *Journal of Public Economics,* 52, 3, 309–328.

—— (1997) R&D cooperation and the stability of international environmental agreements. In C. Carraro (ed.), *International Environmental Negotiations. Strategic Policy Issues* (chapter 5, pp. 71–96). Cheltenham, UK: Edward Elgar.

—— (1998) International environmental agreements: Incentives and political economy. *European Economic Review,* 42, 3, 561–572.

Cesar, H. S. J. and de Zeeuw, A. (1996) Issue linkage in global environmental problems. In A. Xepapadeas (ed.), *Economic Policy for the Environment and Natural Resources: techniques for the management and control of pollution* (chapter 7, pp. 158–173). Cheltenham, UK: Edward Elgar.

Chander, P. and Tulkens, H. (1995) A core-theoretic solution for the design of cooperative agreements on transfrontier pollution. *International Tax and Public Finance,* 2, 2, 279–294.

—— (1997) The core of an economy with multilateral environmental externalities. *International Journal of Game Theory*, 26, 3, 379–401.

Chander, P., Tulkens, H., van Ypersele, J.-P. and Willems, S. (1999) The Kyoto Protocol: An economic and game theoretic interpretation. *Discussion Paper 9925*, CORE, Louvain-la-Neuve.

Chayes, A. and Chayes, A. H. (1995) *The New Sovereignty*. Cambridge, MA: Harvard University Press.

Congleton, R. D. (1992) Political institutions and pollution control. *Review of Economics and Statistics*, 74, 412–21.

—— (1995) Toward a transaction cost theory of environmental treaties: Substantive and symbolic environmental agreements. *Economia delle scelte pubbliche*, 13, 2–3, 119–139.

Copeland, B. R. and Taylor, M. S. (2000) Free trade and global warming: A trade theory view of the Kyoto Protocol. *NBER Working Paper 7657*, Cambridge, MA.: National Bureau of Economic Research.

Currarini, S. and Tulkens, H. (1998) Core-theoretic and political stability of international agreements on transfrontier pollution. *Discussion Paper 9793* Louvain-la-Neuve: CORE, Université Catholique de Louvain.

Dasgupta, P. (1982) *The Control of Resources*. Oxford: Basil Blackwell.

d'Aspremont, C., Jacquemin, A., Gabszewicz, J. J. and Weymark, J. A. (1983) On the stability of collusive price leadership. *Canadian Journal of Economics*, 16, 1, 17–25.

de Zeeuw, A. (1998) International dynamic pollution control. In H. Folmer and N. Hanley (eds), *Game Theory and the Environment*, (chapter 12, pp. 237–254). Cheltenham, UK: Edward Elgar.

Demsetz, H. (1967) Toward a theory of property rights. *American Economic Review*, 57, 347–59.

Downs, G. W., Rocke, D. M. and Barsoom, P. N. (1996) Is the good news about compliance good news about cooperation? *International Orpanization*, 50, 379–406.

Elster, J. (1989) Social norms and economic theory. *Journal of Economic Perspectives*, 3, 4, 99–117.

Eyckmans, J., Proost, S. and Schokkaert, E. (1993) Efficiency and distribution in greenhouse negotiations. *Kyklos*, 46, 3, 363–397.

Farrell, J. and Maskin, E. (1989) Renegotiation in repeated games. *Games and Economic Behavior*, 1, 4, 327–360.

Finus, M. and Rundshagen, B. (1998) Toward a positive theory of coalition formation and endogenous instrumental choice in global pollution control. *Public Choice*, 96, 1–2, 145–186.

Folmer, H., v. Mouche, P. and Ragland, S. (1993) Interconnected games and international environmental problems. *Environmental and Resource Economics*, 3, 4, 313–335.

Fredriksson, P. G. and Gaston, N. (1999) The importance of trade for the ratification of the 1992 Climate Change Convention. *Seminar Paper 99–03*. Adelaide: Centre for international economic studies, University of Adelaide.

Friedman, J. W. (1971) A non-cooperative equilibrium for supergames. *Review of Economic Studies*, 38, 113, 1–12.

Fudenberg, D. and Maskin, E. (1986) The folk theorem in repeated games with discounting or with incomplete information. *Econometrica*, 54, 3, 533–554.

Gastil, R. D. (1987) *Freedom in the World: Political Rights and Liberties 1986–87*. New York: Greenwood Press.

Grubb, M. (2000a) The Kyoto Protocol: an economic appraisal. *Nota di lavoro 30.2000*. Milano: Fondazione Eni Enrico Mattei.

—— (2000) Optimal climate policy versus political and institutional realities: The Kyoto Protocol and its follow-up. In H. Siebert (ed.), *The Economics of International Environmental Problems* (pp. 223–235). Tübingen: Mohr.

Heal, G. M. (1993) Formation of international environmental agreements. *Nota di lavoro 28.93*. Milano: Fondazione Eni Enrico Mattei.

Heister, J. (1993) Who will win the ozone game? *Kiel Working Paper 579*. Kiel: Kiel Institute of World Economics.
—— (1997) *Der internationale CO₂-Vertrag*, Vol. 282 of *Kieler Studien*. Tübingen: J. B. C. Mohr.
Heister, J., Klepper, G. and Stähler, F. (1992) Strategien globaler Umweltpolitik – die UNCED-Konferenz aus ökonomischer Sicht. *Zeitschrift für angewandte Umweltforschung*, 5, 4, 455–465.
Heister, J., Mohr, E., Stähler, F., Stoll, P.-T. and Wolfrum, R. (1997) Strategies to enforce compliance with an international CO_2 treaty. *International Environmental Affairs*, 9, 1, 22–53.
Hoel, M. (1991) Global environmental problems: The effects of unilateral actions taken by one country. *Journal of Environmental Economics and Management*, 20, 1, 55–70.
—— (1992) International environmental conventions: The case of uniform reductions of emissions. *Environmental and Resource Economics*, 2, 3, 141–159.
—— (1994) Efficient climate policy in the presence of free riders. *Journal of Environmental Economics and Management*, 27, 3, 259–274.
Hoel, M. and Schneider, K. (1997) Incentives to participate in an international environmental agreement. *Environmental and Resource Economics*, 9, 2, 153–70.
Mäler, K.-G. (1990) International environmental problems. *Oxford Review of Economic Policy*, 6, 1, 80–108.
Meyne, I. (1997) International environmental agreements as two-level games. *Discussion Paper 13*, Wirtschaftswissenschaftliche Fakultät, Martin-Luther-Universität Halle-Wittenberg, Halle (Saale).
Missfeldt, F. (1999) Game-theoretic modelling of transboundary pollution. *Journal of Economic Surveys*, 13, 3, 287–321.
Mohr, E. (1988) On the credibility of perfect threats in repeated games: Note. *International Economic Review*, 29, 3, 551–555.
—— (1995) International environmental permit trade and debt: The consequences of country sovereignty and cross-default policies. *Review of International Economics*, 3, 1, 1–19.
Mohr, E. and Thomas, J. P. (1998) Pooling sovereign risks: The case of environmental treaties and international debt. *Journal of Development Economics*, 55, 173–190.
Murdoch, J. C. and Sandler, T. (1997) The voluntary provision of a pure public good: The case of reduced CFC emissions and the Montreal Protocol. *Journal of Public Economics*, 63, 331–49.
Murdoch, J. C., Sandler, T. and Sargent, K. (1997) A tale of two collectives: Sulphur versus nitrogen oxides emission reduction in Europe. *Economica*, 64, 281–301.
Myerson, R. B. (1991) *Game Theory — Analysis of Conflict*. Cambridge, MA: Harvard University Press.
Nash, J. F. (1950) The bargaining problem. *Econometrica*, 18, 2, 155–162.
—— (1953) Two-person cooperative games. *Econometrica*, 21, 1, 128–140.
Nordhaus, W. D. (1998) Is the Kyoto Protocol a dead duck? Are there any live ducks around? Comparison of alternative global tradable emissions regimes. *Mimeo*. New Haven, CT: Yale University.
Nordhaus, W. D. and Boyer, J. G. (1998) Requiem for Kyoto: An economic analysis of the Kyoto Protocol. *Cowles Foundation Discussion Paper 1201*. New Haven, CT: Yale University.
Paltsev, S. V. (2000) The Kyoto agreement: Regional and sectoral contributions to the carbon leakage. *Working Paper 00–5*. Boulder, CO: University of Colorado.
Pezzey, J. C. V. (1992) Analysis of unilateral CO_2 control in the European Community and OECD. *Energy Journal*, 13, 3, 159–172.
Putnam, R. D. (1988) Diplomacy and domestic politics: the logic of two-level games. *International Organization*, 42, 3, 427–460.

Raiffa, H. (1982) *The Art and Science of Negotiation*. Cambridge, MA: Harvard University Press.

Rothfels, J. (1997) Die Entstehung internationaler Umweltabkommen. *Forschungsreihe 8/97*. Halle/Saale: Institut für Wirtschaftsforschung.

Schelling, T. C. (1960) *The Strategy of Conflict*. Cambridge, MA: Harvard University Press.

Sebenius, J. K. (1983) Negotiation arithmetic: Adding and subtracting issues and parties. *International Organization*, 37, 2, 281–316.

Shapley, L. S. (1953) A value for *n*-person games. In H. Kuhn and A. W. Tucker (eds), *Contributions to the Theory of Games*, Vol. II, (pp. 307–317). Princeton: Princeton University Press.

Siebert, H. (1998) *The Economics of the Environment*, fifth edn. Heidelberg: Springer.

Springer, K. (2001) The Kyoto Protocol: Implications of international capital mobility on trade and regional welfare. In A. Fossati and W. Wiegard (eds), *Policy Evaluation with Computable General Equilibrium Models*. London: Routledge, forthcoming.

Stähler, F. (1995) Optimal transfer policies. *Kiel Working Paper 702*. Kiel: Kiel Institute of World Economics.

—— (1996) Reflections on multilateral environmental agreements. In A. Xepapadeas (ed.), *Economic Policy for the Environment and Natural Resources: techniques for the management and control of pollution* (chapter 8, pp. 174–196). Cheltenham, UK: Edward Elgar.

Tollison, R. D. and Willett, T. D. (1979) An economic theory of mutually advantageous issue linkage in international negotiations. *International Organization*, 33, 4, 425–449.

Tulkens, H. (1998) Cooperation versus free-riding in international environmental affairs: two approaches. In N. Hanley and H. Folmer (eds), *Game Theory and the Environment* (chapter 2, pp. 30–44). Cheltenham, UK: Edward Elgar.

USEPA (1988) *Regulatory Impact Analysis: Protection of Stratospheric Ozone*. Washington, DC: United States Environmental Protection Agency.

van Damme, E. (1989) Renegotiation-proof equilibria in repeated prisoners' dilemma. *Journal of Economic Theory*, 47, 1, 206–217.

Wagner, U. J. (2000) The economics of global environmental agreements. *Diplomarbeit in Theoretischer Volkswirtschaftslehre*. Kiel: Christian-Albrechts-Universität.

CHAPTER 6

THE ECONOMICS OF TROPICAL DEFORESTATION

E. B. Barbier and J. C. Burgess

University of Wyoming

Abstract. This paper provides a survey of 'first wave' economic studies of tropical deforestation and land use. These studies of tropical forest land conversion are generally at the cross-country level. We also conduct a synthesis cross-country analysis of tropical agricultural land expansion. The results show that agricultural development is the main factor determining land expansion, but institutional factors have an important influence. Income effects tend to vary from region to region, and do not always display an 'Environmental Kuznets Curve' relationship.

This paper also provides a review of the more recent 'second wave' economic studies of tropical deforestation that model and analyze the economic behaviour of agricultural households, timber concessionaires and other agents within tropical forest countries who affect deforestation through their land use decisions. Further work in this area requires more country-level and local case studies into tropical deforestation and land use.

1. Introduction

Although global forest loss has occurred for centuries, rapid rates of tropical deforestation have only become an international concern in the last twenty-five years or so. As is the usual case with such phenomena, it was not economists but natural scientists who initially called the world's attention to the potential consequences of tropical forest destruction, whether it be biodiversity loss, climate change or the loss of traditional livelihoods of indigenous peoples.[1] Economists began studying such problems in the mid-1980s, and since then, there has been steady progress in the economic analysis of tropical forest loss.

The 'first wave' of studies focused on the economic causes of tropical deforestation, and tended to be dominated by statistical analyses across tropical countries, or for selective countries and regions. More recently, a 'second wave' of studies has focused on modeling and analyzing the economic behavior of agricultural households, timber concessionaires and other agents within tropical countries who affect deforestation through their land use decisions. In some cases, the modeling has centered on a single representative agent of a sector (e.g. an agricultural household or a timber concessionaire). In others, the use of general equilibrium models has facilitated the integration of several key economic sectors (e.g. commercial agriculture, subsistence agriculture and forestry) to analyze both their individual and collective impacts on deforestation.

The following paper provides a review of the 'first wave' cross-country studies of tropical forest land use and deforestation and presents a synthesis analysis of tropical agricultural land expansion at the cross-country level. Improving the statistical analysis of the factors determining tropical forest loss is still an important area of research. More importantly, insights gained from cross-country analysis of tropical deforestation may inform case study analyses of the economic behavior determining land use decisions within specific tropical forest countries and regions. This paper also provides a review of the more recent 'second wave' economic studies of tropical deforestation at the household and firm level. These newer economic modeling approaches and case studies can improve our understanding of the underlying causes and the key processes determining deforestation, and thus can in turn support cross-country studies of tropical deforestation.

The outline of this paper is as follows. Section 2 provides a brief summary of global tropical forest land use trends. This is followed by an overview of cross-country analyses of tropical deforestation, highlighting the main factors and causes identified by such studies. Four key economic approaches to cross-country analysis are then discussed in Section 4, and from this a synthesis analysis is proposed and applied to a new cross-country data set in Section 5. Section 6 provides a review of economic studies of tropical deforestation at the household and firm level. The implications and findings of this survey of economic studies of tropical deforestation are discussed in the concluding section.

2. Overview of tropical deforestation and land use trends

The 1990 Global Forest Resource Assessment (FAO, 1993) indicated that the annual deforestation rate across tropical countries over 1981–90 was approximately 0.8%, or 15.4 million hectares (ha) per annum (see Table 1). Although the highest rate of deforestation occurs in Asia (1.2%), the area of tropical forests cleared on average each year in Latin America, 7.4 million ha, is almost as much as the forest area cleared in Asia and Africa put together. The largest amount of deforestation is currently occurring in tropical South America (6.4 million ha) followed by Insular South East Asia (1.9 million ha), but the highest rates of deforestation are being experienced in Continental South East Asia (1.6% annually) and Central America and Mexico (1.5% annually).

In the last few years, several countries have been investing in the establishment of plantation forests, most notably India, Indonesia and Brazil. However, the current level of reafforestation of 2.7 mn ha/yr falls far short of the extent of deforestation. In addition, although plantations may partially compensate for the loss of timber supply from natural tropical forests, they do not provide the wide range of use and non-use benefits that these natural forest ecosystems provide,

Table 1. Global tropical deforestation trends, 1980–90.

Region	Number of countries	Land area (million ha)	Forest cover		Annual deforestation	
			1980 (million ha)	1990 (million ha)	1981–90 (million ha)	1981–90 (% per annum)
Africa	**40**	**2,236.1**	**568.6**	**527.6**	**4.1**	**0.7**
West Sahelian Africa	6	528.0	43.7	40.8	0.3	0.7
East Sahelian Africa	9	489.7	71.4	65.5	0.6	0.9
West Africa	8	203.8	61.5	55.6	0.6	1.0
Central Africa	6	398.3	215.5	204.1	1.1	0.5
Trop. Southern Africa	10	558.1	159.3	145.9	1.3	0.9
Insular Africa	1	58.2	17.1	15.8	0.1	0.8
Asia & Pacific	**17**	**892.1**	**349.6**	**310.6**	**3.9**	**1.2**
South Asia	6	412.2	69.4	63.9	0.6	0.8
Continental S.E. Asia	5	190.2	88.4	75.2	1.3	1.6
Insular S.E. Asia	5	244.4	154.7	135.4	1.9	1.3
Pacific	1	45.3	37.1	36.0	0.1	0.3
Latin America & Caribbean	**33**	**1,650.1**	**992.2**	**918.1**	**7.4**	**0.8**
C. America & Mexico	7	239.6	79.2	68.1	1.1	1.5
Caribbean	19	69.0	48.3	47.1	0.1	0.3
Trop. South America	7	1,341.6	864.6	802.9	6.2	0.7
Total	**90**	**4,778.3**	**1,910.4**	**1,756.3**	**15.4**	**0.8**

Source: FAO (1993).

such as biodiversity maintenance, recreation, carbon storage and watershed protection.

Table 2 shows trends in land area and use for different regions of the world since 1980. Over the last fifteen years in most tropical areas dominated by developing economies, the decline in forest and woodlands is mainly the result of land conversion, in particular agricultural expansion. The loss of permanent pasture (i.e. land used for five or more years for forage, including both natural and cultivated crops) may be the result of both the serious degradation problems posed by over-grazing, and also the conversion of pasture land to cropland. Table 3 suggests that the land expansion occurring in tropical regions could be related to structural features of the agricultural sectors of developing economies, such as low irrigation and fertilizer use as well as poor crop yields.

Table 2. Global trends in land area and use, 1980–95.

	Land Area	Population Density	Land Use								
			Cropland			Permanent Pasture			Forest and Woodlands		
	1995 mn ha	1995 per '000 ha	1995 mn ha	% change since 1980		1994 mn ha	% change since 1980		1994 mn ha	% change since 1980	
Africa	2964	243	193	10.3%		884	−1.1%		713	−2.0%	
Asia	2678	1284	472	3.5%		792	14.1%		537	−2.7%	
Europe	473	1541	135	−4.3%		79	−8.1%		157	1.0%	
North and Central America	2137	213	277	1.1%		366	2.2%		824	2.1%	
Oceania	849	33	53	8.2%		429	−5.3%		200	−0.3%	
South America	1753	181	121	19.8%		495	4.2%		932	0.5%	
USSR (former)	2195	134	226	NA		355	NA		810	NA	
World	13 048	436	1,476	3.4%		3,399	3.5%		4,172	−2.9%	

NA = Not available.
Source: FAO (1997).

Table 3. Global trends in agricultural productivity and input use, 1979–95.

	Cropland (million ha)	Cropland per capita	Cereal Yields (kg/ha)		Irrigated Land as a % of Cropland		Fertilizer Use (kg) per ha of Cropland	
	1995	1995	1980	1995	1979–81	1995	1979–81	1995
Africa	193	0.27	1124	1128	6	6	18	18
Asia	472	0.14	2072	3060	29	35	67	144
Europe	135	0.19	3655	4316	10	12	225	156
North and Central America	277	0.61	3260	3918	10	11	91	89
Oceania	53	1.87	1089	1886	4	5	37	46
South America	121	0.38	1710	2606	7	8	45	54
USSR (former)	226	0.77	NA	1301	8	9	80	19
World	1476	0.26	2160	2752	15	17	81	89

NA = Not available.
Source: FAO (1997).

Increasing agricultural productivity and input use reflect greater agricultural intensification and development, which in turn mean less pressure is put on conversion of forests and other marginal lands for use in agriculture (Barbier, 1997).

3. Overview survey of cross-country analyses of tropical deforestation

As noted above, an important area of economic research into tropical deforestation consists of cross-country, regional and selective country-level statistical analyses of the factors determining declining forest cover. Several surveys have illustrated and synthesized the important findings of this growing literature (Brown and Pearce, 1994; Kaimowitz and Angelsen, 1998; van Kooten, Sedjo and Bulte, 1999). These surveys suggest that the following key factors have an important influence on tropical deforestation both within and across countries:

Income
Population growth/density
Agricultural prices/returns
Agricultural yields
Agricultural exports/export share
Logging prices/returns/production
Roads and road building
Scale factors (size of forest stock, land area, etc.)
Institutional factors (political stability, property rights, rule of law, etc.).

The results of these surveys indicate that increases in incomes, population pressure, agricultural prices, access to markets, tenure insecurity and political instability are associated with greater deforestation. In general, countries with larger forest stocks also display higher rates of deforestation. The analyses have offered more mixed results with respect to the relationship between deforestation and agricultural productivity, logging prices and exports.

However, the literature has also pointed out a number of problems confronting cross-country analyses of deforestation. First, the United Nations Food and Agricultural Organization (FAO), which has been the international agency responsible for compiling forest area data across all countries, based its 1990 Global Forest Resource Assessment on population growth projections in order to overcome an inadequate forest data base for some countries and regions. This means that the FAO country forest cover data are inappropriate for cross-country analyses of deforestation that use demographic factors as explanatory variables. As the list above indicates, the latter are considered important variables explaining global deforestation. This in turn means that cross-country analyses that employ the FAO forest cover data since 1990 are unreliable.[2] An alternative source of forest area data is the FAO Production Yearbook. This includes data on forest, crop and pasture land, but does not specify land area under 'closed broadleaved forest'. The data are drawn from national government responses to surveys rather than using primary data sources and are generally considered to be less reliable than the Global Forest Resource Assessment data.

In addition, times series data on some of the factors listed above, especially agricultural and logging returns or roads and road investments, are simply unavailable across many tropical countries. Thus these factors are more readily incorporated into deforestation analyses for single countries than across tropical regions or countries. The data sets for many other variables across countries also tend to be incomplete. For example, it may be possible to obtain export unit values for logs for a tropical country, but it may be more difficult to get an average domestic stumpage value for that country. Agricultural prices for specific crops may be available, but a reliable food or cereal price index for a country may not exist. Data on key institutional factors generally exist for a relatively small number of developing countries, and these factors tend to be averages over long periods of time.

Finally, some approaches to cross-country analyses have a tendency to be ad hoc. The danger with analyzing deforestation across countries is that too much emphasis can be placed on trying to discover factors that explain trends in changes in forest cover rather than on examining a plausible hypothesis as to why certain economic factors might be correlated with deforestation. However, not all studies suffer from an ad hoc approach to cross-country analysis. In recent years, there have been a number of studies that have attempted to develop a specific model or approach to explaining deforestation, and then have tested the resulting hypothesis. The following section identifies four such approaches in the literature.

4. Survey of four approaches to cross-country analyses

Environmental Kuznets Curve Analyses

The Environmental Kuznets Curve (EKC) hypothesizes that an environmental 'bad' first increases, but eventually falls, as the per capita income of a country rises. Although the EKC model has generally been applied to pollution problems, there have been a number of recent studies that have also examined whether this hypothesis also holds for global deforestation (e.g. Antle and Heidebrink, 1995; Cropper and Griffiths, 1994; Koop and Tole, 1999; Panayotou, 1995; Shafik, 1994). The basic EKC model for deforestation is usually

$$F_{it} - F_{it-1} = F(Y_{it}, Y_{it}^2; \mathbf{z_{it}}) = \alpha_1 Y_{it} - \alpha_2 Y_{it}^2 + \mathbf{z_{it}}\beta + \varepsilon_{it} \tag{1}$$

where $F_{it} - F_{it-1}$ is the change in the forest stock over the previous period (which is negative if deforestation is occurring), Y_{it} is per capita income and $\mathbf{z_{it}}$ is a $1 \times n$ vector that includes other explanatory variables, such as population density or growth and other macroeconomic variables.[3]

The application of such an EKC model to explain deforestation trends across countries has produced mixed results. When the model is tested for both temperate and tropical countries, it is inconclusive (Antle and Heidbrink, 1995; Panayotou, 1995; Shafik, 1994). When applied to just tropical countries, the inverted-U relationship tends not to hold for all countries but may apply to specific regions. For example, Cropper and Griffiths (1994) find some evidence that the EKC model is relevant to Latin America and Africa. However, for each of these regions the turning point — the per capita income level at which the deforestation rate is zero and is about to decline — is generally two to four times higher than the average per capita income for that region.

In addition, the EKC relationship is likely to vary considerably from country to country. Through employing a random coefficients panel analysis, Koop and Tole (1999) were unable to reject the hypothesis that country-specific coefficients are likely to vary compared to cross-country averages (i.e. in Equation (1) $\alpha_1 = \alpha_{1i}$, $\alpha_2 = \alpha_{2i}$ for all $i = 1, ..., N$ countries in the sample). This in turn implies that each tropical forest country or region is likely to have its own unique EKC relationship, which explains why obtaining a single relationship across all countries may be difficult or implausible.

Competing Land Use Models

Some empirical analyses have taken as their starting point the hypothesis that forest loss in tropical countries is the result of competing land use, in particular between maintaining the natural forest and agriculture (e.g. Barbier and Burgess, 1997; Ehui and Hertel, 1989). As indicated in Table 2, the evidence across tropical regions is that substantial conversion of forest and woodlands to agriculture is occurring. From an economic standpoint, given the time and effort required to reestablish tropical forest (where this is ecologically feasible) such conversion implies that potential timber and environmental benefits from forest land are irreversibly lost. Therefore, competing land use models usually include some measure of the 'price' or opportunity cost of agricultural conversion and deforestation in terms of the foregone benefits of timber production and environmental benefits from forest land

$$F_{it} - F_{it-1} = A^D(v_{it};\ \mathbf{z_{it}}),\ \partial A^D/\partial v_{it} < 0 \tag{2}$$

where v_{it} is the opportunity cost or 'price' of agricultural conversion, A^D is the demand for converting forest land to agriculture, and as before $\mathbf{z_{it}}$ is a vector containing exogenous economic factors (e.g. income per capita, population density, agricultural yields).

A cross-country analysis of (2) was conducted by Barbier and Burgess (1997) for tropical countries for the five-year change in forested area over 1980–85. The results indicated that increased population density increases forest clearance, whereas rising income per capita and agricultural yields reduce the demand for forest conversion. The latter effects suggest that as countries develop economically and the productivity of their existing agricultural land improves there is less pressure for deforestation.

However, there were some problems with the analysis that illustrate the general difficulty of applying a competing land use model across tropical forest countries. First, the authors had to use a 'proxy' for v_{it}, as preferred measures of the 'opportunity cost' of conversion (e.g. land values, timber rents) are not available across countries. Although several proxies were employed, including export unit values for timber, only roundwood production per capita proved to be significant. This variable turned out to be positively related to the five-year change in forest area, which the authors concluded was not surprising, given that over the 1980–85 period much agricultural conversion occurred in tropical forests that were first 'opened up' by timber operations.

The competing land use model is not necessarily inconsistent with a possible EKC relationship between deforestation and income. To test for the latter hypothesis, Burgess (2000) re-analysed the original data set used by Barbier and Burgess (1997), but did not find any evidence of a significant EKC relationship for tropical countries as a group over the 1980–85 period.

Forest Land Conversion Models

Many country-level studies of tropical deforestation have focused on the forest land conversion decision of agricultural households (e.g. Barbier, 2000; Barbier and Burgess, 1996; Chomitz and Gray, 1996; Cropper, Mani and Griffiths, 1999; López, 1997; Nelson and Hellerstein, 1996; Panayotou and Sungsuwan 1994). Such approaches model the derived demand for converted land by rural smallholders, and assume that the households either use available labor to convert their own land or purchase it from a market. This in turn allows the determinants of the equilibrium level of converted land to be specified. In such models, the aggregate equilibrium level of cleared land across all households is usually hypothesized to be a function of output and input prices and other factors affecting aggregate conversion

$$A_{it}^D = A^D(p_{it}, w_{L_{it}}, \mathbf{w_{it}}; \ \mathbf{x_{it}}, \mathbf{z_{it}}), \ \frac{\partial A^D}{\partial p_{it}} > 0, \ \frac{\partial A^D}{\partial w_{L_{it}}} < 0, \ \frac{\partial A^D}{\partial x_{it}} > 0. \qquad (3)$$

where p is the price of agricultural output, w_L is rural wage (labor is a key component in land clearing), $\mathbf{w}$ is a vector of other inputs, $\mathbf{x}$ are factors influencing the 'accessibility' of forest areas (e.g. roads, infrastructure, distance to major towns and cities), and as before $\mathbf{z_{it}}$ represents other economic explanatory variables.

Studies for representative countries in Asia, Africa and Latin America have tended to confirm the hypothesis suggested in (3) that agricultural conversion is positively related to agricultural output prices and decreases with rural wage rates (Barbier, 2000; Barbier and Burgess, 1996; López, 1997; Panayotou and Sungsuwan, 1994). Cropper, Mani and Griffiths (1999) also provide evidence from Thailand that the accessibility of forest areas, in this case measure by distance from Bangkok, increases forest land conversion to agriculture. Chomitz and Gray (1996) and Nelson and Hellerstein (1996) include location-specific input and output prices to investigate the impact of roads on the agricultural land conversion decision.

Although the land conversion model appears to work well for specific tropical forest countries, it is difficult to obtain time series data on agricultural input and output prices (especially rural wage rates) for many tropical countries. Cross-country data on important 'x' variables, such as rural road expansion and road building investments, are also hard to find. This means that applying the model to a cross-country panel data set is very problematic.

To date, cross-country analyses of agricultural land conversion have tended to leave out prices and 'x' factors. For example, Southgate (1994) used annual population growth, agricultural export growth, crop yield growth and a land constraint dummy to explain annual agricultural land growth across Latin America over 1982–87. He found that population and agricultural export growth were positively related to land expansion, whereas yield growth and the land constraint were negatively related. Although the results clearly suggest that structural agricultural, economic and geographic factors are significant in explaining land conversion, data constraints meant that the analysis was unable to test the key relationships of the complete forest land conversion model (3).

Institutional Models

In recent years, a variety of empirical analyses at both the country and cross-country level have explored the impact on tropical deforestation of institutional factors, such as land use conflict, security of ownership or property rights, political stability, and the 'rule of law' (e.g. Alston, Libecap and Mueller, 1999, 2000; Deacon, 1994, 1999; Godoy et al., 1998). The main hypothesis tested is that such institutional factors are important factors explaining deforestation

$$F_{it} - F_{it-1} = F(\mathbf{q_{it}}; \; \mathbf{z_{it}}) \tag{4}$$

where $\mathbf{q_{it}}$ is a vector of institutional factors and and $\mathbf{z_{it}}$ represents other economic explanatory variables.

Deacon (1999) has applied such an approach to explain the 1980–85 change in forest cover as a fraction of land area across all countries, omitting those countries with forests less than 5% of land area or with more than 50% of their forests classified as 'open'. The main institutional variable, ownership security, proved to be significant and positive in all models, suggesting that greater security reduces forest loss.[4] Excluding agricultural yield variables from the models increased the ownership security coefficient by 25–30%, which indicates that the latter effect operates partly through agricultural yields.

Although such models have demonstrated the importance of institutional factors in determining deforestation, an important question is how much weight should be given to such factors compared to explanatory variables identified by other approaches to cross-country analyses of forest loss. Nevertheless, by excluding institutional indices, other models applied to cross-country analyses of deforestation may have omitted a potentially important explanatory variable.

However, cross country data sets on institutional factors exist for only a small sub-set of tropical developing countries. In addition, those indices on political stability, corruption, ownership security and other institutional factors that are available for tropical countries tend not to vary much over time, or are constructed as averages over long time periods. Thus the inclusion of institutional indices means the use of a time-invariant variable in a panel analysis explaining forest loss in only a representative sample of tropical countries.

5. Towards a synthesis model

Although each of the above four approaches encounter specific difficulties when applied to cross-country analyses of tropical land use conversion, each model also has produced its own unique insight into the possible factors explaining this land use change. An interesting issue is whether it is possible to construct a synthesis model based on the above approaches. The following model discusses briefly one possible synthesis model and its application to the cross-country analysis of tropical land use change. However, in constructing such a synthesis model, the following points need to be kept in mind:

First, given the problems with recent (i.e. post-1985) FAO forest stock data highlighted above, the synthesis model should concentrate on explaining agricultural land expansion, $A_{it} - A_{it-1}$, rather than deforestation across tropical countries. This would mean that the model would be able to explain tropical forest loss at least, under the assumption that

$$F_{it} - F_{it-1} = -(A_{it} - A_{it-1}) \tag{5}$$

That is, as discussed in the introduction, in most developing countries the major cause of forest loss is presumed to be conversion to agriculture, although the relationship between deforestation and agricultural land expansion may not be as exact as implied by (5) (see Table 2).

Second, any synthesis model should be able to test for more than one key factor explaining land use change identified by the above four approaches, provided that the factors chosen are not mutually exclusive. For example, it should be possible to construct a model that can test for the EKC hypothesis as well as examine the possible influence of institutional factors. On the other hand, given the difficulty in obtaining cross-country time series data on key variables, such as rural wages, roads, other input prices, it is difficult to include variables representing agricultural returns or 'accessibility' of forest lands in the model. Thus the problem of applying the forest land conversion model across countries, let alone combining this model with an analysis of a possible EKC influence or institutional factors, still remains.

However, as some studies have demonstrated, structural agricultural, economic and geographic factors that vary from country to country are significant in explaining the different land conversion trends across countries (e.g. Barbier and Burgess, 1997; Deacon, 1999 and Southgate, 1994). These factors may be particularly significant explanatory variables in a cross-country analysis, if variables representing agricultural returns or 'accessibility' of forest lands cannot be included due to data limitations. Thus, the synthesis model should include certain 'structural' variables (s_{it}), such as agricultural yield, cropland share of land area, agricultural export share, and arable land per capita, to capture country-by-country differences in agricultural sectors and land use patterns, as well as other exogenous explanatory variables, z_{it}.

Thus a possible synthesis model might look like:

$$A_{it} - A_{it-1} = A(Y_{it}, Y_{it}^2, s_{it}, z_{it}; q_i)$$ (6)

Finally, as institutional factors (q_i) tend to be invariant with time, two versions of the model can be tested, one without and one including q_i.

Model (6) was applied to a panel analysis of tropical agricultural land expansion over 1961–94, with the dependent variable being the percentage annual change in agricultural land area.[5] The EKC variables (Y_{it}, Y_{it}^2) are represented by gross domestic product (GDP) per capita in constant purchasing power parity (1987 \$) and by GDP per capita squared, respectively. The structural variables (s_{it}) are cereal yield, cropland share of total land area, agricultural export share of total merchandise exports and arable land per capita. The additional explanatory variables (z_{it}) are population and GDP growth. The source of data used for these variables was the World Bank's *World Development Indicators*, which has the most extensive data set for key land, agricultural and economic variables for developing countries over the period of analysis.

Table 4 indicates the results without institutional factors, q_i. Both one-way and two-way fixed and random effects models were tested for the sample of all tropical

Table 4. Panel analysis of tropical agricultural land expansion, 1961–94.

Dependent Variable: Agricultural land expansion (% annual change)[a]

| | Elasticity estimates:[b] | | | |
| | All Countries ($N = 656$) | Africa ($N = 168$) | Latin America ($N = 319$) | Asia ($N = 169$) |
Explanatory Variables				
GDP per capita[c]	0.270	−0.980	−0.388	3.068
(PPP, constant 1987 $)	(0.199)	(−1.315)	(−0.109)	(2.667)**
GDP per capita squared	−0.708	0.271	0.050	−1.391
	(−2.035)*	(1.228)	(0.036)	(−3.370)**
GDP growth	0.012	0.023	0.009	−0.132
(% annual change)	(0.177)	(0.456)	(0.127)	(−0.502)
Population growth	−0.603	0.259	−0.734	−0.538
(% annual change)	(−1.027)	(0.278)	(−1.234)	(−0.445)
Cereal yield	−2.248	−0.250	−2.632	−1.678
(kg per hectare)	(−2.846)**	(−0.479)	(−2.028)*	(−1.644)†
Cropland share of land	7.112	0.923	5.565	−0.452
(% of land area)	(3.550)**	(4.249)**	(2.485)**	(−0.694)
Agricultural export share	4.351	0.078	0.462	0.395
(% of merchandise exports)	(2.079)*	(0.496)	(2.098)*	(0.967)
Arable land per capita	0.355	−0.695	−0.263	0.406
(hectares per person)	(0.163)	(−1.659)†	(−0.163)	(0.665)
Kuznets Curve	**No**	**No**	**No**	**Yes**
(Turning point estimate)	($858)	($3706)	($17 359)	($6182)
F-test for pooled model	3.077**	1.398	3.323**	2.245**
Breusch-Pagan (LM) test	51.69**	5.90*	11.23**	0.29
Hausman test	31.97**	2.07	15.52*	10.88
Adjusted R^2	0.212	0.183	0.215	0.176
Preferred model	**One way fixed effects**	**One way random effects**	**One way fixed effects**	**One way random effects**

Notes: [a] Mean for all countries is 0.64%, for Africa 0.26%, for Latin America 0.75% and for Asia 0.80%.

[b] t-ratios are indicated in parentheses.

[c] Mean for all countries is $2863, for Africa $1230, for Latin America $3654 and for Asia $3029. PPP is purchase power parity.

** Significant at 1% level, * significant at 5% level, † significant at 10% level.

countries, as well as for the regional sub-samples for Africa, Latin America and Asia. Table 4 displays the results for the preferred models and the relevant statistics. In the table, the parameter estimates are reported as elasticities, in order to facilitate comparison of the effects of the different variables, which are in different units.

Across all tropical countries, the structural variables appear to be the more important explanatory factors determining agricultural expansion. Growth in agricultural land area increases with the share of total land area that cropland accounts for and with agricultural export share but declines with cereal yield. GDP per capita squared also has a negative impact on agricultural expansion, although this effect is smaller than for the other significant variables. These results are pretty much replicated for the Latin America sub-sample, with the exception that neither per capita income variable is significant. In Africa, agricultural expansion is explained by cropland share of total land area only, although it is possibly negatively affected by the amount of arable land per capita. The regression for Asia is the only estimation that cannot reject the EKC hypothesis. However, the level of per capita income at which agricultural expansion peaks in Asia is estimated to be $6,182, which is approximately double the sample mean. Increases in cereal yields may also possibly slow agricultural land expansion in Asia.

Table 5 repeats the same regressions, but with the inclusion of three institutional variables: a corruption index, a property rights index and a political stability index. These indices were obtained from the Levine-Loayza-Beck data set used in Beck, Levine and Loayza (1999) and Levine, Loayza and Beck (1999), which are available from the Economic Growth Research Group of the World Bank. The corruption and property rights indices are directly from the Levine-Loayza-Beck data set and are averaged over 1982–95. The political stability index was created as a composite index of the average number of revolutions and coups (averaged over 1960–90), average number of assassinations per million population (averaged over 1960–90), and an index of ethnic fractionalization (averaged over 1982–95). As these indices were not available for all tropical countries in the original sample, the inclusion of these institutional factors reduced the sample sizes of the regressions considerably. In addition, the three indices are time invariant, and with their inclusion in addition to the original explanatory variables of the model, fixed effects regressions cannot be run.[6]

Table 5 indicates that the inclusion of institutional factors has a considerable influence on the analysis.[7] For all tropical countries, the EKC hypothesis can no longer be rejected, although the estimated EKC turning point is nearly double the mean per capita income for the sample. Population growth, the ratio of cropland to total land area, the share of agricultural exports and political instability all appear to have a significant and positive impact on agricultural expansion across all tropical countries. The regression for Latin American countries yields similar results, which is not surprising as this region dominates the sample of all countries. However, the estimated EKC turning point for Latin America is only one third larger than the average per capita income of $3,675 for the sub-sample. This suggests, that if agricultural land growth does start to slow down as GDP per capita increases, we are likely to observe this phenomenon occurring in tropical Latin America first. For Asia, population growth and lower corruption appear to have a significant and positive influence on agricultural expansion. The latter effect may seem counter-intuitive, although López (1998) has argued that reduced corruption and improved bureaucratic efficiency may actually facilitate the implementation of land and credit policies that stimulate a 'race for property rights' to convert forest and other common resource land to agriculture. Finally, given the small number of

Table 5. Panel analysis of tropical agricultural land expansion, 1961–94 including institutional factors.

Dependent Variable: Agricultural land expansion (% annual change)[a]

Explanatory Variables	Elasticity estimates:[b]			
	All Countries (N = 383)	Africa (N = 48)	Latin America (N = 233)	Asia (N = 102)
GDP per capita[c]	4.125	−25.214	7.943	0.749
(PPP, constant 1987 $)	(3.443)**	(−1.388)	(2.595)**	(0.200)
GDP per capita squared	−1.519	13.984	−3.499	−0.699
	(−2.461)**	(1.651)†	(−2.328)*	(−0.528)
GDP growth	−0.066	−0.088	−0.066	0.010
(% annual change)	(−0.778)	(−0.463)	(−0.862)	(0.032)
Population growth	1.152	2.945	1.421	4.635
(% annual change)	(2.153)*	(0.803)	(2.271)*	(2.510)**
Cereal yield	−0.309	−0.270	−0.623	−2.267
(kg per hectare)	(−0.577)	(−0.180)	(−0.929)	(−0.783)
Cropland share of land	0.433	5.364	0.789	3.541
(% of land area)	(2.064)*	(0.648)	(2.343)*	(1.474)
Agricultural export share	0.654	−1.168	0.383	−0.282
(% of merchandise exports)	(5.658)**	(−1.217)	(2.948)**	(−0.421)
Arable land per capita	−0.043	−0.970	0.358	−2.842
(hectares per person)	(−0.174)	(−0.334)	(0.83)	(−1.087)
Corruption index	0.840	2.779	0.249	4.447
(high = 0, low = 10)	(1.703)†	(0.105)	(0.345)	(2.251)*
Property rights index	−0.395	−5.266	−0.363	9.440
(high = 5, low = 1)	(−0.590)	(−0.214)	(−0.425)	(1.046)
Political stability index	0.613	−5.266	0.494	−1.429
(high = 0, low = 1)	(1.896)**	(0.150)	(2.220)*	(−0.948)
Kuznets Curve	**Yes**	**No**	**Yes**	**No**
(Turning point estimate)	($5445)	($1211)	($4946)	($1815)
Durbin-Watson statistic[d]	2.009	2.372	2.045	1.998
Adjusted R^2	0.191	0.073	0.128	0.450
Preferred model	**OLS with AC[d]**	**OLS with AC[d]**	**OLS**	**OLS with AC[d]**

Notes: [a] Mean for all countries is 0.61%, for Africa 0.14%, for Latin America 0.66% and for Asia 0.72%

[b] t-ratios are indicated in parentheses.

[c] Mean for all countries is $2986, for Africa $1211, for Latin America $3675 and for Asia $2246. PPP is purchase power parity.

[d] After autocorrelation correction (AC) by Cochrane-Orcutt procedure, if required.

** Significant at 1% level, * significant at 5% level, † significant at 10% level.

observations for the African sub-sample, the separate regression for the African region has poor explanatory power and should be ignored.

The above results for the synthesis model provide interesting additional results to the 'first wave' cross-country analyses of tropical land use and deforestation.

First, the pattern of agricultural development, as represented by such structural variables as cropland share of total land area, agricultural export share of total exports, and to some extent, cereal yields, appears consistently to influence tropical agricultural land expansion. Population growth could be an additional factor, especially in Asia. Corruption and political stability may also be important institutional influences, but their significance may vary from region to region. The existence of an EKC effect for agricultural expansion appears to be highly sensitive to the model specification, and the impact of changes in GDP per capita on agricultural expansion is likely to differ considerably across tropical regions.

In the next section we provide a brief review of the existing 'second wave' economic studies of tropical deforestation that model and analyze the economic behavior of agricultural households, timber concessionaires and other agents within tropical forest countries who affect tropical deforestation. The new advances and insights provided by the 'first wave' studies need to be incorporated into the analysis of the behavior of the key agents who are directly responsible for forest conversion decisions. This is best reflected in the forest land conversion models and competing forest land use models that have recently been developed for cross-country analyses.

6. Survey of household and firm level studies of tropical deforestation

Comparatively few studies have focused on the agents of forest land clearing and how the agents' decision to maintain or convert forest land is influenced by the agents' socio-economic characteristics, such as income level, size of household, and land holding (Parks et al., 1998). For example, López and Nicklitschek (1991) model the role of natural biomass (vegetation cover) in tropical agricultural production at the farm level, including the influence of property rights and international trade. These relationships are also examined empirically by López (1998 and 1997) in Côte d'Ivoire and Ghana. Several authors have developed models of frontier agricultural expansion, including the decision to abandon existing agricultural land and convert frontier forests to agriculture (Barbier, 2000; Larson, 1991; Mendelsohn, 1994; Southgate, 1990; Schneider, 1994).

Several studies indicate that increasing agricultural output prices, tenure insecurity and accessibility to markets through road building may be correlated with increasing deforestation, whereas increasing off-farm wages and employment are correlated with reduced deforestation. For example, Barbier and Burgess (1996) and Panayotou and Sungsuwan (1994) show for Mexico and Thailand respectively that deforestation increases with higher agricultural prices. Road building and deforestation appear to be highly correlated in Belize (Chomitz and Gray, 1996) and Brazil (Reis and Guzmán, 1994). Tenure insecurity appears to be a major factor in Ecuador (Southgate, Sierra and Brown, 1991), and across tropical countries generally (Deacon, 1995). There is also empirical evidence that increases in rural wages and off-farm employment reduces the pressure on forest clearance (Barbier and Burgess, 1996; Boyd, 1994; Bluffstone, 1995).

Until the advent of widely available geographic information systems technology, most studies of forest land use emphasized the extent of forest area (e.g. size in hectares), and did not specifically consider spatial features (e.g. size, shape, and location of forest habitats), and consideration of the human decisions that drive land use change. A few recent economic and policy analyses of land use decisions have been integrated with landscape ecological analyses in order to quantify spatial aspects of these changes (Bockstael, 1996). For example, location (i.e. relative to roads) has begun to be included in economic models of forest and agricultural land use development, and Pfaff (1999), Chomitz and Gray (1996), and Nelson and Hellerstein (1997) have included location to help explain deforestation in Brazil, Belize, and Mexico, respectively.

Certain factors influencing deforestation, such as increasing agricultural input prices, timber output prices, tenure security, credit availability and technological progress, tend to be determined by local conditions, such as the availability of 'idle' land, open access frontier conditions and labor or capital constraints (Barbier and Burgess, 1996; Kaimowitz and Angelsen, 1998, Larson, 1991; Mendelsohn, 1994, Schneider, 1994; Southgate, 1990). There is more limited evidence of the role of economy-wide foreign debt, macroeconomic policies and trade policies in influencing forest conversion (Capistrano, 1994; Kahn and MacDonald, 1994; Shafik, 1994). Ehui, Hertel and Preckel (1990) construct a two-sector dynamic model for agriculture and forestry in a developing country. Ehui and Hertel (1989) use this model to estimate the socially optimal steady-state forest stock in Côte d'Ivoire and show that the long run stock is negatively affected by the social rate of discount and by technological change.

The studies show that agricultural and forest sector policies and investments are more directly related to deforestation. For example, in Southeast Asia, forest and industrialization policies, combined with poor monitoring and enforcement of concession agreements, are contributing to excessive timber-related deforestation and forest conversion rather than reinforcing the valued added incentives of the forest products trade in encouraging sustainable management of production forests (Barbier et al., 1995; Hyde and Sedjo, 1992; Repetto and Gillis, 1988; Vincent and Binkley, 1991). In the Brazilian Amazon, direct costs of harvesting and converting forests are often subsidised by various government policies (Schneider and Mahar, 1994). Land titling regulations which essentially acknowledge forest clearing as evidence of effective occupation for both agriculture and livestock raising have also been documented as a major factor in frontier agricultural conversion in Latin America (Peuker, 1992; Schneider, 1994; Southgate, Sierra and Brown, 1991; Sunderlin and Rodrígez, 1996).

Pricing and economic policies influencing tropical forest land use decisions rarely take into account the forgone environmental benefits of forest conversion, such as biodiversity maintenance, carbon storage, micro-climatic maintenance, watershed protection, amenity values and non-timber products, even though non-market valuation studies show that these may be highly significant (Georgiou et al., 1997; Peters, Gentry and Mendelsohn, 1989; Ruitenbeek, 1992). For example, based on an extensive survey of valuation studies, Pearce (1998) determined a general consensus of the estimate of annual values of tropical forests, such that potential extractive benefits amount to $50/ha, recreation benefits $5–10/ha, ecological benefits $30/ha, carbon benefits $600–4,400/ha and non-use benefits $2–27/ha.

7. Conclusion

As we have discussed in this paper, the economics of tropical deforestation and land use has consisted of two distinct 'waves' of analysis. We have provided a brief overview of the cross-country analyses of the causes of tropical deforestation that typify the 'first wave', and have attempted a synthesis analysis of the factors influencing agricultural land expansion across countries. The results suggest that the pattern of agricultural development across these countries appears to affect the growth in agricultural land area, which tends to be the predominant cause of forest loss in tropical regions. Population growth may also matter, especially in Asia. Institutional factors are also important influences, although their inclusion in cross-country analyses is still constrained by the lack of data for some countries as well as the limited appropriateness of those institutional indices that are available. Finally, the impact of changes in per capita GDP on agricultural expansion varies considerably from region to region, and does not always exhibit an EKC-type relationship.

We have also provided a brief review of the 'second wave' country case studies of tropical deforestation that are able to investigate in much more detail other key factors that influence the economics of tropical deforestation and land use. Such studies have included new methods, such as spatial analysis, to illustrate the importance of location, the 'accessibility' of forests and other geographical factors in explaining forest land use patterns in tropical countries. Other studies have demonstrated how computable general equilibrium (CGE) modeling can be an effective tool for investigating a variety of economy-wide and sectoral policy impacts on agricultural expansion and deforestation. Still other studies focus on how external market forces may affect the land clearing decisions of farmers, who can be highly responsive to changes in regional and national crop prices as well as off- farm employment opportunities. The role of the state in influencing both local patterns of deforestation in remote frontier forested areas and forest degradation by major state-supported activities, such as the timber industry, is important and needs more careful analysis.[8]

As we have illustrated in this paper, recent work in tropical regions has begun to include the influences of competing uses on forests. Most studies show that public policies, property rights systems, and government are the principal factors determining forest land use decisions and thus the composition of the forest landscape in most regions (Southgate, 1990; Deacon, 1994, 1995). Nongovernmental institutions may also influence land quality, particularly when lands are managed as commons (Larson and Bromley, 1990). More research is needed on how policies, property rights systems, and social institutions change land use frontiers in tropical regions.

In sum, innovative economic models can be used effectively to investigate a range of important influences on tropical land use changes in a variety of representative developing countries. What we need is more of these novel and insightful studies into the economics of tropical deforestation and land use.

Acknowledgements

The authors would like to thank Nick Hanley for inviting them to contribute to this Special Issue and for his helpful advice and comments. All errors remain the responsibility of the authors.

Notes

1. One of the first to popularize the scientific concerns over tropical deforestation was Myers (1979).
2. The inappropriateness of using the FAO 1990 assessment based country forest cover estimates in cross-country deforestation analyses has been pointed out by Barbier and Burgess (1997), Cropper and Griffiths (1994) and Deacon (1999).
3. Strictly speaking, deforestation is defined as (minus) the percentage change in forested area, or $(F_{it-1} - F_{it})/F_{it-1}$. However, deforestation is clearly related to the change in forest stock variable, $F_t - F_{t-1}$, in equation (1). In fact, various cross-country analyses have tended to use either specification as the dependent variable to represent forest loss. To simplify notation, $F_t - F_{t-1}$ is used in equation (1) and subsequent equations as a short-hand expression for deforestation.
4. The measure of ownership risk in the study was an index derived by Bohn and Deacon (1997). The index was formed from an estimated investment function that relates investment rates in a cross-country panel to macroeconomic variables and political attributes, including measures of government instability and regime type.
5. Following Barbier and Burgess (1997), topical countries were defined as those countries with the majority of their land mass lying between the tropics.
6. Including the three time-invariant institutional indices in a fixed effects regression leads to collinear regressors (Baltagi, 1995). As the institutional indices are in themselves 'weighted' country-specific dummy variables, including the indices in an OLS regression will essentially imitate a fixed effects model. Of course, the estimated coefficients on the institutional variables may also be including the influence of other slow-changing factors that vary across countries.
7. The failure of the property rights index to be significant in any of the regressions reported in Table 5 may reflect the fact that this variable indicates the degree of protection of private property rights across all sectors of the economy rather than the security of land tenure in the agricultural sector.
8. Examples of these different type of economic case studies can be found in a forthcoming special issue of *Land Economics* on 'The Economics of Tropical Deforestation and Land Use' that we have had had the privilege of editing (Barbier and Burgess, 2000).

References

Alston, L. J., Libecap, G. D. and Mueller, B. (1999) *Titles, Conflicts And Land Use: The Development Of Property Rights And Land Reform In The Brazilian Amazon Frontier*. Ann Arbor: University of Michigan Press.

Alston, L. J., Libecap, G. D. and Mueller, B. (2000) Land reform policies, the sources of violent conflict, and implications for deforestation in the brazilian amazon. *Journal of Environmental Economics and Management*, 39, 2, 162–188.

Angelsen, A. (1999) Agricultural expansion and deforestation: modelling the impact of population, market forces and property rights. *Journal of Development Economics*, 58, April, 185–218.

Antle, J. M. and Heidebrink, G. (1995) Environment and development: theory and international evidence. *Economic Development and Cultural Change*, 43, 3, 603–625.

Baltagi, B. H. (1995) *Econometric Analysis of Panel Data*. Chichester: John Wiley.

Barbier, E. B. (1997) The economic determinants of land degradation in developing countries. *Philosophical Transactions of the Royal Society Series B*, 352, 1356, 891–899.

Barbier, E. B. (2000) Institutional constraints and deforestation. Paper presented at the 2000 Royal Economic Society/Scottish Economic Society Conference, St Andrews, Scotland, July 10–13, 2000.

Barbier, E. B. (2000) Rural poverty and natural resource degradation. In *Rural poverty in Latin America*, ed. R. López and A. Valdés. New York: St Martin's Press, pp. 152–184.

Barbier, E. B., Bockstael, N., Burgess, J. C. and Strand, I. (1995) The linkages between the timber trade and tropical deforestation – Indonesia. *World Economy*, 18, 3, 411–442.

Barbier, E. B. and Burgess, J. C. (1996) Economic analysis of deforestation in Mexico. *Environment and Development Economics*, 1, 2, 203–240.

Barbier, E. B. and Burgess, J. C. (1997) The economics of tropical forest land use options. *Land Economics*, 73, 2, 174–95.

Barbier, E. B. and Burgess, J. C. eds. (2000) Special issue on the economics of tropical deforestation and land use. *Land Economics*, forthcoming.

Beck, T., Levine, R. and Loayza, N. (1999) Finance and the sources of economic growth. Economic Growth Research Group, The World Bank, forthcoming in *Journal of Financial Economics*.

Bockstael, N. E. (1996) Modeling economics and ecology: the importance of a spatial perspective. *American Journal of Agricultural Economics*, 78, 5, 1168–1180.

Bohn, H. and Deacon, R. T. (1997) Ownership risk, investment and the use of natural resources. Working paper, Department of Economics, University of California, Santa Barbara.

Brown, K. and Pearce, D. W. eds. (1994) *The Causes of Tropical Deforestation: The Economic and Statistical Analysis of Factors Giving Rise to the Loss of the Tropical Forests*. London: University College London Press.

Burgess, J. C. (2000) The economics of tropical forest land use. Ph.D. diss., Economics Dept, University College London.

Capistrano, A. D. (1994) Tropical forest depletion and the changing macroeconomy, 1967–85. In *The Causes of Tropical Deforestation*, eds. K. Brown and D. W. Pearce. London: University College London Press.

Chomitz, K. M. and Gray, D. P. (1996) Roads, land markets and deforestation: A spatial model of land use in belize. *The World Bank Economic Review*, 10, 3, 487–512.

Cropper, M. and Griffiths, C. (1994) The interaction of population growth and environmental quality. *American Economic Review*, AEA Papers and Proceedings, 84, 2, 250–254.

Cropper, M., Mani, M. and Griffiths, C. (1999) Roads, population pressures, and deforestation in thailand, 1976–1989. *Land Economics*, 75, 1, 58–73.

Deacon, R. T. (1994) Deforestation and the rule of law in a cross-section of countries. *Land Economics*, 70, 4, 414–430.

Deacon, R. T. (1995) Assessing the relationship between government policy and deforestation. *Journal of Environmental Economics and Management*, 28, 1–18.

Deacon, R. T. (1999) Deforestation and ownership: evidence from historical accounts and contemporary data. *Land Economics*, 75, 3, 341–359.

Ehui, S. K. and Hertel, T. W. (1989) Deforestation and agricultural productivity in the Côte d'Ivoire. *American Journal of Agricultural Economics*, 71, August, 703–711.

Ehui, S. K., Hertel, T. W. and Preckel, P. V. (1990) 'Forest resource depletion, soil dynamics, and agricultural development in the tropics. *Journal of Environmental Economics and Management*, 18, 2, 136–154.

Food and Agricultural Organization (FAO) (1993) *Forest Resources Assessment 1990: Tropical Countries*. Rome: FAO.

Food and Agricultural Organization of the United Nations (FAO) (1997) *State of the WorldBs Forests 1997*. Rome: FAO.

Gergiou, S., Whittington, D., Pearce, D. and Moran, D. (1997) *Economic Values and the Environment in the Developing World*. London: Edward Elgar.

Godoy, R., Jacobson, M., De Castro, J., Aliaga, V., Romero, J. and Davis, A. (1998) The role of tenure security and private preference in neotropical deforestation. *Land Economics*, 74, 2, 162–170.

Hyde, W. F. and Sedjo, R. A. (1992) Managing tropical forests: reflections on the rent distribution discussion. *Land Economics*, 68, 3, 343–50.

Kahn, J. and MacDonald, J. (1994) International debt and deforestation. In *The Causes of Tropical Deforestation*, eds. K. Brown and D. W. Pearce. London: University College London Press.

Kaimowitz, D. and Angelsen, A. (1998) *Economic Models of Tropical Deforestation: A Review*. Bogor, Indonesia: Center for International Forestry Research.

Koop, G. and Tole, L. (1999) Is there an environmental Kuznets curve for deforestation? *Journal of Development Economics*, 58, July, 231–244.

Kooten, van G. C., Sedjo, R. A. and Bulte, E. H. (1999) Tropical deforestation: issues and policies. In *The International Yearbook of Environmental and Resource Economics 1999/2000*, eds. H. Folmer and T. Tietenberg. London: Edward Elgar, pp. 199–248.

Larson, B. A. (1991) The causes of land degradation along 'spontaneously' expanding agricultural frontiers in the Third World: comment. *Land Economics*, 67, 2, 260–66.

Larson, B. A. and Bromley, D. W. (1990) Property rights, externalities and resource degradation: locating the tragedy. *Journal of Development Economics*, 33, 2, 235–260.

Levine, R., Loayza, N. and Beck, T. (1999) Financial intermediation and growth: causality and causes. Economic Growth Research Group, The World Bank, forthcoming in *Journal of Monetary Economics*.

López, R. (1997) Environmental externalities in traditional agriculture and the impact of trade liberalization: the case of Ghana. *Journal of Development Economics*, 53, July, 17–39.

López, R. (1998) Where development can or cannot go: the role of poverty-environment linkages. In *Annual Bank Conference on Development Economics 1997*, eds. B. Pleskovic and J. E. Stiglitz. Washington DC: The World Bank, pp. 285–306.

López, R. and Niklitschek, M. (1991) Dual economic growth in poor tropical areas. *Journal of Development Economics*, 36, 189–211.

Myers, N. (1979) *The Sinking Ark: A New Look at the Problem of Disappearing Species*. Oxford: Pergamon Press.

Nelson, G. C. and Hellerstein, D. (1997) Do roads cause deforestation? Using satellite images in econometric analysis of land use. *American Journal of Agricultural Economics*, 79, 2, 80–88.

Panayotou, T. (1995) Environmental degradation at different stages of economic development. In *Beyond Rio: The Environmental Crisis and Sustainable Livelihoods in the Third World*, eds. I. Ahmed and J. A. Doeleman. London: MacMillan Press.

Panayotou, T. and Sungsuwan, S. (1994) An econometric analysis of the causes of tropical deforestation: the case of Northeast Thailand. In *The Causes of Tropical Deforestation: The Economic and Statistical Analysis of Factors Giving Rise to the Loss of the Tropical*

Forests, eds. K. Brown and D. W. Pearce. London: University College London Press, pp. 192–210.

Parks, P. J., Barbier, E. B., Burgess, J. C. (1998) The economics of forest land use in temperate and tropical areas. *Environmental and Resource Economics*, 11, 3–4, 473–487.

Pearce, D. W. (1998) Can non-market values save the tropical forests? In F. B. Goldsmith (ed.), *Tropical Rain Forest: A Wider Perspective*, Chapman and Hall, London.

Peters, C., Gentry, A. and Mendelsohn, R. (1989) Valuation of an Amazonian rainforest.' *Nature*, 339, 655–656.

Peuker, A. (1992) *Public Policies and Deforestation: A Case Study of Costa Rica*. Latin America and the Caribbean Technical Department, Regional Studies Program, Report No. 14. The World Bank, Washington DC.

Pfaff, A. (1999) What drives deforestation in the Brazilian Amazon? Evidence from satellite and socioeconomic data. *Journal of Environmental Economics and Management*, 37, 26–43.

Reis, E. and Guzmán, R. (1994) An econometric model of Amazonian deforestation. In *The Causes of Tropical Deforestation*, eds. K. Brown and D. W. Pearce. London: University College London Press.

Repetto, R. and Gillis, M. (1988) *Public Policies and the Misuse of Forest Resources*. Cambridge: Cambridge University Press.

Ruitenbeek, H. J. (1992) The rainforest supply price: a tool for evaluating rainforest conservation expenditures. *Ecological Economics*, 6, 1, 57–78.

Schneider, R. R. (1994) *Government and the Economy on the Amazon Frontier*. Latin America and the Caribbean Technical Department, Regional Studies Program, Report No. 34. The World Bank, Washington DC.

Shafik, N. (1994) Economic development and environmental quality: an econometric analysis. *Oxford Economic Papers*, 46, October, 757–773.

Southgate, D. (1990) The causes of land degradation along 'spontaneously' expanding agricultural frontiers. *Land Economics*, 66, 1, 93–101.

Southgate, D. (1994) Tropical deforestation and agricultural development in Latin America. In *The Causes of Tropical Deforestation: The Economic and Statistical Analysis of Factors Giving Rise to the Loss of the Tropical Forests*, eds. K. Brown and D. W. Pearce. London: University College London Press, pp. 134–145.

Southgate, D, Sierra, R. and Brown, L. (1991) The causes of tropical deforestation in Ecuador: a statistical analysis. *World Development*, 19, 9, 1145–1151.

Sunderlin, W. D. and Rodrígez, J. A. (1996) *Cattle, Broadleaf Forests and the Agricultural Modernization Law of Honduras*. CIFOR Occasional Paper No. 7, Center for International Forestry Research, Jakarta, Indonesia.

Vincent, J. R. and Binkley, C. S. (1991) *Forest Based Industrialization: A Dynamic Perspective*, Development Discussion Paper No. 389, Harvard Institute for International Development (HIID), Cambridge, Massachusetts

CHAPTER 7

CHOICE MODELLING APPROACHES: A SUPERIOR ALTERNATIVE FOR ENVIRONMENTAL VALUATION?

Nick Hanley
University of Glasgow

Susana Mourato
Imperial College, London

Robert E. Wright
University of Stirling, CEPR and IZA, Bonn

Abstract. In this paper, we examine some popular 'choice modelling' approaches to environmental valuation, which can be considered as alternatives to more familiar valuation techniques based on stated preferences such as the contingent valuation method. A number of choice modelling methods are consistent with consumer theory, their focus on an attribute-based theory of value permits a superior representation of many environmental management contexts. However, choice modelling surveys can place a severe cognitive burden upon respondents and induce satisficing rather than maximising behavioural patterns. In this framework, we seek to identify the best available choice modelling alternative and investigate its potential to 'solve' some of the major biases associated with standard contingent valuation. We then discuss its use in the light of policy appraisal needs within the EU. An application to the demand for rock climbing in Scotland is provided as an illustration.

1. Introduction

Although still controversial, the contingent valuation method has managed to gain increased acceptance amongst both academics and policy makers as a versatile and powerful methodology for estimating the monetary value of environmental changes. Contingent valuation (Mitchell and Carson, 1989) is a direct survey approach to estimating consumer preferences. By means of an appropriately designed questionnaire, a hypothetical market is described where the good or service in question can be traded. This contingent market defines the good itself, the institutional context in which it would be provided, and the way it would be financed. Respondents are then asked to express their maximum willingness to pay (WTP) or minimum willingness to accept for a hypothetical change in the level of provision of the good. Theoretically, contingent valuation is well rooted in welfare economics, namely in the neo-classical concept of economic value based on individual utility maximisation. This assumes that stated WTP amounts are related to respondents' underlying preferences in a consistent manner.

The choice of elicitation formats for willingness to pay questions in contingent valuation surveys has already passed through a number of distinct stages. In the early years, open-ended elicitation formats were predominant amongst practitioners. The answers were informative and statistically straightforward to analyse. Nonetheless, dissatisfaction with this approach gradually grew as evidence mounted of the incidence of protest bids possibly resulting from the associated cognitive burden, and of the potential for strategic bidding. During the 1980s, following the seminal work of Bishop and Heberlein (1979), there was a shift towards the use of dichotomous choice elicitation, which not only provided incentives for the truthful revelation of preferences but also simplified the cognitive task faced by respondents. After receiving the endorsement of the NOAA panel in 1993 (Arrow *et al.*, 1993) the use of dichotomous choice questions substantially increased particularly in US-based applications. However, an increasing number of empirical studies started to reveal that dichotomous choice results seemed to be significantly larger than open-ended values, possibly due to yeah saying. Moreover, neither approach is ideally suited to deal with cases where changes are multidimensional.

Partly as a response to these problems, valuation practitioners are increasingly developing an interest in alternative stated preference formats such as Choice Modelling (CM).[1] CM is a family of survey-based methodologies for modelling preferences for goods, where goods are described in terms of their attributes and of the levels that these take. Respondents are presented with various alternative descriptions of a good, differentiated by their attributes and levels, and are asked to rank the various alternatives, to rate them or to choose their most preferred. By including price/cost as one of the attributes of the good, willingness to pay can be indirectly recovered from people's rankings, ratings or choices. As with contingent valuation, CM can also measure all forms of value including non-use values. The conceptual microeconomic framework for CM lies in Lancaster's (1966) characteristics theory of value which assumes that consumers' utilities for goods can be decomposed into utilities for composing characteristics. Empirically, CM has been widely used in the market research and transport literatures (e.g. Green and Srinivasan, 1978; Henscher, 1994), but has only relatively recently been applied to other areas such as the environment.

This paper is organised as follows. Section two contains a descriptive analysis of the main CM techniques. An example of a recent CM experiment is presented in Section three. Section four summarises the advantages and disadvantages of CM and compares its performance with contingent valuation. The last section discusses the potential to use CM techniques to aid policy decisions in the environmental arena.

2. Choice Modelling Techniques

A typical CM exercise is characterised by a number of key stages. These are described in Table 1.

As mentioned in Table 1, individual preferences can be uncovered in CM surveys by asking respondents to rank the options presented to them, to score

Table 1. Stages of a Choice Modelling Exercise

Stage	Description
Selection of attributes	Identification of relevant attributes of the good to be valued. Literature reviews and focus groups are used to select attributes that are relevant to people while expert consultations help to identify the attributes that will be impacted by the policy. A monetary cost is typically one of the attributes to allow the estimation of WTP.
Assignment of levels	The attribute levels should be feasible, realistic, non-linearly spaced, and span the range of respondents' preference maps. Focus groups, pilot surveys, literature reviews and consultations with experts are instrumental in selecting appropriate attribute levels. A baseline 'status quo' level is usually included.
Choice of experimental design	Statistical design theory is used to combine the levels of the attributes into a number of alternative scenarios or profiles to be presented to respondents. *Complete factorial designs* allow the estimation of the full effects of the attributes upon choices: that includes the effects of each of the *individual* attributes presented (main effects) and the extent to which behaviour is connected with variations in the *combination* of different attributes offered (interactions). These designs often originate an impractically large number of combinations to be evaluated: for example, 27 options would be generated by a full factorial design of 3 attributes with 3 levels each. *Fractional factorial designs* are able to reduce the number of scenario combinations presented with a concomitant loss in estimating power (i.e. some or all of the interactions will not be detected). For example, the 27 options can be reduced to 9 using a fractional factorial. These designs are available through specialised software.
Construction of choice sets	The profiles identified by the experimental design are then grouped into choice sets to be presented to respondents. Profiles can be presented individually, in pairs or in groups. For example, the 9 options identified by the fractional factorial design can be grouped into 3 sets of four-way comparisons.
Measurement of preferences	Choice of a survey procedure to measure individual preferences: ratings, rankings or choices.
Estimation procedure	OLS regression or maximum likelihood estimation procedures (logit, probit, ordered logit, conditional logit, nested logit, panel data models, etc.). Variables that do not vary across alternatives have to be interacted with choice-specific attributes.

them or to choose their most preferred. These different ways of measuring preferences correspond to different variants of the CM approach. There are four main variants: choice experiments, contingent ranking, contingent rating and paired comparisons. As will be shown in this section, these techniques differ in the quality of information they generate, in their degree of complexity and also in their ability to produce WTP estimates that can be shown to be consistent with the usual measures of welfare change. Table 2 summarises the various approaches.

The next section provides a detailed analysis of each of the main CM variants depicted in Table 2.[2]

Table 2. Main Choice Modelling Alternatives

Approach	Tasks	Welfare consistent estimates?
Choice Experiments	Choose between two or more alternatives (where one is the status quo)	Yes
Contingent Ranking	Rank a series of alternatives	Depends
Contingent Rating	Score alternative scenarios on a scale of 1–10	Doubtful
Paired Comparisons	Score pairs of scenarios on similar scale	Doubtful

2.1. *Choice Experiments*

In a choice experiment (CE) respondents are presented with a series of alternatives, differing in terms of attributes and levels, and asked to choose their most preferred. A baseline alternative, corresponding to the status quo or 'do nothing' situation, is usually included in each choice set. This is because one of the options must always be in the respondent's currently feasible choice set in order to be able to interpret the results in standard welfare economic terms. Table 3

Table 3. Illustrative Choice Experiment Question

WHICH ROUTE WOULD YOU PREFER TO VISIT IN THE SUMMER, GIVEN THE TWO ROUTES DESCRIBED BELOW?

Characteristics of route	Route A	Route B
Length of climb	100 metres	200 metres
Approach time	3 hours	2 hours
Quality of climb	2 stars	0 stars
Crowding at route	Crowded	Not crowded
Scenic quality of route	Not at all scenic	Not at all scenic
Distance of route from home	160 miles	110 miles

PREFER ROUTE A?:	☐
PREFER ROUTE B?:	☐
STAY AT HOME? (CHOOSE NEITHER)?:	☐

presents an example used in a recent study of rock climbing in Scotland. In this study, described in detail in the next section, the good is a climb, defined in terms of its attributes such as length and congestion. Each respondent is asked a sequence of these questions.

The choice experiment approach was initially developed by Louviere and Hensher (1982) and Louviere and Woodworth (1983). Choice experiments share a common theoretical framework with dichotomous-choice contingent valuation in the Random Utility Model (Luce, 1959; McFadden, 1973), as well as a common basis of empirical analysis in limited dependent variable econometrics (Greene, 1997). According to this framework, the indirect utility function for each respondent $i(U)$ can be decomposed into two parts: a deterministic element (V), which is typically specified as a linear index of the attributes (X) of the j different alternatives in the choice set, and a stochastic element (e), which represents unobservable influences on individual choice. This is shown in equation (1).

$$Uij = Vij(Xij) + eij = bXij + eij \qquad (1)$$

Thus, the probability that any particular respondent prefers option g in the choice set to any alternative option h, can be expressed as the probability that the utility associated with option g exceeds that associated with all other options, as stated in equation (2).

$$P[(Uig > Uih)\forall h \neq g] = P[(Vig - Vih) > (eih - eig)] \qquad (2)$$

In order to derive an explicit expression for this probability, it is necessary to know the distribution of the error terms (e_{ij}). A typical assumption is that they are independently and identically distributed with an extreme-value (Weibull) distribution:

$$P(e_{ij} \leqslant t) = F(t) = \exp(-\exp(-t)) \qquad (3)$$

The above distribution of the error term implies that the probability of any particular alternative g being chosen as the most preferred can be expressed in terms of the logistic distribution (McFadden, 1973) stated in equation (4). This specification is known as the conditional logit model:

$$P(Uig > Uih, \forall h \neq g) = \frac{\exp(\mu Vig)}{\sum_j \exp(\mu Vij)} \qquad (4)$$

where μ is a scale parameter, inversely proportional to the standard deviation of the error distribution. This parameter often cannot be separately identified and is therefore typically assumed to be one. An important implication of this specification is that selections from the choice set must obey the Independence from Irrelevant Alternatives (IIA) property (or Luce's Choice Axiom; Luce, 1959), which states that the relative probabilities of two options being selected are unaffected by the introduction or removal of other alternatives. This property follows from the independence of the Weibull error terms across the different options contained in the choice set.

This model can be estimated by conventional maximum likelihood procedures, with the respective log-likelihood function stated in equation (5) below, where y_{ij} is an indicator variable which takes a value of one if respondent i chose option j and zero otherwise.

$$\log L = \sum_{i=1}^{N} \sum_{j=1}^{J} yij \log \left[\frac{\exp(Vij)}{\sum_{j=1}^{J} \exp(Vij)} \right] \tag{5}$$

Socio-economic variables can be included along with choice set attributes in the X terms in equation (1), but since they are constant across choice occasions for any given individual (e.g. income is the same when the first choice is made as the second), they can only be entered as interaction terms, i.e. interacted with choice specific attributes.

Once the parameter estimates have been obtained, a WTP compensating variation welfare measure that conforms to demand theory can be derived for each attribute using the formula given by (6) (Hanemann, 1984; Parsons and Kealy, 1992) where V^0 represents the utility of the initial state and V^1 represents the utility of the alternative state. The coefficient b_y gives the marginal utility of income and is the coefficient of the cost attribute.

$$WTP = b_y^{-1} \ln \left\{ \frac{\sum_i \exp(V_i^1)}{\sum_i \exp(V_i^0)} \right\} \tag{6}$$

It is straightforward to show that, for the linear utility index specified in (1), the above formulae can be simplified to the ratio of coefficients given in equation (7) where b_C is the coefficient on any of the attributes. These ratios are often known as implicit prices.

$$WTP = \frac{-b_C}{b_y} \tag{7}$$

Choice experiments are therefore consistent with utility maximisation and demand theory, at least when a status quo option is included in the choice set.[3]

Notice however that specifying standard errors for the implicit price ratios is more complex. Although the asymptotic distribution of the maximum likelihood estimator for the parameters b is known, the asymptotic distribution of the maximum likelihood estimator of the welfare measure is not, since it is a non-linear function of the parameter vector. One way of obtaining confidence intervals for this measure is by means of the procedure developed by Krinsky and Robb (1986). This technique simulates the asymptotic distribution of the coefficients by taking repeated random draws from the multivariate normal distribution defined by the coefficient estimates and their associated covariance matrix. These are used to generate an empirical distribution for the welfare measure and the associated confidence intervals can then be computed.

If a violation of the IIA hypothesis is observed, then more complex statistical models are necessary that relax some of the assumptions used. These include the multinomial probit (Hausman and Wise, 1978), the nested logit (McFadden, 1981) and the random parameters logit model (Train, 1998). IIA can be tested using a procedure suggested by Hausman and McFadden (1984). This basically involves constructing a likelihood ratio test around different versions of the model where choice alternatives are excluded. If IIA holds, then the model estimated on all choices should be the same as that estimated for a sub-set of alternatives (see Foster and Mourato, 2000, for an example).

Appendix 1 summarises some choice experiment applications in environmental economics.

2.2. Contingent Ranking

In a contingent ranking experiment respondents are required to rank a set of alternative options, characterised by a number of attributes, which are offered at different levels across options. As with CE, a status quo option is normally included in the choice set to ensure welfare consistent results. An example is provided in Table 4.

As before, the random utility model provides the economic theory framework for analysing the data from a ranking exercise. Under the assumption of an independently and identically distributed random error with a Weibull distribution, Beggs, Cardell and Hausman (1981) developed a rank-order logit model capable of using all the information contained in a survey where alternatives are fully ranked by respondents. Their specification is based on the repeated application of the probability expression given in equation (4) until a full ranking of all the alternatives has been obtained. The probability of any particular ranking of alternatives being made by individual i can be expressed as:

$$Pi(U_{i1} > U_{i2} > \cdots > U_{ij}) = \prod_{j=1}^{J} \left[\frac{\exp(Vij)}{\sum_{k=j}^{J} \exp(Vik)} \right] \quad (8)$$

Clearly, this rank ordered model is more restrictive than the standard conditional logit model in as much as the extreme value (Weibull) distribution governs not only the first choice but all successive choices as well. As before, the model relies critically on the IIA assumption, which in this case is what permits the multiplication of successive conditional logit probabilities to obtain the probability expression for the full ranking.

Table 4. Illustrative Contingent Ranking Question

RANK THE ALTERNATIVES FOR A SUMMER VISIT BELOW ACCORDING TO YOUR PREFERENCES, ASSIGNING 1 TO THE MOST PREFERRED, 2 TO THE SECOND MOST PREFERRED, 3 TO THE THIRD MOST PREFERRED AND 4 TO THE LEAST PREFERRED.

Characteristics of route	Route A	Route B	Route C	Stay at home
Length of climb	200 metres	250 metres	250 metres	
Approach time	3 hours	2 hours	2 hours	
Quality of climb	2 stars	1 stars	0 stars	
Crowding at route	Crowded	Not crowded	Crowded	
Scenic quality of route	Scenic	Not at all scenic	Not scenic	
Distance of route from home	160 miles	70 miles	30 miles	
RANKING:	☐	☐	☐	☐

The parameters of the utility function can be estimated by maximising the log-likelihood function given in equation (9).

$$\log L = \sum_{i=1}^{N} \sum_{j=1}^{J} \log \left[\frac{\exp(Vij)}{\sum_{k=j}^{J} (\exp Vik)} \right] \qquad (9)$$

Contingent ranking can be seen as a series of choices in which respondents face a sequential choice process, whereby they first identify their most preferred choice, then, after removal of that option from the choice set, identify their most preferred choice out of the remaining set and so on. In other words, one can decompose a contingent ranking exercise into a set of choice experiments (Chapman and Staelin (1982); Foster and Mourato, 2000). Welfare values can therefore be estimated as in the choice experiment example. Ranking data provides more statistical information than choice experiments, which leads to tighter confidence intervals around the parameter estimates.

One of the limitations of this approach lies in the added cognitive difficulty associated with ranking choices with many attributes and levels. Previous research in the marketing literature by Ben-Akiva et al. (1991), Chapman and Staelin (1982), and Hausman and Ruud (1987) found significant differences in the preference structure implicit across ranks. In other words, choices seem to be unreliable and inconsistent across ranks. A possible explanation is that responses may be governed by different decision protocols according to the level of the rank (Ben-Akiva et al.,1991). Alternatively, the results could indicate increasing noise (random effects) with the depth of the ranking task as, in general, lower ranks seem to be less reliable than higher ranks (Hausman and Ruud, 1987). Foster and Mourato (1997) developed a number of tests of logicality, rank consistency and transitivity by including in the ranking sets dominated alternatives and repeated pairs of options.

More importantly, the fact that a baseline alternative is necessarily not present in all the trade-offs presented to respondents may result in welfare estimates that do not conform with standard consumer theory. In other words, once the baseline alternative is chosen, subsequent choices do not convey information about a respondent's real demand curve but reflect instead a conditional demand, conditional on the choices remaining in the choice set (Louviere, Hensher and Swait, 2000). To ensure welfare consistent results, once the status quo is chosen, any subsequent rankings should be discarded from the estimation procedure.

Used initially by Beggs, Cardell and Hausman (1981) and Lareau and Rae (1987), contingent ranking approaches have also been applied to environmental valuation. A summary of recent studies is included in Appendix 2.

2.3. Contingent Rating

In a contingent rating exercise respondents are presented with a number of scenarios and are asked to rate them individually on a semantic or numeric scale. This approach does not involve a direct comparison of alternative choices and consequently there is no formal theoretical link between the expressed ratings and economic choices. An example is provided in Table 5.

Rating data have been analysed within the framework of the random utility model with ratings being first transformed into a utility scale. In this context, the indirect utility function is assumed to be related to individual's ratings via a transformation function:

$$Rij(Xij) = \phi[Vij(Xij)] \tag{10}$$

where R represents the rating of individual i for choice j and ϕ is the transformation function. In marketing applications these data are typically analysed using OLS regression techniques which imply a strong assumption about the cardinality of the ratings scale. An alternative approach, which allows the data to be analysed in a random utility framework, is to use ordered probit and logit

Table 5. Illustrative Contingent Rating Question

ON THE SCALE BELOW, PLEASE RATE YOUR PREFERENCES FOR A SUMMER VISIT TO THE FOLLOWING ROUTE?

Characteristics of route	Route A
Length of climb	300 metres
Approach time	30 min
Quality of climb	2 stars
Crowding at route	Crowded
Scenic quality of route	Not at all scenic
Distance of route from home	200 miles

1	2	3	4	5	6	7	8	9	10

Very low preference	Very high preference

models that only imply an ordinal significance of the ratings. However, there remains the implicit assumption that ratings are comparable across individuals.

Roe et al. (1996) have shown how to estimate compensating variation measures from ratings data based on ratings differences. The approach consists in subtracting a monetary cost from income until the ratings difference is made equal to zero:

$$R^1ij(X^1ij, M - WTP) - R^0ij(X^0ij, M) = 0 \qquad (11)$$

where R^0 is the rating of the baseline choice, R^1 the rating attributed to the alternative choice, and M is income.

Despite its popularity amongst marketing practitioners, rating exercises are much less used in environmental economics (see Appendix 3 for a summary of existing studies). The main reason for this lack of popularity lies in the strong assumptions that need to be made in order to transform ratings into utilities. These assumptions relate either to the cardinality of rating scales or to the implicit assumption of comparability of ratings across individuals: both are inconsistent with consumer theory. Hence, contingent rating exercises do not produce welfare consistent value estimates.

2.4. Paired Comparisons

In a paired comparison exercise respondents are asked to choose their preferred alternative out of a set of two choices and to indicate the strength of their preference in a numeric or semantic scale. This format is also known as graded or rated pairs. Table 6 provides an example.

The graded pairs approach is an attempt to get more information than simply identifying the most preferred alternative and, as such, combines elements of choice experiments (choosing the most preferred alternative) and rating exercises (rating the strength of preference). If the ratings are re-interpreted as providing an indication about choices only, then this approach collapses into a choice experiment and the comments and procedures described previously in Section 2.1 also apply in this case. Note that a status quo option must always be present in the pairs for the resulting estimates to be welfare consistent. But if only choice information is used from the ratings then why specify a graded pair rather than a CE in the first place? If instead it is assumed that a change in rating is related to a change in utilities, then the resulting data can be analysed using ordered probit or logit techniques, similarly to the contingent rating procedure, and the caveats described in Section 2.3 become relevant.

Pairwise comparisons are extremely popular amongst marketing practitioners, especially after the introduction of computerised interviewing techniques and the development of specialised computer software such as Adaptive Conjoint Analysis (Green et al., 1991; Sawtooth Software, 1993) which determines attributes, levels and pairwise comparisons, tailor-made for each respondent. It should however be noted that these computer generated designs do not necessarily conform with standard optimality criteria. Some applications of paired comparisons exist in the environmental field and are summarised in Appendix 4.

Table 6. Illustrative Paired Comparisons Question

WHICH ROUTE WOULD YOU PREFER TO VISIT IN THE SUMMER, GIVEN THE TWO ROUTES DESCRIBED BELOW?

Characteristics of route	Route A	Route B
Length of climb	150 metres	50 metres
Approach time	3 hours	2 hours
Quality of climb	3 stars	1 stars
Crowding at route	Not crowded	Not crowded
Scenic quality of route	Not at all scenic	Very scenic
Distance of route from home	200 miles	110 miles

1	2	3	4	5	6	7	8	9	10

Strongly prefer Route A   Strongly prefer Route B

3. An Illustration: Modelling the Demand for Rock Climbing Sites in Scotland

Mountaineering is an increasingly popular sport in Scotland. Figures from Highlands and Islands Enterprise[4] suggest that 767 000 mountaineers from the UK visited the Highlands and Islands for hillwalking, technical climbing, ski mountaineering or high level cross-country ski-ing in 1996 (HIE, 1996). Spending by mountaineers is an important source of income for many areas of the Highlands. For rock-climbing (defined here to include both summer and winter climbing), participation is harder to estimate. In the HIE survey, mountaineers classified the main purpose of their trips to the area as hillwalking (77.2%); rock-climbing (10.8%); ski-mountaineering (5.5%) and ski-touring (6.5%). Using a mean of 14 trips per annum implies a total participation of between 82 836–153 400 total climbers, and 1 159 704–2 147 600 climbing days in Scotland per year.

Rock climbs are classified according to two grading systems in Britain, which between them describe both the overall difficulty and exposure of a route, and the degree of difficulty in making the hardest move on the climb (the crux). Climbers' appreciation of routes though extends beyond this technical grading, to include aspects such as length of climb, quality, and degree of crowding on a route. One may thus think of individual climbs as different bundles of a given set of attributes, although it may be hard for the researcher to completely describe a particular climb using this set. Climbers make choices from the set of all climbs in Scotland in deciding on where to go on a particular trip: a natural way to model this choice problem is thus to make use of random utility theory. In this section, a choice experiment applied to climbers' choices of rock climbing sites is described.[5] Results from this approach are then compared with results from a standard multinomial site choice model based on revealed preference data from the same sample of users.

3.1. *Study Design*

The initial steps in this study were to identify the choice sets and their relevant attributes. To accomplish this, focus groups were conducted with climbers from university mountaineering clubs in Edinburgh and Stirling. Eight principal climbing areas were identified. These were: Northern Highlands, Creag Meagaidh, Ben Nevis (including Glen Nevis), Glen Coe (including Glen Etive), Isle of Arran, Arrochar, the Cullins of Skye and the Cairngorms. The attributes and levels selected to describe these sites were:

Length of climbs: 50, 100, 200 and 300 metres
Approach time from the road to the base of the climb: 1/2, 1, 2 and 3 hours
Crowding on the climbing route: 'crowded' versus 'not crowded'
Quality of climbs, as measured by the star rating system popularised in SMC area guidebooks: 0, 1, 2 and 3 stars
Scenic quality of area: 'very scenic', 'scenic', 'not scenic' and 'not at all scenic'
Travel distance from home: 30, 70, 110, 160, 200 and 250 miles

The chosen attributes and levels produced a full factorial design with $2^1 4^4 6^1 = 3072$ possible climbing routes. A fractional factorial design reduced the number of route alternatives to 36. These alternatives were then grouped into 4 or 8 choice pairs to be presented to respondents. A baseline alternative ('staying at home') was added to each choice pair.

The sampling frame was provided through a list of climbing club members in Scotland. A random sample of addresses was selected, and a mail questionnaire was implemented. As a response incentive, a donation of £2 was promised to the John Muir Trust (a charity which exists to conserve wilderness areas in Scotland) for every questionnaire returned. To widen the sample in terms of representativeness, questionnaires were also administered at climbing walls in Edinburgh, Glasgow and Falkirk. A sample of 267 useable responses from climbers was acquired.

Climbers were asked questions relating to their total trips in the last twelve months (summer and winter) to each of the 8 areas; to score each area in terms of the 6 attributes used; to complete a number of choice experiments, ranging from 4 to 8 choice pairs; to provide a ranking of attributes in summer and in winter; to provide information on spending related to rock-climbing; to provide information on their climbing abilities and experience; and finally, to provide us with standard socio-economic information. An example choice set was given in Table 3.

3.2. *Results*

The majority of respondents ranked the star rating of the climb as the most important attribute in the summer and 50% ranked it as most important also in winter. In summer the largest group (27%) identified travel time as least important attribute with 26% of respondents stating that the scenic quality of the site was least important in winter.

Table 7. Choice Experiment Estimates

Attribute	Coefficient	Correct sign?	T statistic
Length of climb	0.00395	Yes	7.25
Approach time	−0.00671	Yes	−7.36
Quality of climb	0.637	Yes	13.72
Crowding at route	−0.618	Yes	−11.85
Scenic quality of route	0.591	Yes	11.83
Travel cost	−0.0321	Yes	−9.50
ASC1	1.723	?	6.83
ASC2	0.3458	?	4.501

L max: −1026.245; L (constants only): −1385.096; Pseudo-R square: 0.259.
N = 3996 choice occasions.

The conditional logit model, set out in equations (4) and (5) in Section 2.1, was used to analyse the survey data. The distance term was converted into a travel cost before estimation by multiplying by (2 ∗ 10p), to allow comparison with the revealed preference data and to allow estimation of welfare measures. Alternative specific constants (ASCs) were included in the estimation to reflect the differences in utilities for each alternative relative to the base. Results are given in Table 7. As may be seen, all signs are in accord with a priori expectations, and all attributes emerge as significant determinants of choice.

As explained above, assuming a linear utility function, the implicit price of any attribute can be calculated by dividing the parameter estimate for that attribute by the parameter estimate on the price term. In the above model, this implies that climbers would be willing to pay an additional £19.23 to climb at a 'not crowded' as distinct from a 'crowded' site and an extra £0.12 per additional metre length of climb.

4. Advantages and Problems

4.1. *Advantages*

As several authors have pointed out, choice modelling approaches possess some advantages relative to the standard contingent valuation (CV) technique. Here, and for the rest of the paper, the focus will be mostly on choice experiments as an example of choice modelling. Principal among the attractions of CE are claimed to be the following:

(i) CE is particularly suited to deal with situations where changes are multi-dimensional and trade-offs between them are of particular interest because of its natural ability to separately identify the value of individual attributes of a good or programme, typically supplied in combination with one another. Whilst in principle CV can also be applied to estimate the value of the attributes of a programme, for example by including a series of CV scenarios in a questionnaire or by conducting a series of CV studies, it is a more costly and cumbersome alternative. Hence CE does a better job than CV in measuring the marginal value of changes in various characteristics of environmental programmes. This is often a more useful focus from a management/policy perspective than focussing on either the gain or loss of the good, or on a discrete change in its attributes. Useful here might mean more generalisable, and therefore more appropriate from a benefits transfer viewpoint (for encouraging evidence on the use of CE in benefits transfer, see Morrison *et al.*, 1998).

(ii) CE are more informative than discrete choice CV studies as respondents get multiple chances to express their preference for a valued good over a range of payment amounts: for example, if respondents are given 8 choice pairs and a 'do nothing' option, they may respond to as many as 17 bid prices, including zero. In fact, CE can be seen as a generalisation of discrete choice contingent valuation concerning a sequence of discrete choice valuation questions where there are two or more goods involved.

(iii) Choice modelling generally avoids an explicit elicitation of respondents' willingness to pay by relying instead on ratings, rankings or choices amongst a series of alternative packages of characteristics from where willingness to pay can be indirectly inferred. As such, CE may minimise some of the response difficulties found in CVM that were mentioned in Section 1 (protest bids, strategic behaviour, yeah saying). But this point has yet to be demonstrated.

4.2. *Problems*

Experience with choice experiments in environmental contexts is still fairly limited, despite the fact that choice modelling in general has been very widely applied in the fields of transport and marketing. Several problem areas seem to be important:

(i) Arguably, the main disadvantage of CM approaches lies with the cognitive difficulty associated with multiple complex choices or rankings between bundles with many attributes and levels. Both experimental economists and psychologists have found ample evidence that there is a limit to how much information respondents can meaningfully handle while making a decision. Swait and Adamowicz (1996) estimated an inverted U-shaped relationship between choice complexity and variance of underlying utility amounts; Mazotta and Opaluch (1995) found that increased complexity leads to increased random errors; Chapman and Staelin (1982) and Hausman and Ruud (1987) found evidence of increasing random effects with the depth of a ranking task; and Ben-Akiva *et al.* (1991) and Foster and Mourato (1997) detected significant numbers of inconsistent responses in even simple ranking tasks.

In addition, since respondents are typically presented with large number of choice sets both learning and fatigue effects can occur that may lead to apparently irrational choices (Tversky and Shaffir, 1992). Handling repeated answers per respondent also poses statistical problems and the correlation between responses needs to be taken into account and properly modelled (Adamowicz, Louviere and Swait, 1998).

This implies that, whilst the researcher might want to include many attributes, and also interactions between these attributes, then unless very large samples are collected, respondents will be faced with daunting choice tasks. The consequence is that, in presence of complex choices, respondents use heuristics or rules of thumb to simplify the decision task. These filtering rules lead to options being chosen that are good enough although not necessarily the best, avoiding the need to solve the underlying utility-maximisation problem (i.e. a satisficing approach rather than a maximising one). Heuristics often associated with difficult choice tasks include maximin and maximax strategies and lexicographic orderings (Tversky, 1972; Foster and Mourato, 1997). Hence, it is important to incorporate consistency tests into CM studies in order to detect the range of problems discussed above (Foster and Mourato, 1997; Hanley, Wright and Koop, 2000).

(ii) In order to estimate the total value of an environmental programme or good from a CE, as distinct from a change in one of its attributes, it is necessary to assume that the value of the whole is equal to the sum of the parts. For example, with a linear utility function, Hanley *et al.* (1998) calculate the value of the Environmentally Sensitive Areas programme as the sum of the values of its component parts. This clearly raises two potential problems. First, that there may be additional attributes of the good not included in the design which generate utility (in practice, these are captured in the constant terms in the estimated model). Second, that the value of the 'whole' is indeed additive in this way. Elsewhere in economics, objections have been raised about the assumption that the value of the whole is indeed equal to the sum of its parts. In order to test whether this is a valid objection in the case of CE, values of a full programme or good obtained from CE should be compared with values obtained for the same resource using some other method such as CV, under similar circumstances. In the transport field, research for London Underground and London Buses among others has shown clear evidence that values of whole bundles of improvements are valued less than the sum of the component values, all measured using CE (SDG, 2000, 1999). Furthermore, Foster and Mourato (1999) found that the estimates from a choice experiment of the total value of charitable services in the UK were significantly larger than results obtained from a parallel contingent valuation survey.

(iii) It is more difficult for CE and other CM approaches to derive values for a sequence of elements implemented by policy or project, when compared to a contingent valuation alternative. Hence, valuing the sequential provision of goods in multi-attribute programmes is probably better undertaken by CV (EFTEC, 2001).

(iv) As is the case with all stated preference techniques, welfare estimates obtained with CE are sensitive to study design. For example, the choice of attributes, the levels chosen to represent them, and the way in which choices are relayed to respondents (e.g. use of photographs vs text descriptions, choices vs ranks) are not neutral and may impact on the values of estimates of consumers' surplus and marginal utilities. Hanley, Wright and Koop (2000) found that changing the number of choice tasks respondents performed produced significant impacts on the model of preferences derived from their responses.

4.3. *Do Choice Experiments Solve Any of the Main Problems of CVM?*

Contingent valuation has been criticised as a means of eliciting environmental preferences by many authors, most famously perhaps by Kahneman and Knetsch (1992) and by Hausman (1993). Moreover, practitioners have been very open about areas of sensitivity in applying the method. Some of the main areas in which difficulties have been encountered include the following:

(i) 'Hypothetical' bias: from early on in the history of the CV, there has been a concern that the hypothetical nature of CV responses might lead respondents to overestimate their true valuations (e.g. Cummings *et al.*, 1986). Many studies that compare actual payments with behavioural intentions as expressed in CV surveys find the latter amounts to be significantly smaller than the former (see Foster, Bateman and Harley, 1997 and Christie, 1999 for reviews of these studies). Conversely, in a large comparative study (616 comparisons) of contingent valuation results and estimates derived from actual markets via revealed preference methods, Carson *et al.* (1996) found that CV estimates were on average lower than revealed preference estimates. Further inspection of the available evidence reveals that the only consistent case where CV estimates are higher than estimates from revealed preference and real payment experiments is when the values result from voluntary contributions. This is because voluntary contributions give respondents the incentive to overbid in the hypothetical market while free-riding in terms of actual payments (Carson, Groves and Machina, 1999). There are very few similar tests at present for CE in the environmental context (Carlsson, 1999). However, given that CE is in effect a generalisation of discrete choice CV, there is little reason to suppose, a priori, that it performs any better than contingent valuation in this regard.

(ii) Sensitivity to scope: one of the recommendations of the NOAA panel (Arrow *et al.*, 1993) was that CV surveys should include tests of scope to assess whether WTP values are sensitive to the size of environmental change being offered. This issue is very relevant from a policy appraisal perspective: in the UK, for example, a debate has been on-going of the extent to which it is acceptable to aggregate up from WTP findings for individual Environmentally Sensitive Areas to all ESAs, in calculating programme benefits.

Sensitivity to scope is typically assessed by one of two methods: either presenting each individual with a number of valuation scenarios which differ according to scope (a within group or internal test) or by presenting different sub-samples of the population with valuation scenarios which differ according to scope (a between groups or external test). One advantage of CE is that it provides a natural internal scope test due to the elicitation of multiple responses per individual. The internal test is however weaker than the external test in as much as the answers given by any particular individual are not independent from each other and thus sensitivity to scope is to some extent forced.

A meta analysis by Carson (1998) has shown that, on the whole, CV studies pass the scope test, although the evidence is mixed: for unfamiliar goods and with external tests scope effects can be less discernible. In one of the few formal tests of sensitivity to scope in both CV and CE, Foster and Mourato (1999) undertook separate CV studies of two nested public goods both of which were explicitly incorporated in a parallel CE survey. The authors found that, while there was evidence that both CV and CE produced results which exhibited sensitivity to scope, the evidence for the CE method was much stronger than that for CV. This result conforms with prior expectations as the scope test used for the CV method was an external test and consequently more demanding than the internal test provided by the CE method.

(iii) Sensitivity of estimates to study design: a common finding in CV studies is that bids can be affected by design choices, for example in terms of the choice of payment mechanism, the amount and type of information provided, and the rules of the market.[6] But, as noted above, design issues are as important in CE as in CVM.

(iv) Ethical protesting: a small percentage of respondents in contingent valuation studies typically refuse to 'play the game' due to ethical objections to the underlying utilitarian model (Spash and Hanley, 1995; Hanley and Milne, 1996). This implies, for example, an un-willingness to pay in principle to prevent environmental degradation.[7] Such responses are usually treated as protests, and are excluded from the analysis. The preponderance of ethical protests may be sensitive to the type and amount of monetary payment requested. Therefore, CE might reduce the incidence of ethical protesting as the choice context can be less 'stark' than direct elicitation of willingness to pay. However, as noted above, this point has yet to be proven.

(v) Expense: CV studies can be hugely expensive, especially when large probabilistic samples and personal interviews are used. If split-samples are required, for example to evaluate various components of a given programme, then the costs can quickly become prohibitive. When valuing multi-attribute programmes, CE studies can reduce the expense of valuation studies, because of their natural ability to value programme attributes in one single questionnaire and because they are more informative than discrete choice CV surveys.

5. Valuation in a Policy Context

Economics should ideally be useful, and one way it can be useful is through the provision of advice to policy makers. In the UK, much of the funding for environmental valuation studies has come from government departments and agencies with responsibilities for environmental policy design and implementation or with responsibility for policies which impact on the environment. This source of funding and interest was also important in the early development of valuation techniques in the US, especially prior to the use of contingent valuation in damage assessments.

Within the UK, a formal commitment to engage in environmental cost-benefit analysis (CBA) exists with respect to the national environment agencies (although varying degrees of importance are then attached to the results of these exercises). Government departments, since the publication of 'Policy Appraisal and the Environment' by the DETR in 1991, have all been encouraged to apply environmental CBA principles to policy design: this encouragement has been moved in the direction of a requirement by recent Cabinet Office guidelines. For policy-making within the European Union, Pearce (1998b) has argued that up until relatively recently, there was no or only little consideration given to comparing the environmental costs and benefits of draft directives, which has probably led to some expensive errors. However, the situation appears to be changing.

In this context, it seems likely that environmental valuation will increasingly be called upon by policy makers to aid improvement in policy design, although it also appears that this is unlikely to be solely or mainly as part of a formal CBA (Hanley, 2001). In many instances, choice modelling may be more useful in policy design than contingent valuation, since the latter does not typically involve the estimation of attribute values as constituents of the value of the whole. For example, in the Environmental Sensitive Areas scheme, farmers are paid subsidies to conserve or improve different environmental features within defined geographic areas of the country. Knowing the relative marginal values of, for example, wetlands compared to farm woodlands, may be very useful in this regard. Also, if a public forestry service is charged with managing forests in a manner which maximises net social benefits, then decisions over species mix, age diversity and the provision of recreation facilities would be helped if managers have estimates of the marginal values of these attributes. By focusing directly on attributes, choice modelling techniques seem to be ideally suited to inform the choice and design of multidimensional policies.

Furthermore, environmental valuation has been increasingly used in the UK for setting eco-taxes, for example with regard to the landfill tax and the potential future tax on quarrying. CV has been used in both justifying a tax, and in determining its level. However, applying an estimate of average external cost at the current level of activity does not constitute the Pigouvian tax which it is made out to be, that would measure the marginal external cost at the optimal level of externality. Here, the crucial issue is to find out how marginal damages vary with level of the externality-causing activity. This is essentially the question of scale in valuation. Whilst, as noted above, most contingent valuation studies are sensitive to scale, it is uncommon for more than a couple of quantities to be valued. Valuation functions can of course be estimated with scale as one independent variable, but choice experiments allow scale itself to be an attribute. Thus, CE may be more useful for eco-tax setting, but again this is unproven at present.

Environmental cost-benefit analysis seems to be under increasing pressure as a technique, in the sense that government appears worried that its focus is too narrow. There is an increasing interest among policy makers to be able to somehow combine environmental CBA with multi-criteria analysis and with participatory approaches, such as citizen juries (Kenyon and Hanley, 2000). Whether and how this can be done is an important area for future research. However, as Pearce (1998a) notes, ignoring CBA altogether is undesirable, since it means governments can end up with very inefficient policy designs. As Alan Randall notes, there is also a very powerful case to be made for continuing to use CBA in environmental decision making, since this is one way of representing peoples' preferences for the environment relative to alternatives (Randall, 1998). In this framework, a crucial question is whether choice modelling techniques are the way forward for environmental valuation, given this debate over the future role of environmental valuation within Europe. The current state of the literature is unable to answer this question adequately: to paraphrase Socrates:

'The only thing we know is that we don't know enough'.

Acknowledgements

This paper was originally prepared for a plenary address to the European Association of Environmental and Resource Economists conference, Oslo, June 1999. We would like to thank Vic Adamowicz for invaluable advice on choice experiments and Richard Carson for very helpful comments on earlier drafts. We are also indebted to Gary Koop and Ceara Nevin for contributions to the rock climbing project and W. Douglass Shaw, Jeff Englin and Scott Shonkwiler for comments on this project. Alistair McVittie compiled some of the appendices. The ESRC provided funding for this research under the Global Environmental Change programme.

Notes

1. This approach is also sometimes known as 'conjoint analysis'.
2. See EFTEC (2001), Louviere, Hensher and Swait (2000) and Morrison *et al.* (1999) for further information on these techniques.
3. It is necessary to include a status quo option in the choice set in order to achieve welfare measures that are consist with demand theory. This is because, if a status quo alternative is not included in the choice set, respondents are effectively being 'forced' to choose one of the alternatives presented, which they may not desire at all. If, for some respondents, the most preferred option is the current baseline situation, then any model based on a design in which the baseline is not present will yield inaccurate estimates of consumer welfare.
4. Based on UK general population sample of 3539 adults; and a sample of 550 readers of High magazine.
5. Other studies which apply recreational demand models to rock climbing are Shaw and Jakus (1996), Hanley *et al.* (2001), Hanley *et al.* (2000), Cavlovic and Berrens (1999) and Cavlovic *et al.* (2000).
6. This sensitivity is desirable in some cases, as it mirrors the picture for market goods: for example, we expect WTP to change when respondents' information sets change (Munro and Hanley, 1999).
7. As many have pointed out, such prioritising of the environment on moral/ethical grounds has opportunity costs (for example, less schools and hospitals get built) which often get forgotten by such ethical protesters.

Appendix 1: Some environmental choice experiment studies in the literature

Year	Authors	Title	Journal	Subject of study
1994	Adamowicz, W., Louviere, J. and Williams, M.	Combining revealed and stated preference methods for valuing environmental amenities	Journal of Environmental Economics and Management 26: 271–292	First environmental application of choice experiments? Freshwater recreation in Alberta.
1996	Boxall, P. C., Adamowicz, W. L., Swait, J., Williams, M., Louviere, J.	A comparison of stated preference methods for environmental valuation.	Ecological Economics, 18(3): 243–253	Recreational moose hunting in Alberta, Canada.
1997	Adamowicz, W., J. Swait, P. Boxall, J. Louviere, M. Williams	Perceptions versus Objective Measures of Environmental Quality in Combined Revealed and Stated Preference Models of Environmental Valuation	Journal of Environmental Economics and Management. (32): 65–84.	Compares objective with perceived measures of attributes in choice modelling for moose hunting
1998	Adamowicz, W., Boxall, P., Williams, M., Louviere, J.	Stated preference approaches for measuring passive use values: choice experiments and contingent valuation.	American Journal of Agricultural Economics, 80(1): 64–75	Woodland caribou habitat enhancement in Alberta, Canada.
1998	Bullock, C. H., Elston, D. A., Chalmers, N. A.	An application of economic choice experiments to a traditional land use — deer hunting and landscape change in the Scottish Highlands.	Journal of Environmental Management, 52(4): 335–351	Preferences for deer stalking trips in Scotland.

1998	Hanley, N., MacMillan, D., Wright, R. E., Bullock, C., Simpson, I., Parsisson, D., Crabtree, B.	Contingent valuation versus choice experiments: estimating the benefits of environmentally sensitive areas in Scotland.	Journal of Agricultural Economics, 49(1): 1–15	Valuation of the Breadalbane ESA, Scotland.
1998	Morrison M, Bennett J, Blamey R and Louviere J	Choice modelling and tests of benefits transfer	Choice Modelling Research Report 8, University of NSW, Camberra	Benefits transfer test of wetlands
1998	Hanley, N., Wright, R. E., Adamowicz, V.	Using choice experiments to value the environment — design issues, current experience and future prospects.	Environmental and Resource Economics, 11(3–4): 413–428	Preferences for different forest landscapes in the UK.
1999	Garrod, G. and Willis, K.	*Economic Valuation of the Environment*	Cheltenham: Edward Elgar	Polluted beaches, polluted rivers and low flow rivers in SW England
1999	Blamey, R., Bennett, J., Louviere, J., Morrison, M. and Rolfe, J.	The use of policy labels in environmental choice modelling studies	Research report 9, Choice Modelling reports, University of NSW, Camberra	Value of remnant vegetation in desert uplands of Central Queensland

Appendix 2: Some environmental contingent ranking studies in the literature

Year	Authors	Title	Journal	Subject of study
1981	Beggs, S., Cardell, S. and Hausman, J.	Assessing the potential demand for electric cars	Journal of Econometrics 16: 1–19	Potential demand for electric cars
1983	Rae, D.	The Value to Visitors of Improving Visibility at Mesa Verde and Great Smoky National Parks	In Rowe, R. and Chestnut, L. (eds) *Managing Air Quality and Scenic Resources at National Parks and Wilderness Areas*, Westview Press	Valuing visibility improvements
1985	Lareau, T. and Rae, D.	Valuing willingness to pay for diesel odor reduction: an application of the contingent ranking technique	Southern Economic Journal 55(3): 728–742	Valuing the benefits of diesel odor reductions
1986	Smith, V. and Desvousges, W.	*Measuring Water Quality Benefits*	Kluwer-Nijhoff, Boston	Valuing river water quality improvements
1997	Garrod, G. and Willis, K.	The Non-use Benefits of Enhancing Forest Biodiversity: A Contingent Ranking Study	Ecological Economics 21: 45–61	Valuing forest landscape attributes
1999	Foster, V. and Mourato, S.	Elicitation Format and Part-Whole Bias: Do Contingent Valuation and Contingent Ranking Give the Same Result?	CSERGE Working Paper GEC 99–17	Measuring the value of the charitable sector in the UK and respective sub-sectors

Year	Author	Title	Source	Description
1998	Garrod, G. and Willis, K.	Using contingent ranking to estimate the loss of amenity value for inland waterways from public utility service structures	Environmental and Resource Economics 12: 241–247	Loss of amenity value for inland waterways from public utility service structures
1998	Bergland, O.	Valuation of landscape elements using a contingent choice method	University of Oslo, Working paper	Valuation of several rural landscape elements
1998	Israngkura, A.	Environmental Valuation: An Entrance Fee System for National Parks in Thailand	EEPSEA Research Report Series, August 1998	Environmental benefits of recreational areas in Thailand
1999	Machado, F. and Mourato, S.	Evaluating the Multiple Benefits of Marine Water Quality Improvements: How Important are Health Risk Reductions?	CSERGE Working Paper GEC 09–99, University College London	Evaluating the choice between alternative beaches, differing in access facility and water quality, in the Lisbon Coast
1999	Maddison, D. and Mourato, S.	Valuing different road options for Stonehenge	CSERGE Working Paper GEC 08–99, University College London	Valuing different road options for the A303 road in the Stonehenge bowl
2000	Atkinson, G., Machado, F. and Mourato, S.	Balancing Competing Principles of Environmental Equity	Environmental and Planning A 32: 1791–1806	Preferences for the different burden sharing rules: polluter pays, beneficiary pays or ability to pay
2000	Foster, V. and Mourato, S	Measuring the Impacts of Pesticide Use in the UK: A Contingent Ranking Approach	Journal of Agricultural Economics 51: 1–21	Value of health and biodiversity impacts of pesticide applications in the UK

Appendix 3: Some environmental contingent rating studies in the literature

Year	Authors	Title	Journal	Subject of study
1993	Mackenzie, J.	A comparison of contingent preference models	American Journal of Agricultural Economics: 593–603	Preferences for recreational hunting
1993	Gan, C. and Luzar, E.	A Conjoint Analysis of Waterfowl Hunting in Louisiana	Journal of Agricultural and Applied Economics 76: 760–771	Analysis of waterfowl hunting
1995	Jacobsson, K., Kennedy, J. and Elliot, M.	Survey Method of Valuing the Conservation of Endangered Species	Agricultural Economics Discussion Paper 26/95, La Trobe University	Preservation of endangered species (bandicoots)
1996	Roe, B., Boyle, K. and Teisl, M.	Using conjoint analysis to derive estimates of compensating variation	Journal of Environmental Economics and Management 31: 145–159	Preferences for recreational fishing
1998	Layton, D. and Lee, S.	From Ratings to Rankings: The Econometric Analysis of Stated Preference Ratings Data	Paper presented at the World Congress of Environmental and Resource Economists, Venice, July 1998	Recreational fishing
2001	Alvarez-Farizo, B. and Hamley, N.	Using conjoint analysis to quantify public preferences over the environmental inputs of wind farms	Energy Policy, forthcoming	Compares CE and CR values for wind farms in Spain

Appendix 4: Some environmental paired comparisons in the literature

Year	Authors	Title	Journal	Subject of study
1974	Sinden, J. A.	A Utility Approach to the Valuation of Recreational and Aesthetic Experiences	American Journal of Agricultural Economics 56(1): 61–72	Valuing recreation and aesthetic experiences
1988	Magat, W., Viscusi, W. and Huber, J.	Paired Comparisons and Contingent Valuation Approaches to Morbidity Risk Valuation	Journal of Environmental Economics and Management 15: 395–411	Valuing morbidity risk reductions
1991	Viscusi, W., Magat, W. and Huber, J.	Pricing Environmental Health Risks: Survey Assessments of Risk-Risk and Risk-Dollar Trade-offs for Chronic Bronchitis	Journal of Environmental Economics and Management 21: 32–51	Valuing morbidity risk reductions
1992	Krupnick, A. and Cropper, M.	The Effect of Information on Health Risk Valuations	Journal of Risk and Uncertainty 5: 29–48	Valuing morbidity risk reductions
1996	Desvousges, W., Johnson, F. R., Hudson, S., Gable, A. and Ruby, M.	Using Conjoint Analysis and Health-State Classifications to Estimate the Value of Health Effects of Air Pollution	Report for Environment Canada, Triangle Research Institute	Valuing morbidity risk reductions
1997	Johnson, F. R. and Desvousges, W. H.	Estimating Stated Preferences with Rated Pair-Data; Environmental, Health and Employment Effects of Energy Programs	Journal of Environmental Economics and Management 32: 79–99	Evaluating different characteristics of electricity programs
1998	Lockwood, M.	Integrated Value Assessment Using Paired Comparisons	Ecological Economics 25: 73–87	Preserving endangered species
1998	Newcombe, J.	The Risks and Environmental Benefits of Investing in Climate Change Projects Under the Kyoto Protocol: An Investor Perspective	Report to CIFOR	Evaluating the characteristics of potential CDM projects

References

Adamowicz, W., Louviere, J. and Swait, J. (1998) *Introduction to Attribute-Based Stated Choice Methods*, Final Report to NOAA, US.

Arrow, K., Solow, R., Portney, P., Leamer, E., Radner, R. and Schuman, H. (1993) Report of the National Oceanic and Atmospheric Administration Panel on Contingent Valuation, *Federal Register*, 58, 4602–4614.

Beggs, S., Cardell, S. and Hausman, J. (1981) Assessing the Potential Demand for Electric Cars, *Journal of Econometrics* 16, 1–19.

Ben-Akiva, M., Morikawa, T. and Shiroishi, F. (1991) Analysis of the Reliability of Preference Ranking Data, *Journal of Business Research* 23, 253–268.

Bishop, R. C. and Heberlein, T. A. (1979) Measuring Values of Extra-market Goods: are Indirect Measures Biased?, *American Journal of Agricultural Economics* 61 5, 926–930.

Carlsson, F. (1999) *Essays on Externalities and Transport*. Economic studies 90, Economics Dept., University of Gothenborg.

Carson, R. T. (1998) Contingent Valuation Surveys and Tests of Insensitivity to Scope. In Kopp, R. J., Pommerehne, W. W. and Schwarz, N. (eds), *Determining the Value of Non-Marketed Goods: Economic, Psychological, and Policy Relevant Aspects of Contingent Valuation Methods*, Boston: Kluwer Academic Publishers.

Carson, R. T., Flores, N. E., Martin, K. M. and Wright, J. L. (1996) Contingent Valuation and Revealed Preference Methodologies: Comparing the Estimates for Quasi-public Goods, *Land Economics*, 72, 80–99.

Carson, R. T., Groves, T. and Machina, M. J. (1999) Incentive and Informational Properties of Preference Questions, *Plenary Address, Ninth Annual Conference of the European Association of Environmental and Resource Economists*, Oslo, June.

Cavlovic, T. and R. Berrens, (1999) A question of standing? Institutional change and rock climbing in wilderness areas mimeo, Department of Economics, University of New Mexico.

Cavlovic, T., R. Berrens, A. Bohara, P. Jakus, and W. D. Shaw, (2000) Valuing the loss of rock climbing access in wilderness areas: a national-level random utility model mimeo, Department of Economics, University of New Mexico.

Chapman, R. G. and Staelin, R. (1982) Exploiting Rank Ordered Choice Set Data Within the Stochastic Utility Model. *Journal of Marketing Research*, 19, 288–301.

Christie, M. (1999) An Examination of Factors affecting the Disparity between Hypothetical and Actual Willingness to Pay, Paper to Agricultural Economics Society conference, Belfast.

Cummings, R. Brookshire, D. and Schulze, W. (eds) (1986) *Valuing Environmental Goods — A State of the Arts Assessment of the Contingent Valuation Method*, Rowman and Allanheld, NJ: Totowa.

EFTEC (Economics for the Environment Consultancy) (2001) *Guidance on using Stated Preference Techniques for the Economic Valuation of Non-market Effects*, report to Department of Environment, Transport and the Regions, London, UK.

Foster, V., Bateman, I. J. and Harley, D. (1997) Real and Hypothetical Willingness to Pay for Environmental Preservation: A Non-experimental Comparison. *Journal of Agricultural Economics*, 48, 2, 123–138.

Foster, V. and Mourato, S. (1997) Behavioural Consistency, Statistical Specification and Validity in the Contingent Ranking Method: Evidence from a Survey on the Impacts of Pesticide Use in the UK, CSERGE Working Paper 97–09.

Foster, V. and Mourato, S. (1999) Elicitation Format and Part-Whole Bias: Do Contingent Valuation and Contingent Ranking Give the Same Result?, CSERGE Working Paper GEC 99–17.

Foster, V. and Mourato, S. (2000) Measuring the Impacts of Pesticide Use in the UK: A Contingent Ranking Approach. *Journal of Agricultural Economics*, 51, 1–21.

Green, P., Krieger, A. and Agarwal, M. (1991) Adaptive Conjoint Analysis: Some Caveats and Suggestions. *Journal of Marketing Research* **28**: 223–225.

Green, P. and Srinivasan, V. (1978) Conjoint Analysis in Consumer Research: Issues and Outlook. *Journal of Consumer Research*, 5, 103–123.

Greene, W. H. (1997) *Econometric Analysis*, 3rd Edition, New York, US: Macmillan.

Hanemann, W. M. (1984) Welfare Evaluations in Contingent Valuation Experiments with Discrete Responses. *American Journal of Agricultural Economics*, 66, 332–341.

Hanley, N. (2001) Cost-benefit analysis and environmental policy-making *Environment and Planning C*, 19, 103–118.

Hanley, N., Koop, G., Wright, R. and Alvarez-Farizo, B. (2001) Go Climb a Mountain: An Application of Recreational Demand Models to Rock Climbing. *Journal of Agricultural Economics*, 52, 1, 36–51.

Hanley, N., Wright, R. and Koop, G. (2000) Modelling Recreation Demand Using Choice Experiments: Climbing in Scotland Discussion papers in Economics 2000–11, University of Glasgow.

Hanley, N., MacMillan, D., Wright, R. E., Bullock, C., Simpson, I., Parsisson, D. and Crabtree, B. (1998) Contingent Valuation versus Choice Experiments: Estimating the Benefits of Environmentally Sensitive Areas in Scotland. *Journal of Agricultural Economics*, 49, 413–428.

Hanley, N. and Milne, J. (1996) Ethical Beliefs and Behaviour in Contingent Valuation. *Journal of Environmental Planning and Management*, 39, 2, 255–272.

Hausman, J. (ed.) (1993) *Contingent Valuation: A Critical Assessment*, Amsterdam: North Holland.

Hausman, J. and McFadden, D. (1984) Specification Tests for the Multi-nomial Logit Model. *Econometrica*, 52, 1219–1240.

Hausman, J. and Ruud, P. (1987) Specifying and Testing Econometric Models for Rank-Ordered Data. *Journal of Econometrics*, 34, 83–104.

Hausman, J. and Wise, D. (1978) A Conditional Probit Model for Qualitative Choice: Discrete Decisions Recognising Interdependence and Heterogeneous Preferences. *Econometrica*, 42, 403–426.

Hensher, D. (1994) Stated Preference Analysis of Travel Choices: The State of Practice. *Transportation*, 21, 107–133.

Highlands and Islands Enterprise (1996) *The Economic Impacts of Hillwalking, Mountaineering and Associated Activities in the Highlands and Islands of Scotland*, Jones Economics, Highlands and Islands Enterprise.

Kahneman, D. and Knetsch, J. (1992) Valuing Public Goods: The Purchase of Moral Satisfaction. *Journal of Environmental Economics and Management*, 22, 57–70.

Kenyon, W. and Hanley, N. (2000) Economic and Participatory Approaches to Environmental Evaluation Discussion Papers in Economics, 2000–15, University of Glasgow.

KPMG (1997) *Experience with the Policy Appraisal and the Environment Initiative*, London: DETR.

Krinsky, I. and Robb, A. (1986) Approximating the Statistical Properties of Elasticities. *Review of Economics and Statistics*, 68, 715–719.

Lancaster, K. (1966) A New Approach to Consumer Theory. *Journal of Political Economy*, 84, 132–157.

Lareau, T. and Rae, D. (1987) Valuing Willingness to Pay for Diesel Odor Reduction: An Application of the Contingent Ranking Technique. *Southern Economic Journal*, 55, 3, 728–742.

Louviere, J. and Hensher, D. (1982) On the Design and Analysis of Simulated Choice or Allocation Experiments in Travel Choice Modelling. *Transportation Research Record*, 890, 11–17.

Louviere, J, Hensher, D. and Swait, J. (2000) *Stated Choice Methods: Analysis and Application*, Cambridge: Cambridge University Press.

Louviere, J. and Woodworth, G. (1983) Design and Analysis of Simulated Consumer Choice or Allocation Experiments: An Approach Based on Aggregate Data. *Journal of Marketing Research*, 20, 350–367.

Luce, R. D. (1959) *Individual Choice Behavior: A Theoretical Analysis*, New York: John Wiley & Sons.

Mazotta, M. and Opaluch, J. (1995) Decision Making when Choices are Complex. *Land Economics*, 71, 4, 500–515.

McFadden, D. (1973) Conditional Logit Analysis of Qualitative Choice Behaviour. In Zarembka, P. (ed.), *Frontiers in Econometrics*, New York: Academic Press.

McFadden, D. (1981) Econometric Models of Probabilistic Choice. In Manski, C and McFadden, D. (eds). *Structural Analysis of Discrete Data with Econometric Applications*, Cambridge: MIT Press.

Mitchell, R. and Carson, R. (1989) *Using Surveys to Value Public Goods: The Contingent Valuation Method*, Baltimore: John Hopkins Press.

Morrison, M., Bennett, J., Blamey, R. and Louviere, J. (1998) Choice Modelling and Tests of Benefit Transfer, Choice Modelling Research Report 8, University College, University of New South Wales, Canberra.

Morrison, M., Blamey, R., Bennett, J. and Louviere, J. (1999) A Review of Conjoint Techniques for Estimating Environmental Values mimeo, University of New South Wales, Camberra.

Munro, A. and Hanley, N. (1999) Information, Uncertainty and Contingent Valuation. In Bateman, I. J. and Willis, K. G. (eds), *Contingent Valuation of Environmental Preferences: Assessing Theory and Practice in the USA, Europe, and Developing Countries*, Oxford University Press.

Parsons, G. R. and Kealy, M. J. (1992) Randomly Drawn Opportunity Sets in a Random Utility Model of Lake Recreation, *Land Economics*, 68, 1, 93–106.

Pearce, D. W. (1998a) Cost Benefit Analysis and Environmental Policy. *Oxford Review of Economic Policy*, 14, 4, 84–100.

Pearce, D. W. (1998b) Environmental Appraisal and Environmental Policy in the European Union. *Environmental and Resource Economics*, 11, 3–4, 489–501.

Randall, A. (1998) Taking Benefits and Costs Seriously. In H. Folmer and T. Tietenberg (eds). *Yearbook of Environmental Economics, 1998*, Edward Elgar.

Roe, B., Boyle, K. and Teisl, M. (1996) Using Conjoint Analysis to Derive Estimates of Compensating Variation. *Journal of Environmental Economics and Management*, 31, 145–159.

Sawtooth Software (1993) *ACA System: Adaptive Conjoint Analysis*, Version 4, Sawtooth Software, Evanston, Illinois.

Shaw, W. D. and Jakus, P. (1996) Travel Cost Models of the Demand for Rock Climbing. *Agricultural and Resource Economics Review*, October: 133–142.

Spash, C. and Hanley, N. (1995) Preferences, information and biodiversity preservation, *Ecological Economics*, 12, 191–208.

Steer Davies Gleave (SDG) (1999) *Bus Station Passenger Preferences*, report for LT Buses.

Steer Davies Gleave (SDG) (2000) *London Underground Customer Priorities Research*, report for London Underground.

Swait, J. and Adamowicz, W. (1996) The Effect of Choice Environment and Task Demands on Consumer Behaviour, paper to 1996 Canadian resource and Environmental Economics Study Group, Montreal.

Train, K. E. (1998) Recreation Demand Models with Taste Differences Across People, *Land Economics*, 74, 2, 230–239.

Tversky, A. (1972) Elimination by Aspects: A Theory of Choice. *Psychological Review*, 79, 281–299.

INDEX